The Intelligent Consumer's

COMPLETE GUIDE
TO DENTAL HEALTH

How to Maintain Your Dental Health

And

Avoid Being Overcharged and Overtreated

- All about dentistry and dental health care
- The safest (and cheapest) way to fill a cavity
- You may not need root canal therapy
- New ways to save your teeth
- Risks, costs, and benefits of cosmetic dentistry
- How to choose a dentist

Jay W. Friedman, DDS, MPH

ISBN: 0-7596-7656-9

T   110931

This book is printed on acid free paper.

This book is a revised edition of the *Complete Guide to Dental Health: How to Avoid Being Overcharged and Overtreated* published by Consumer Reports Books, 1991.

Library of Congress Cataloging-in-Publication Data
Friedman, Jay W.

1stBooks - rev. 4/24/02

To my wife, Judith-Ann, for her support and assistance in the completion of this work, and my father, Carl I. Friedman, DDS, by whose example I became a consumer advocate early in life and chose my career.

When last we spoke of what we wrote
The world took little note -
No different now, but still
We hope.

Figure 2-2 (pages 16-17) from I. Schour and M. Massler, University of Illinois College of Dentistry and the American Dental Association. Adapted from *Dental Science Handbook*, U.S. Department of Health, Education, and Welfare, Public Health Service. Washington, D.C.: Government Printing Office, 1969.

Figure 2-3 (page 19), Figure 3-2 (page 25), Figure 6-1 (page 71), Figure 8-1 (page 98), and Figure 8-2 (page 106) from *Dental Science Handbook*, U.S. Department of Health, Education, and Welfare, Public Health Service. Washington, D.C.: Government Printing Office, 1969. (A joint project of the American Dental Association and the National Institutes of Dental Health.)

Figure 4-1 (page 34) courtesy of West Los Angeles College Dental Hygiene Program.

Figure 9-1 (page 115) courtesy of Dr. Alan Samuel.

Contents

COMPLETE GUIDE
TO DENTAL HEALTH

Introduction

Not many books have been written *for the consumer* about dental problems and diseases. A few attempt to explain in everyday language what dentistry is all about. Others are exposés of bad dental care. Most lead to the seemingly inevitable conclusion that in the end the consumer must rely on the competence and goodwill of his or her dentist, leaving readers with pretty much the same problem they hoped to solve by reading the book.

Though you will not be able to practice dentistry after reading this book, you will know more about how decisions affecting your dental health are made by dentists and others in the dental health field, and you will have a better sense of where and when your interests are being compromised in the dental care offered you. Recommendations are made to help you avoid unnecessary treatment, protecting both your dental and your financial health. You will be advised on how to be more assertive in demanding a role in managing your dental care. And, you will save the purchase price of the book many times over if you follow the guidelines for the frequency of examinations and X-rays alone. You will also save yourself and your family the physical, psychological and financial risks that go along with all unnecessary treatment.

Such advice is not always easy to follow. No matter how hard we work to improve our technical knowledge, we all become laypersons when we turn into patients. We want to and need to trust our doctors, much as children need to trust their parents when in trouble. Although intellectually we know that doctors are not infallible, emotionally we want to believe that they are, that they always know what they are doing and are capable of doing it. The most skeptical of us longs to leave such skepticism in the waiting room.

Dentists, like physicians and other health care providers, are better trained to treat disease, injuries, and disabilities than to prevent them. Some conditions are treated more easily than others. Relief for acute conditions, such as pain from injuries or infected teeth, is relatively easy to accomplish, but the more subtle chronic and degenerative diseases defy the dramatic cures that have given doctors their reputation as demigods. The fact is that neither medical nor dental science can cure every infirmity or restore every diseased and defective part of our anatomy to full use. We cannot reverse all the ravages of time, and there are situations in which attempting such dramatic reversals may actually introduce greater risks to health than treating the condition conservatively. Doctors need to protect their demigod status by promising too much, and we as patients want to believe them.

When you pay all or most of the cost of treatment out-of-pocket, you are more likely to participate in the determination of treatment based on the doctor's recommendations, which may include a number of alternatives. These days, many people have dental insurance to cover at least part of the cost of treatment. As the amount of insurance coverage increases, the deterrence of cost decreases, and the decision-making process passes into the hands of dentists, physicians and review consultants at insurance companies. In effect, the doctor becomes the consumer of health care services, deciding what will be done to the raw material-the patient-in the office or hospital. This occurs even though dental insurance is seldom complete and large out-of-pocket expenses remain to be borne by the patient. There is a tendency to believe that if an insurance company will pay from 50 to 80 percent of the cost of a treatment, the patient would be losing out by not going ahead and having the treatment done. Of course, insurance payments to dentists are not gifts to patients. The money comes from all of us, as direct or indirect wage contributions.

Certainly one does not question the value of emergency treatment that saves lives and reduces pain and suffering. But most treatment and expense in dentistry is not for emergency care. Much of it can be avoided by preventive behavior on the part of the patient. Nonetheless, we need periodic examination and treatment to discover and assess those conditions that cannot be prevented entirely. What we don't need is the expense, the discomfort and the risk of **FUN**-functionally unnecessary treatment that benefits not the patients but the doctors who provide it. This book, then, is about adequate and appropriate dental treatment and how you-the consumer-can arrive at informed decisions.

Dental students are not trained sufficiently in preventive techniques. Even more distressing is the failure of dental schools to communicate an understanding of the rate of progression of each of the dental diseases and the limitations of treatment. Technical perfection in the restoration and replacement of teeth, albeit impossible to achieve, is emphasized at the expense of learning what is necessary and adequate treatment. This training makes it difficult for a dentist to accept a patient's rejection of recommended treatment or the choice of a less expensive but adequate service.

Another problem with dental care is overspecialization. Dentistry is in fact a specialty restricted to treatment of the oral mechanism-the teeth and connected structures of the jaws and mouth. Further specialization deprives the general dentist of sufficient training in such areas as pedodontics (treatment of children), periodontics (treatment of pyorrhea or inflammatory gum and bone diseases), exodontics (removal of teeth), endodontics (root canal treatment), and orthodontics (straightening of teeth), to name the most common dental specialties. Thus, the general dentist, already a specialist, is further restricted by current trends in dental education. No wonder a specialist is sometimes defined as a person who knows more and more about less and less.

The average dentist is well intentioned and capable of providing adequate dental care. By training and the imperatives of market place economics, however, the dentist is more than likely to provide too much care. It is therefore important for you to learn enough about good dental health and common problems to make informed choices about treatment.

I do not expect or even intend that you read this book from start to finish. Some chapters are essential to a general understanding of what dentistry is all about. Others should be studied when you need to learn more about specific problems.

It is hoped that you will conclude that there is much about modern dental care that is valuable. However, you must also assume the responsibility for self-care that can prevent or minimize dental disease, and thereby reduce the need for treatment.

Ut Prosim

Lifetime Dental Health

Dental health is dependent on good heredity, diligent home care, proper diet, and periodic maintenance treatment. Heredity goes a long way in determining if we will have strong teeth and healthy bones. We cannot choose our parents, but even if one has inherited "soft teeth" or susceptibility to pyorrhea, primary preventive measures can avoid or minimize most dental diseases. And with secondary prevention or treatment, most if not all your teeth can last a lifetime.[1-2]

PRIMARY PREVENTION

Water Fluoridation

In the 1930s it was discovered that fluoride naturally present in community water supplies significantly reduces tooth decay. Since that time, artificial fluoridation of water has resulted in a 50 to 60 percent reduction in dental caries in these communities, without requiring any change in human behavior. If you already live in a community with fluoridated water, both you and your children are benefiting. If you don't, you should actively support the dental associations and your state and local public health departments in their attempts to introduce fluoridation to your community.[*]

---

[*] It is a sad commentary that anti-fluoridationists have successfully prevented fluoridation in many large cities. They ignore basic epidemiological studies over the past 80 years, which have conclusively documented the safety of minute amounts of fluoride in the water, ranging from 0.7 to 1.5 parts fluoride per million parts of water. Instead the antifluoridationists refer to toxic doses and repudiated studies of brittle bones and cancer, making up in volume of repeated falsehoods for the lack of a scientific basis for their opposition. It is the poor who suffer the most, those who cannot afford early visits to the dentist to have cavities filled before the teeth have to be extracted. Millions of children, as well as adults, denied the benefits of fluoridation suffer gross decay, abscessed teeth and infections that would be prevented by fluoridation.

Brushing and Flossing

Daily brushing with a fluoride toothpaste and flossing between the teeth minimize dental plaque that causes dental decay and periodontal disease. Parents can brush the teeth of infants and, as the children develop sufficient dexterity, supervise their brushing. Flossing should begin in early adolescence when permanent teeth have fully erupted. From then on, flossing should be a daily habit along with toothbrushing.

Defensive Diets

Every dentist says, "Don't eat sugar. Reduce your carbohydrates." In our culture that is like saying, "Don't eat!" Most processed foods contain large amounts of fermentable carbohydrates (sugars such as glucose, fructose, sucrose, and cooked starches). Many dry cereals contain 20 to 50 percent sugar, as much or more than many candy bars. Nondairy creamers are more than 50 percent sugar. Chewing gums, cough drops, and cough syrups range in sugar content from 20 to 65 percent, although a few-very few-contain none. Ketchup and salad dressings are about one-third sugar. Did you ever wonder why salt "pours when it rains?" It is because the grains are glazed with sugar to prevent absorption of moisture and clumping.

Sugar content can be determined by reading the label on the can or package. Although the label does not tell the amount of sugar, it lists contents in the order of the most to the least amounts. You will usually find one or more of the following sugars high on the list: sugar, corn syrup, caramel, molasses, honey, dextrose, fructose, glucose, lactose and sucrose.

From a nutritional viewpoint, sugar and sugar substitutes represent empty calories, replacing foods that provide important nutrients: proteins, vitamins, and minerals. Everyone knows that fruits and vegetables are not only good for meals but also make excellent snacks. But it is easy to be diverted by the constant bombardment of radio, TV, and magazine advertisements that stress reaching for highly refined carbohydrate foods and sugared carbonated drinks.

Fermentable carbohydrates are bad for your teeth because they are food for the bacteria that produce acids that dissolve enamel and dentin, resulting in dental decay. Although the natural flow of saliva can clear the mouth in 20 minutes, it cannot remove the sugars that are bound by plaque and retained against the tooth surface, thus providing a steady diet for these bacteria.

The more frequently one snacks, the longer foods are present in the mouth, the more likely one is to develop cavities. Some foods are more damaging than others, although the difference is slight if one is snacking or drinking all day long. A highly sticky caramel or dried fruit, for instance, holds sugar against the teeth longer than sugared gum. But if you chew sugared gum for hours on end,

2

snack on cookies, suck on lozenges, or drink sugared coffee or soft drinks throughout the day, the effect will be equally damaging. The important point to remember is that excessive sugar in any form, including natural sugars such as honey or the concentrated sugar in dried fruits, is bad for your teeth.

There is little evidence to support the belief that fibrous or nonsticky foods such as fresh fruits and vegetables prevent plaque formation. They do require more chewing, however, which stimulates salivary flow, which in turn dilutes sugars and clears the mouth of debris more quickly.

If you avoid frequent snacking, especially sticky carbohydrates and sugared drinks, a single episode of *thorough* daily brushing and flossing will rid the mouth of most retained food and minimize plaque deposits. If you eat a lot of junk food and are prone to caries or have spaces between teeth from periodontal disease, brushing, flossing and rinsing after meals is advisable. If you cannot brush and floss after eating, at least rinse away loose food particles with water. And, if you are addicted to chewing gum, make sure it is sugar-free and, preferably, contains xylitol, which recent studies indicate reduces the amount of acid-producing bacteria in the mouth.[3-4]

Dental Prophylaxis

Bacterial plaque that cannot be removed by toothbrushing and flossing begins to mineralize into tartar or calculus soon after it forms. Periodic prophylaxis by a dentist or dental hygienist is necessary to remove these hard, calcified deposits, prevent gingivitis, and reduce the risk of periodontal disease.

Sealants

Although fluoride is very helpful in lessening tooth decay, it is not effective against defective pits and fissures that are particularly common in molar teeth. These defective areas can be sealed with a special plastic to prevent decay. To be most effective, the sealant needs to be placed by a dentist, a dental hygienist, or a trained assistant soon after the tooth erupts.

Many states, however, do not allow assistants to apply sealants, which is hardly more difficult that a manicurist applying fingernail polish. By restricting the procedure to dentists and hygienists, the cost is significantly increased at the expense of poor kids who need it the most but cannot afford it.

SECONDARY PREVENTION

Because not all dental disease is completely preventable, *secondary* prevention or treatment to prevent further damage is often necessary. Tooth decay has to be removed, inflamed gums treated, diseased pulps eliminated. Sooner or later, most people, especially those who have not benefited from fluorides, require fillings, crowns, root canal treatment, periodontal therapy, and other procedures to restore damaged teeth and prevent tooth loss.

TERTIARY PREVENTION

Replacement of teeth to restore lost function and prevent further tooth loss is referred to as *tertiary* prevention. It is not necessary to replace every missing tooth. However, multiple loss of teeth may overburden the remaining teeth and lead to periodontal breakdown and more extractions. Missing teeth such as incisors and bicuspids appear as visible gaps between other teeth and are usually replaced for cosmetic reasons. Multiple missing posterior teeth should also be replaced when it is necessary to stabilize the dental arches and provide adequate chewing for good digestion. As a rule of thumb, if two-thirds of the teeth are in functional occlusion, replacement of non-visible missing teeth is not necessary.

BEGINNING WITH BABIES

Baby teeth start to form as early as the sixth week of embryonic life. Permanent tooth buds are evident by the fourth month in the womb. Thus, the future strength of teeth is dependent on a healthy pregnancy. If the mother develops a high fever during pregnancy, if tetracycline is administered, or if adequate maternal nutrition is not maintained, both baby teeth and permanent teeth may be damaged, discolored, or malformed.

The first baby teeth enter the mouth at about 6 months of age, and the full complement of 10 upper and 10 lower baby teeth has erupted by the second or third year of infancy, all of which are replaced with permanent teeth by age 11 or 12. Eruption continues until age 20 or 25, by which time the 32 permanent teeth have fully developed. (*See* Eruption of Teeth in chapter 2.) Infant teething can be quite uncomfortable for babies as well as discomforting to parents. The gums may become inflamed and minor infections can occur at the site of eruption. Fortunately, the condition is self-correcting as the teeth fully emerge through the tissue.   In adolescents and young adults, teething discomfort frequently accompanies the eruption of the last molars, the wisdom teeth. If there is insufficient room for full eruption, wisdom teeth sometimes, *but not always*, need to be removed.

One does not ordinarily think of babies having bad eating habits, but this is actually one of the major causes of tooth decay in infants. Rampant decay of the front teeth is frequently caused by allowing the infant to fall asleep with a nursing bottle containing milk, fruit juice, or sweetened water, or at the mother's breast where there is a constant flow of milk over the teeth. This condition, known as *baby bottle tooth decay,* is preventable by avoiding excessive nursing with cariogenic liquids. If you feel the baby needs a bottle at sleep time, fill it with water, not milk, fruit juice or soda pop.

The major effect of fluoride in preventing tooth decay is obtained by its topical effect on the outer tooth surface.[5] Dental decay may also be diminished by the addition of fluoride to the infant's diet, usually in combination with prescribed vitamin drops. But as soon as the child is old enough, it is more effective to chew fluoride tablets and, especially, to begin toothbrushing with a pea-sized dollop of fluoridated toothpaste as soon as the teeth appear in the mouth. Dietary fluoride should be continued to at least age 16 if community water is not fluoridated. If water is fluoridated, then dietary supplements should be reduced or eliminated, depending on the level of fluoride. Too much dietary fluoride can cause slight to unsightly discoloration of teeth known as *mottled enamel* but is otherwise harmless. (*See* chapter 4.)

Parents and pediatricians are responsible for looking at the baby's teeth as well as other parts of the oral cavity. Cavities can begin as early as age 1. If white, brown or black spots are noticed on the baby teeth, a trip to the dentist is advisable. (Use a flashlight to view the back teeth.) Fluoride varnishes, introduced in the United States in 1994, though long used in Europe, can be applied to the infant's teeth every six months to inhibit cavities.[6] Since a prophylaxis is not necessary, this could easily be done by a pediatric nurse in the medical office. The teeth need only be dried with a cotton guaze, with immediate application of the fluoride, which dries virtually on contact. Unless suspected cavities or some other problem is present, there is no need for a dental examination before age two or two and a half, or until all the baby teeth are in; once a year is sufficient thereafter unless special problems develop. As long as the baby teeth are spaced so that all surfaces are visible to the naked eye, X-rays are unnecessary. Unless the teeth are stained, a baby prophylaxis (cleaning of teeth) serves no purpose and is a needless expense. For most children the first trip to the dentist can be a fun visit, an early orientation to a lifelong behavior pattern.

WHAT TO DO WITH ADOLESCENTS

Already programmed by thousands of hours of advertising to crave sugared cereals, carbonated drinks, and all other varieties of junk food, adolescents need parental guidance to develop and maintain sensible health care habits. Too often, however, parents have also succumbed and thus serve as poor role models for their children's diets.

Outward appearance becomes a dominating influence in the early teens. While the appearance of teeth is important, adolescents are probably more concerned with the sweetness of their breath than with the health of their gums. They will chew gum incessantly, suck on candy, snack interminably, grind and clench their teeth, just like the adults they will become. If their teeth are crooked, they will want them straightened.

Poor diet and inadequate toothbrushing contribute to dental decay and gingivitis. Newly erupted teeth may have defective grooves that need to be sealed or, if decayed, filled. Harmful habits such as excessive chewing gum and snacking need to be modified.

While preventive measures can effectively reduce most adolescent dental problems, annual examinations are necessary to detect cavities, gingivitis and, occasionally, more serious conditions that require treatment. An annual prophylaxis is sufficient for most adolescents, particularly if they have good oral hygiene habits including daily brushing and flossing.

Straight teeth are important cosmetically, but not every crooked tooth needs straightening. Orthodontics has become very popular, but its value as an esthetic treatment should not be confused with functional necessity. Rarely does a "bad bite" adversely effect chewing or contribute to malnutrition, or cause other oral problems. Severely crooked teeth, however, can affect an adolescent's emotional well being and self-image. Orthodontic correction can greatly improve appearance and personality if there is a significant problem. Otherwise, the expense of treatment may be better allocated to more serious family needs.

ADULT DENTAL HEALTH-
PAST AND FUTURE BEHAVIOR

It is surprising how many adults fear dental treatment, many because of bad childhood experiences at the hands of insensitive dentists or of woeful tales recounted by others. But even among those who have never had a bad experience, many people become more anxious and fearful as they grow older. The thought of the needle instills chills. The sound of the drill, quiet as it has become, resonates through the brain. Even scaling teeth to remove tartar sends chills up and down the spine. For most of us these anxieties are easily overcome. We do what we have to do. We go to the dentist for periodic checkups. We accept the prick of the needle to avoid the pain of the drill. We tolerate the mild discomfort of tooth scaling for the pleasure of clean teeth and healthy gums.

But some put off the trip to the dentist out of fear not only of dental treatment itself but also of its cost, fears that can be overcome by a dentist sensitive to the patient's problem. The modern dental office is attractive, clean, and nonthreatening. The patient reclines comfortably in a contour chair. Anesthetic injections are given virtually painlessly to make further treatment painless. The financial pain can be minimized by budgeting the cost.

As one ages, fillings occasionally need replacement, new cavities can develop, a nerve may degenerate, a tooth may crack or fracture, teeth wear down, and periodontal disease becomes more common. Most of these problems are now treatable if they are not ignored too long, and few persons need ever lose all their teeth.

SPECIAL PROBLEMS OF THE ELDERLY

Before the full impact of fluoridation, fluoride toothpastes, and improved oral hygiene and dental care, three-fourths of the population eventually ended up toothless. That solved the problems of dental decay and periodontal disease, but the elderly were hardly more comfortable with dentures. While 4 out of 10 adults over the age of 65 still lose all their teeth, many more are now retaining at least some of their natural teeth into their final years.

With aging comes a decrease in dexterity and, not infrequently, less concern with oral hygiene. Diets tend to become softer and food debris and plaque accumulate around the natural teeth, contributing to root decay and advancing periodontal disease. Teeth become more brittle and fracture. Drugs, radiation therapy, and aging may decrease salivary flow. "Dry mouth" accelerates tooth decay and reduces denture stability and comfort. At a time when more frequent professional care is necessary—for prophylaxis, periodontal therapy, fillings, crowns, root canal treatment, bridges and dentures—the elderly are often without funds and, increasingly, are immobilized in nursing homes. Still, the problem is not so much that the elderly require substantially different dental care than the younger adult population but that they lack the means and access to obtain it.

Some of the difficulty of the elderly in maintaining oral hygiene can be relieved by use of electric toothbrushes and oral irrigation devices. Fluoride rinses, gels and varnishs and antimicrobial agents can be administered by nursing home personnel to inhibit root caries. If we could rid ourselves of archaic licensing board restrictions, we could train nurses and nurse's aides to apply fluoride varnishes, which is easier to apply than traditional topical fluoride application and is as effective in inhibiting root decay. Institutions for the aged can arrange for visiting dentists and hygienists to perform periodic examinations, prophylaxis, and fillings using portable equipment. That these types of dental care programs are not better organized and funded simply reflects the low priority society places on dental health care for the elderly.

WHAT TO EXPECT FROM YOUR DENTIST

Tender, competent care. Tender loving care (TLC) is a much heralded but unrealistic expectation when it comes to most medical and dental care. What you are entitled to is competent diagnosis and treatment delivered with concern for your comfort and sensitivities by dentists, dental hygienists, and well-trained assistants using up-to-date equipment.

What you are at risk of, particularly as an adult, is being viewed as a financial target. Practice management courses teach the dentist how to appeal to your vanity and sell you the most expensive treatment. Articles are written in prestigious dental journals advocating a panoramic X-ray for all patients not because of their diagnostic value, which is limited, but because "they are highly educational to the patient," which translated means they help the dentist sell you more treatment.[7] At an extra $40 to $60, these films, taken just to show you an x-ray picture of your teeth, are highly lucrative to the dentist. Dental assistants and hygienists are also taught to participate in the diagnosis and treatment plan, combining with the dentist to make a powerful sales force to entice you, the consumer, to buy more, and more expensive, treatment than you need.

Cleanliness and sterilization. The office should be clean and neat. Instruments should be sterilized and stored properly. Personnel should wear protective eyeglasses, masks and plastic, latex or vinyl gloves when treating patients.[*]

Thorough examination. A good oral examination, whether performed by the dentist or the hygienist, includes an inspection of the hard and soft tissues of the mouth: teeth, gums, top and sides of the tongue, inner lining of the cheeks, and palate. In adults, a periodontal probe should be inserted gently between the gum and the tooth to measure the depth of the gingival crevice or pocket. Measurements exceeding three millimeters should be recorded on the dental chart. This type of examination takes no more than five minutes. If periodontal disease is detected, an additional five minutes will be required to record the amount of bone loss-the depths of all the pockets-around the teeth.

Unless there are special problems, the dental examination need not be repeated more than once a year. For persons with no obvious problems, an 18-month interval between exams is sufficient.

Frequency of dental X-rays (radiographs). X-rays should not be taken at every examination. As already noted, children seldom need X-rays before the age of five, and often not even then. In the event the baby molars are too close together to inspect visually, one bitewing film on each side is sufficient to detect

---

[*] Patients allergic to latex should notify the dentist and make sure the staff uses vinyl gloves for them.

cavities. Bitewing X-rays are also sufficient for adolescents. At approximately age 16, a full set of periapical and bite-wing X-rays may be taken to assess the condition of the teeth and to determine if there are any unusual conditions warranting further examination.

Adults may expect a complete dental examination to include full- mouth X-rays at their first dental appointment. These X-rays are recommended not only for current diagnosis but also as a baseline for comparison in future years. This is particularly important in evaluating the progress of periodontal disease. It is rarely necessary to repeat full-mouth radiographs more than once in five or eight years. Bite-wing X-rays are sufficient every 12 to 18 months for routine examinations. Additional X-rays should be taken only for specific diagnostic reasons.

At the completion of the examination, the dentist should explain his or her findings and treatment recommendations. Unless special problems require more complex treatment planning, an estimate of costs can also be provided at this visit.

Prophylaxis. Children seldom require a complex prophylaxis. Until tartar begins to form, a child's cleaning is simply that-the removal of stains from the teeth. Since surface stains are harmless, the value of the visit lies in the opportunity to impart good oral hygiene instruction-toothbrushing, flossing, diet- that should be reinforced at each subsequent prophylaxis. A topical fluoride solution may also be applied to the child's teeth at this visit, but it has minimal value for a child using fluoride toothpastes and ingesting dietary fluorides, or living in a fluoridated area. Because these procedures are totally painless, they provide an excellent introduction to dental care.

Children and young adolescents rarely need more than one prophylaxis visit a year. Those adolescents who develop heavy stains and tartar may require prophylaxis every six months. Likewise, if gums are puffy, inflamed or bleed easily, a prophylaxis every six months is beneficial in teaching and reinforcing personal oral hygiene practices.

Not all adults require prophylaxis every 6 months. Again, it depends on the rate of formation of tartar, stains, and gingival inflammation. For those individuals with no special problems, a prophylaxis every 12 to 18 months is sufficient. For adults with heavy calculus formation and poor oral hygiene, however, semiannual prophylaxis is in order. Many adults with moderate to advanced periodontal disease require more frequent visits, as often as every 3 or 4 months, not merely for a prophylaxis but to have the roots of the teeth cleaned (scaling and root planning or SRP). But be wary of the dentist who recommends SRPs at extra cost without documenting that you have periodontal disease, and he is only doing a prophylaxis. And don't pay extra for "medicinal or antimicrobial irrigation" of the gums that has little value as applied in most dental offices. (See Antimicrobial Rinses in Chapters 4 and 8.) It is the removal of soft and hard plaque with scaling instruments by dentists and hygienists, and keeping it off by conscientious toothbrushing, flossing and periodic professional scaling that is of real value.

Treatment. The first priority is always to relieve pain and eliminate infections. Less urgent treatment can then be phased in at everyone's convenience. If treatment needs are complex, a patient should be given a choice of alternative treatment plans to match his or her preferences and budget. Do not be reluctant to express your anxieties and fears; a good dentist wants to hear all the patient's concerns. The dentist should be receptive to your questions and be willing to explain recommendations to your satisfaction. Then he or she should provide the agreed-upon treatment in a relaxed manner with a minimum of pain and discomfort.

Maintenance (recall) care. A good dentist will assess the frequency of cavity formation, the rate and amount of tartar deposits, the condition of the gums and periodontal bone, and other special problems, and determine the frequency for examination, radiographs, prophylaxis, and root planing based on these findings. When all current treatment has been completed, the patient will be placed on a recall schedule and receive a telephone call or a postcard reminder at the proper time to return for maintenance care. Many patients are automatically placed on 6 month recall even though an annual recall would be sufficient. Regardless, if the patient does not respond, a conscientious office will follow up with further reminders at 12 and 18 month intervals. If one had a choice of only one recall, the 18 month recall would be the most important since that is how long it usually takes for a small cavity to get so large that the nerve may become infected or for the gums to become more seriously diseased.

The key to dental health is vigilant personal and professional maintenance care. If you and your family are concerned enough to practice daily oral hygiene, have good diets, avoid harmful habits, and have periodic dental checkups and maintenance treatment, your teeth will be yours to enjoy for a lifetime.

Dental Anatomy

STRUCTURE OF THE MOUTH AND JAWS

The mouth is a remarkable mechanism. Like all parts of the body, it is subjected to wear, tear, and aging. The powerful muscles of mastication prepare food for swallowing by a shearing and grinding action. To withstand these chewing forces, the lower jaw or mandible is connected to the skull by the temporomandibular joints (TMJs), ball-and-socket hinges on either side. The teeth are protected by a shell of enamel, which is the hardest substance in the body.[1]

In order to cushion chewing forces that can exceed 150 pounds of pressure per square inch, each tooth is attached to its socket in the jaw by a thin, tough, elastic periodontal ligament. The TMJs are also attached to the skull sockets by elastic ligaments and cushioned by discs of cartilage. These TMJ hinges are uniquely mobile, allowing both up and down movement and slight sideways or semi-rotary action. Only the lower jaw moves within the bilateral sockets of the skull.

Both upper and lower jaws are composed of the body or base bone and the alveolar bone. Alveolar bone contains the sockets for the teeth. When teeth are lost, the remnant alveolar bone or ridge is gradually resorbed (dissolved), presenting great difficulty for denture wearers, especially in the lower jaw, as the remaining bone becomes flat.

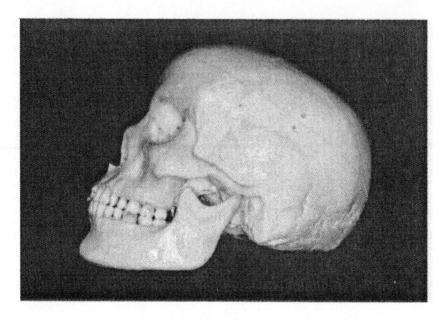

Figure 2-1 A.   Lateral view of the human skull and jawbones

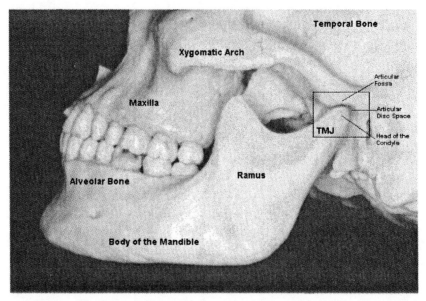

Figure 2-1 B.   Upper (maxilla) and lower (mandible) jaws and the temporomandibular joint (TMJ)

Bone and muscle must be covered by skin. In the mouth this skin is a mucous membrane called the **oral mucosa**. The roof of the mouth or **hard palate** is covered by firm, thick mucosa that bears the brunt of food movement and the swallowing action of the tongue.Thinner, softer tissue covers the muscles of the soft palate, and curves back toward the throat and the inside of the cheeks and lips, where it blends into the tougher gingival (gum) tissue. The gingiva or gum consists of attached and unattached sections. **Attached gingiva** covers alveolar bone to just beneath the crown of the tooth where it folds over and connects directly to the tooth, leaving a small crevice, much like the cuticle of your fingernail. In a healthy mouth this crevicular fold or sulcus, the **unattached gingiva**, may be from one to three millimeters deep, depending on the location in the mouth. The attachment of the gingiva directly to the teeth is what prevents food and microorganisms from penetrating more deeply. When the gingiva is infected or breaks down, you have the beginning of periodontal disease or what is commonly known as pyorrhea.

Then there is the **tongue**, that ubiquitous muscle with which we swallow as much as 1,500 to 2,000 times a day and which is also essential for speech, taste, and touch. The shape, size, and action of the tongue help to mold the contours of the mouth, forming an inner wall opposite the outer wall of the cheeks and lips, separated by the rows of upper and lower teeth. When these inner and outer muscles are in balance, the dental arches are maintained evenly. If the tongue misbehaves, as when it is positioned improperly in swallowing, thrusting forward between the front incisor teeth, then an open bite and protruding teeth may result.

All of this activity requires constant lubrication by **saliva**. Food not only requires chewing and grinding into particles small enough to be mushed into a small, round bolus, it also must be lubricated to pass easily down the throat into the stomach. The constant movement of the jaws and tongue in speaking and in day and night dreaming causes continuous rubbing of mucosa, teeth, and lips. Without adequate, continuous lubrication, the soft tissues erode and ulcerate. Saliva is produced by the myriad mucous and serous glands of the mouth, the large parotid glands in the cheeks, and the submandibular and sublingual glands under the tongue from which secretions flow into the oral cavity, as much as 1.5 liters (1.4 quarts) a day. Saliva is a complex fluid with many protective elements as well as enzymes that begin the digestion of food even as it is being chewed. The mouth is home for many microorganisms-bacteria, viruses, and fungi or yeasts-most of which become normal inhabitants soon after we are born. These microorganisms live in a harmless, symbiotic relationship in your mouth provided that good health and resistance are maintained. When resistance is lowered, these same organisms multiply out of control to produce a variety of diseases including gingivitis, Vincent's infection ("trench mouth"), periodontitis (pyorrhea), and moniliasis (yeast infection). Thus, most oral diseases are not the result of an invasion of new microorganisms but the acting up of our daily companions. It also should be noted that many systemic diseases, such as diabetes and leukemia, can cause the breakdown of gingival tissue and the loss of alveolar bone.

ERUPTION OF TEETH

Human beings grow two sets of teeth. The table below outlines the average eruption/replacement process in detail. A delay of two or more years beyond these averages may be an indication of hormonal deficiencies, although more often the cause remains unknown. In addition to mastication, the baby molars protect the space for the permanent bicuspids developing in the bone underneath. The roots of the baby teeth gradually resorb and the teeth exfoliate (fall out) to make room for the permanent teeth to erupt. If a permanent tooth, most frequently a mandibular second bicuspid, is genetically missing, the deciduous tooth will last into adulthood.

ERUPTION OF TEETH			
Primary Teeth	*Months*	*Permanent Teeth*	*Years*
Central Incisors	6-8	Central incisors	5-6
Lateral Incisors	7-9	Lateral incisors	7-9
First molars	12-14	First premolars (bicuspids)	10-11
Canines (cuspids)	16-18	Canines (cuspids)	9-11
Second molars	20-24	Second premolars (bicuspids)	10-12
		First molars	6-7
		Second molars	11-13
		Third molars (wisdom teeth)	16-25

THE SHAPE OF TEETH

Every tooth is distinctly divided into a **crown** and a **root**. The crown is what we see in our mouth; the root is below the gum, attached to the jawbone. Within the center of the crown is a pulp chamber that houses the large part of the nerve or pulp tissue. Within each root is a canal through which pulp tissue connects to the larger nerves and blood vessels running through the jawbones.

Each crown is shaped to serve a specialized function by which the tooth receives its name. For example, the front central and lateral **incisors** have a single cutting edge to incise or shear food. The third tooth from the center is called the **canine**, **cuspid**, or **eyetooth**. It is longer than the other teeth, allowing it to grasp and tear. Behind the cuspids are the two **premolars** or **bicuspids** (first and second baby molars up to age 10-12) followed by the three permanent molars. The bicuspids assist the cuspid in grasping and tearing, whereas the back **molars** have a broad surface composed of four or five cusps for grinding and mashing the food in preparation for swallowing.

Incisors and cuspids have single, cone-shaped roots. Premolars may have one or two roots. Lower molars usually have two large roots, whereas the upper molars have three.

WHAT TEETH ARE MADE OF

Teeth consist of enamel, dentin, cementum, and pulp tissue. Enamel is the hardest substance in the body. It is 95 percent calcified (mineralized), as compared with dentin at 70 percent and cementum at 50 percent. Enamel is almost as hard as topaz, a semiprecious stone, and cementum is about the same hardness as normal bone, with dentin approximately in between. Well-calcified enamel is translucent, usually yielding a light yellow color, a reflection of the natural color of the underlying dentin. White enamel may appear prettier to some people but it is quite uncommon. In its extreme form, it represents hypoplastic or less calcified, softer enamel, which is more susceptible to decay and fracture.

Enamel covers the entire crown of the tooth, forming a hard protective shell. It varies in thickness from less than one-half millimeter on the sides to one and a half millimeters on the cutting or chewing surfaces. It does not contain any nerve endings and is therefore totally insensitive to touch or dental drilling.

In cultures with tough, gritty diets or where teeth are used to soften leather and fibers, people wear through the enamel by early adulthood. By mid-life the dentin may be worn through and the pulp tissue exposed and infected. In our society, diet and other factors have become less abrasive for teeth. Nonetheless, some people still wear through the enamel at an early age by grinding away (bruxism), often involuntarily, during waking hours and while asleep.

DECIDUOUS TEETH

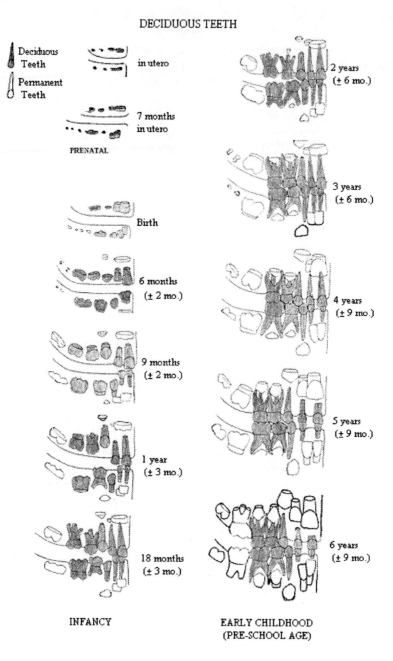

Figure 2-2 A. Development of the human dentition from birth to 6ᵗʰ year

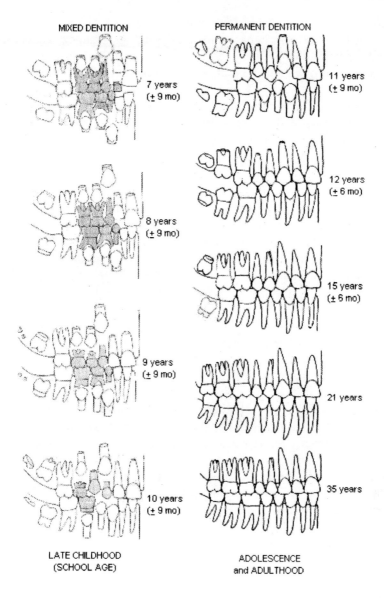

MIXED DENTITION

PERMANENT DENTITION

7 years
(± 9 mo)

8 years
(± 9 mo)

9 years
(± 9 mo)

10 years
(± 9 mo)

11 years
(± 9 mo)

12 years
(± 6 mo)

15 years
(± 6 mo)

21 years

35 years

LATE CHILDHOOD
(SCHOOL AGE)

ADOLESCENCE
and ADULTHOOD

Figure 2-2 B. Development of the Human Dentition from 7th Year to Maturity

Although extremely hard, enamel is not impermeable. Calcium, phosphorus, and fluoride ions in the saliva can pass into and through the enamel. This process allows limited repair of enamel damaged from early decay, but the tooth cannot grow new enamel to replace enamel that is worn away by attrition (grinding) and abrasion.

Dentin forms about 70 percent of the bulk of an adult tooth, including both crown and root portions. Although highly calcified, it is a live tissue containing specialized cells sensitive to temperature changes and touch. The thickness of dentin increases throughout life, gradually filling in part or all of the pulp chamber and root canals. Because of the increasing density of dentin, the color of the tooth gradually becomes a deeper yellow. As the pulp chamber decreases with age, teeth become less sensitive to heat, cold, and touch.

Cementum overlays the outer surface of dentin, covering the entire surface of the root. It is light yellow in color, barely distinguishable from dentin. Cementum is very thin, ranging from .05 millimeter to .2 millimeter, which is about the thickness of a fingernail. Not counting the pulp, it is the softest part of a tooth, yet has the hardness of bone. As its name implies, cementum attaches the root to the alveolar bone of the jaw by means of the periodontal ligament. The periodontal ligament contains special fibers that fasten to the cementum on one side and the alveolar bone on the other. The ligament functions like a shock absorber, providing a slightly elastic attachment of each tooth. This prevents the bone socket from breaking down under the forces of chewing, grinding, and clenching.

Cementum, like dentin, has a limited capacity to grow. As a tooth wears down, cementum adds on at the apex or tip of the root, causing the tooth to erupt and thus maintain contact with its opposite in the other jaw. Because cementum formation is limited, continuous eruption cannot keep pace with excessive wear on the occlusal or chewing surfaces of teeth. That is why the clinical crowns-the portion of the teeth in the mouth-eventually become shorter. Shorter crowns decrease the separation of lower and upper jaws, shortening the face and giving it an aged appearance.

Pulp is the technical name given to the connective tissue and the minute blood vessels and nerves in the center of the tooth, the part of the tooth most people call the **nerve** because of its extreme sensitivity. The vessels and nerves in the pulp connect with the larger arteries, veins, and nerves of the jaws through very small openings in the root tips. The larger vessels join with the major arteries and veins of the body. Blood circulating from the heart to the tooth and back to the heart again takes 10 to 15 seconds for the round trip.

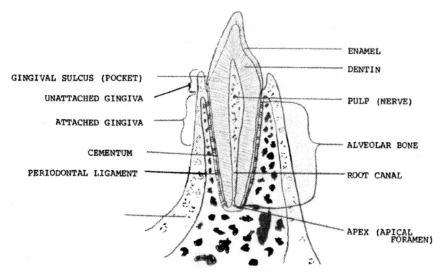

ENAMEL

DENTIN

GINGIVAL SULCUS (POCKET)

UNATTACHED GINGIVA

ATTACHED GINGIVA

PULP (NERVE)

CEMENTUM

PERIODONTAL LIGAMENT

ALVEOLAR BONE

ROOT CANAL

APEX (APICAL FORAMEN)

Figure 2-3   Diagrammatic representation of the dental tissues

Although the pulp decreases in size with age, its vitality is essential to provide nutrients for ongoing dentin formation.   This process not only strengthens the tooth but also protects the pulp from irritation and penetration as the overlying enamel and dentin are worn away.   If the pulp becomes nonvital ("dies" in popular vernacular), and the dead pulp tissue is not thoroughly removed by good root canal treatment, the tooth may turn dark yellow, gray, or black.

The mouth is an enormously complex organ with many functions.   Small wonder, then, that everyone experiences dental problems occasionally, and many persons continuously, throughout life.   Compared to many medical diseases, it would seem that dental problems are relatively simple.   Yet there have been no miracle cures for the common dental diseases.   Even though we are reasonably sure how to prevent some of them, the cure lies not in miracle drugs but in behavioral change of the individual and of society.   The chemicals that we put in our mouths, including food, carbonated drinks, alcohol, tobacco, and drugs, the stresses and strains of life and ineffective oral hygiene, all combine to work against our resistance to disease and toward functional breakdown.   That we— and our mouths and teeth—survive as well as we do is perhaps the miracle.

3

Dental Caries (Decay)

Through the centuries, dental decay has been a scourge of mankind. Foul breath, excruciating toothaches, swollen jaws, and severe infections leading to death have been commonplace. Biographies of pioneers describe how tooth infections put them to bed for weeks. Explorers have been known to abandon their expeditions because of pain and infections resulting from abscessed teeth. All this seems in the past, but only for those fortunate enough to be caries-free or to have access to good dental care.

It is largely true that a clean tooth does not decay. The problem is that teeth cannot be kept completely clean, completely free of plaque. Even though the incidence of dental caries has declined significantly, 50 percent of 5 to 9 year old children in the United States still has at least one cavity or filling, increasing to 78 percent by age 17.[1] Early childhood caries (ECC), including *baby bottle tooth decay*, remains one of the most common childhood diseases, particularly among low income families. Twenty-five percent of children account for 80 percent of ECC. Caries rates for children enrolled in Head Start or Women, Infants and Children (WIC) programs can exceed 50 percent.[2]

It is estimated that children lose 51 million school hours a year due to dental-related illness.[3] Many adults continue to develop cavities throughout life; the elderly are particularly at risk of root decay as the roots are exposed to plaque and bacteria by gum recession. Over $53 billion is spent annually on dental care, much of which is to restore or replace teeth damaged or lost from dental decay.[4] How such a relatively simple disease affects us all is the subject of this chapter.

THE CAUSE OF DENTAL DECAY

Dental caries or decay is an **infectious microbial plaque disease** caused by bacteria (mutans streptococci and lactobacilli) that are transmitted to the infant by the contaminated saliva of parents and other caregivers.[5] Since it would be impossible to prevent infecting infants without outlawing kissing, researchers are looking towards development of dental vaccines, which are proving as elusive as vaccines to prevent AIDS.

Bacteria require a protected environment-dental plaque-to do their dirty work. **Plaque** is a sticky, nearly invisible, gelatinous substance deposited on the teeth by bacteria and their products in combination with dietary carbohydrates and salivary components. Plaque takes about 24 hours to reach a detectable thickness. A large variety of bacteria colonize the plaque, creating acids as they metabolize fermentable carbohydrates. The plaque concentrates these acids against the tooth surface, resulting in demineralization of enamel and cavity formation in susceptible people. But teeth can remineralize and many very early cavities heal spontaneously, a process aided by the presence of fluoride.[6-7]

TYPES OF DENTAL DECAY

Dental caries develop on three distinct areas of the tooth: enamel pits and fissures, smooth enamel surfaces, and the root.

Pit and fissure caries occur on the occlusal (chewing) surfaces and the outsides of teeth that fail to form perfectly during development, most commonly in molars. In children, pits and fissures account for about 60 percent of all cavities. When these areas are defective, decay begins soon after the tooth erupts into the mouth and usually progresses rapidly.

Pit and fissure caries can be detected by visual examination, in which the defect appears as a darkly stained brown or black *dot* or *crevice*. In the United States dentists habitually and forcibly probe these areas with a pinpoint explorer, a steel instrument actually capable of creating a defect that otherwise would not require filling. When the explorer sticks and holds in a pit or fissure, the area is generally defined as a cavity, whether or not decay is present. To avoid this type of *iatrogenic* diagnosis, you should ask your dentist to probe pits and fissures with an explorer with only light to moderate pressure, or better yet, to rely on visual examination of air-dried teeth.[8]

When decay is present, however, it must be removed. If not, the enamel of the crown will be eaten through, the pulp will become infected, and the tooth may eventually have to be extracted. This kind of decay can be prevented by sealants applied to the tooth soon after eruption (See chapter 4.). Caries will not be prevented from developing in defective pits and fissures by tooth brushing or fluorides.

Remember, not all of these defects require filling. Even though a defect is observable to the naked eye or an explorer sticks in a pit or a groove, filling is not necessary unless decay has penetrated through the enamel into dentin. If the dark stain is only in the enamel, the pit or fissure can still be sealed instead of filled.

Smooth surface decay occurs most often on the proximal sides of the teeth, the surfaces that contact each other, and is best seen in the bitewing X-ray film.

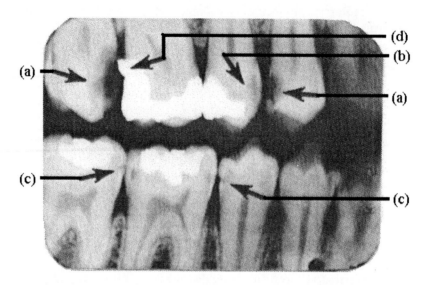

Figure 3-1 Stages of interproximal tooth decay. (a) Gross decay extending close to or into the nerve. (b) Medium dental decay. (c) Early but definite decay that should be filled. (d) Overhang or excess amalgam filling material. This patient is highly susceptible to caries and at risk of losing many teeth.

Normally, there are no irregularities on these surfaces, but when dental plaque forms here, it cannot be removed easily because toothbrush bristles do not reach between the teeth. This is one of the reasons dental flossing is necessary. The other is to inhibit periodontal disease. Passing the string through the contact points of the teeth and rubbing each surface up and down breaks up the plaque that holds the acid against the enamel. Smooth surface caries also occur on the cheek and tongue surfaces teeth, especially when oral hygiene is poor. Caries on these surfaces are also referred to as gum line cavities because they commonly occur where food debris and plaque accumulate easily near the gum or just beneath it.

One of the worst forms of smooth surface decay occurs in infants who fall asleep nursing at the breast or are left to suckle continuously on bottles of milk or fruit juice. This is called **baby bottle tooth decay** (also called nursing caries and early childhood caries), because the entire enamel surfaces, particularly of the front teeth, are literally dissolved by the acids formed from these liquids. Whether due to the bottle or a high sugar diet, early childhood caries (ECC) occurs in infants as young as one year.[9]

Besides using sugar to feed the bacterial plaque that produces and holds acids against the teeth, there is another way to dissolve the enamel of healthy teeth. Directly bathing the tooth in acids leads to a form of erosion. Sucking on lemons dissolves enamel rapidly, as will excessive consumption of soft drinks, fruit juices, and other acidic fluids. Erosion is also facilitated by frequent regurgitation of stomach acids, as occurs in *bulimia nervosa*, an illness characterized by binge eating and self-induced vomiting.

Another common type of erosion occurs along the gum line where an area of the enamel has dissolved. It usually involves a number of teeth simultaneously. The eroded surface is smooth, hard and shiny. The cause is not known. Although erosion is not always followed by decay, the area may become more susceptible to it. In addition, there may be more sensitivity to hot and cold liquids and to touch where the enamel has dissolved away.

Root caries, as the name states, are found on the roots of teeth. In order for a root surface to decay, it must be exposed to the oral environment. Therefore, root caries are usually found only in older people who have experienced gum recession and periodontal bone loss. Cancer patients who have had radiation therapy of the head and neck are particularly prone to root caries. Radiation damages the salivary glands, markedly reducing the flow of saliva, a condition known as xerostomia or **dry mouth**. Salivary flow also decreases as a side effect of many medications, in diseases of the salivary glands and, to a limited extent, in normal aging. Without an adequate flow of saliva to lubricate and protect the mouth and provide essential ingredients for remineralization, exposed root surfaces are subject to rapid and severe decay.

HOW DECAY INFECTS THE NERVE AND CAUSES TOOTHACHE

Sometimes a tooth becomes sensitive to touch, to temperature changes (hot and cold), and to certain types of foods, particularly sweets. There are many causes of this sensitivity—erosion or attrition (grinding) of the enamel, exposing the underlying dentin; gum recession that exposes root surfaces; excessive gum chewing or tooth grinding, called bruxism, that irritates the dental pulp; and dental decay, which also exposes sensitive parts of the tooth.

Cavities, including very large ones, do not always cause pain, at least not until the decay reaches the nerve. As with any infection, body defenses are activated when bacteria from decay invade the pulp tissue. The blood supply to the tooth increases to provide more of the special cells that destroy bacteria. But the pulp is encased within the rigid walls of the pulp chamber and root canals. The tissue swells as the blood supply increases, exerting pressure on the nerve fibers to produce a toothache. Eventually the pulp dies, literally by strangulation within its rigid chamber. Bacteria continue to feast on this dead tissue, multiplying, invading, and destroying the bone at the tip or apex of the root, resulting in a dental abscess.

The *acute* stage of pulp infection—**pulpitis**—causes not only toothache but also pain on biting or even just closing the teeth together. The reason is that the periodontal ligament, the elastic membrane holding the root in its bony socket, is also infected. As it swells at the apex, the tooth actually extrudes slightly from its socket. The extruded tooth becomes very sensitive to biting or to light tapping, called *percussion*. A dentist will use percussion to locate and assess the extent of the infection.

Sometimes the pulp degenerates slowly without passing through an acute stage. The most common symptom of chronic pulpitis is a dull ache, frequently brought on by hot liquids such as coffee and soup. The pulp still has some live nerves, although the tissue has become gangrenous. Some bacteria produce gas, and the heat causes the gas to expand in the tight pulp chamber, putting pressure on the small nerve fibers.

It is often difficult for a patient to know exactly which tooth is hurting, especially when the pulp degeneration is not due to obvious decay. For example, the pulp might already have been infected even though the visible decay was removed and replaced with a filling. Or the dentist may have inadvertently overheated the tooth while drilling, or the drill may have nicked the nerve, causing it to degenerate after a filling was placed. The patient may show up in the dental office free of pain, reporting only an occasional ache when drinking a hot liquid. One way for the dentist to find out which tooth is at fault is to apply heat to a single tooth for a second or two. A normal tooth will respond to the heat immediately and momentarily. A chronically infected pulp will respond very differently. Even when the heat is removed, the pain will increase, slowly at first and then more rapidly and intensely until a severe toothache is experienced. The pain may be relieved quickly by swishing cold water in the mouth, cooling and contracting the gas within the tooth and thus relieving the pressure on the nerves.

Figure 3-2   Dental abscess from advanced caries.

The progress of decay:

A. *The bacteria have penetrated the enamel and attacked the softer dentin.*
B. *The bacteria have penetrated the dentin and killed the pulp (dental nerve), causing an abscess to form at the apex (tip) of the root. This condition may often be treated successfully by endodontic treatment, (root canal therapy) or the tooth may have to be removed and replaced with an artificial tooth.*

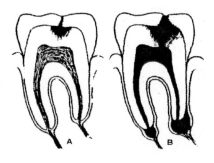

Failure to treat an infected dental nerve usually leads to breakdown of the bone around the root with the formation of an abscess or cavity filled with pus. The abscess is called acute or chronic, depending on how rapidly it forms and how effectively the body defends itself. An **acute abscess** is characterized by pain, swelling, and fever. A **chronic abscess** may be painless, with the patient completely unaware of its presence even as it continues to grow inside the jawbone. Or the area of infection may be walled off by a fibrous sac, forming a **granuloma**, which contains noninfectious (sterile) tissue but not pus.

Most of the pathological lesions at the tips of roots are granulomas, but it is common practice to refer to all such conditions as abscesses. Since granulomas are usually painless and very slow-growing, they are discovered only by means of a dental X-ray examination. Unless the whole tooth is very badly broken down or the roots have lost most of the bone support, the tooth can be saved by root canal therapy. (See chapter 11.) Failure to treat an acute abscess immediately can lead to serious infection as the pus spreads. Fever and malaise intensify when infection penetrates the bone marrow of the jaw, producing an osteomyelitis. Further extension of bacteria and pus into the throat and bloodstream can eventually cause death. Today, death rarely occurs because the pain and illness force the individual to seek treatment. Prompt antibiotic therapy and surgical intervention in more extreme cases are usually successful in limiting the abscess or osteomyelitis, although often not before extensive and permanent damage has been done.

From this brief review of the disease process, it is clear that dental caries, though not completely preventable, are controllable. The disease itself is relatively simple-a dissolution of enamel and dentin by acids produced by specific types of bacteria lodged in plaque deposits clinging to tooth surfaces. Untreated, decay progresses into the dental pulp; infection of the pulp destroys the nerve. Abscesses develop when the infection extends into the jawbone and bloodstream. If treated too late, the infection can result in death. This ubiquitous disease can be contained as long as people assume responsibility for maintaining oral hygiene and for obtaining periodic professional treatment.

4

Prevention and Treatment of Dental Caries (Decay)

THE ROLE OF FLUORIDES

Until the 1970s, 95 percent of the population experienced dental decay, beginning in childhood and continuing throughout life. Nearly one-half of children 5 to 17 years of age in the United States are now caries-free, more so in fluoridated areas than in nonfluoridated ones. According to *Oral Health in America,* the year 2000 report of the Surgeon General of the United States, about 145 million people, or 62 percent of the population served by public water supplies, consume water with optimal fluoride levels. Forty-three of the 50 largest cities are fluoridated. Yet, over one third of the population (100 million people) does not have access to community water fluoridation, most of whom live in the other seven largest unfluoridated cities.[1] This deficiency is partly compensated by the addition of fluoride to over 90 percent of the toothpastes sold in this country, with an overall 48 to 70 percent reduction in dental decay.

Important as fluorides are, other factors may be contributing to the decline in dental decay. Environmental hygiene has been improving, and better nutrition has built healthier bodies with more resistance to acute diseases.[2] Thus, many factors-improved sanitation and nutrition, vaccines, antibiotics-result in fewer people dying in childhood, adolescence, and young adulthood. With increased life expectancy, however, we also suffer more from chronic diseases and the breakdown of tissues and organs with aging.

So it is with dental health. Whether it is because the organisms causing dental diseases have changed or because our resistance through fluoridation and better oral hygiene has increased, fewer teeth are lost in early age from dental decay. But since we keep our teeth longer, we suffer more from chronic dental problems, including not only periodontal disease but also a different type of decay that occurs later in life-root caries.

SAFETY OF FLUORIDATION

There are no health hazards to the normal population in either naturally or artificially fluoridated public water supplies.[3] The issue has been researched extensively for over half a century. The only negative effect occurs if community supplies exceed two to three parts per million (ppm) of fluoride to water. If this concentration is ingested during the teeth's formative years, a slight mottling or minor discoloration of the enamel occurs. As the concentration increases, the severity of mottling increases and becomes more unsightly, but it is otherwise harmless. Since approximately one ppm of fluoride is all that is necessary to reduce cavities, public water supplies are adjusted to try to maintain that level. In practice, the concentration may vary from .7 to 1.5 ppm, depending on climate. Where natural fluoride concentrations are excessive, about 4 ppm and sometimes registering as high as 7 or 8 ppm, the concentration is reduced to levels that will avoid mottling.

The cost of fluoridating public water is extremely small, about 68 cents per person per year in most large communities. Since many other chemicals are added to water in treatment plants to make it safe for drinking and cooking, the mechanism can be adapted easily for the addition of fluorides.

DIETARY FLUORIDES FOR INFANTS AND CHILDREN

Dietary fluoride supplementation is not as effective as daily topical application through water and toothpastes.[4] Nonetheless, dietary fluorides are still recommended by the dental profession in areas that lack optimally fluoridated water supplies.[5] The reason children should ingest fluorides from 6 months to 16 years of age is to make the enamel more resistant to dental decay as the crowns are being formed. Pediatricians should prescribe vitamins containing fluorides for infants living in communities with less than the optimal level in the public water supply. The dosage, measured in milligrams (mg), varies according to the child's age and the amount of fluoride present in drinking water. In infants and young children, fluorides should be in liquid form, as in liquid vitamin supplements, or as drops on the tongue or in food. Older children can use chewable tablets that provide a topical as well as systemic effect. The following table provides the recommended daily dietary supplement.

SUPPLEMENTAL DAILY FLUORIDE DOSAGE SCHEDULE*

Fluoride Concentration in Water Supply	Recommended Daily Dietary Fluoride Supplement			
	Birth To 6 Months	6 Months to 3 years	Ages 3-6	Ages 6-16
Less than 0.3 ppm†	0	0.25 mg‡	0.50 mg	1.00 mg
0.3 to 0.6 ppm	0	0	0.25 mg	0.50 mg
More than 0.6 ppm	0	0	0	0

* American Dental Association, 1995.[5]
† ppm: parts per million
‡ mg: milligrams - 2.2 mg sodium fluoride = 1 mg fluoride ion

Fluoride Toothpaste

Daily brushing with a fluoride toothpaste reduces smooth surface decay by as much as 30 percent.[6] While studies of fluoride toothpaste have been done mostly on children, there is accumulating evidence that adults also benefit. Most commercial toothpastes now contain fluoride; therefore, your choice comes down to a matter of taste. Toothpastes approved by the American Dental Association are recommended to ensure quality control.

Children should be taught to spit out the toothpaste after brushing to avoid swallowing the fluoride, which could cause minor mottling of the enamel of the permanent teeth. However, it is likely that very young children swallow most, if not all, of the toothpaste.[7] Therefore, no more than a "pea-sized" amount of toothpaste should be placed on the brush. Further, do not buy fruit flavored toothpastes that a child might like to swallow.

More concentrated fluoride toothpastes and gels that reduce hypersensitivity to hot and cold temperature changes are also available. They are recommended for adults following periodontal treatment that often leaves teeth sensitive along the gum line.

SELF-APPLIED FLUORIDE MOUTH RINSES AND GELS

Mouth rinses containing safe concentrations of fluorides are available over the counter for those individuals experiencing a high rate of decay. Rinses are not recommended for very young children because they cannot avoid swallowing. Older children should be closely supervised to prevent swallowing of the solution. Higher concentration fluoride rinses and gels to reduce thermal sensitivity and inhibit root caries can be obtained on prescription from a dentist. The dentist may also construct form-fitted plastic trays for use at home to hold the gel against the teeth for maximum effectiveness.

Many dentists are unaware that the most common topical fluoride—acidulated phosphate fluoride (APF)—can damage some sealants, composite fillings, and porcelain crowns and veneers.[8] An APF topical fluoride contains a dilute phosphoric acid that combines with sodium fluoride to form hydrofluoric acid. Hydrofluoric acid, used for etching or dissolving glass, is powerful stuff. Most composite sealants and fillings contain a glass filler to increase hardness and durability, and, of course, porcelain is a form of glass. Frequent use of APF can damage or etch these restorations; therefore, a nonacidulated sodium fluoride should be used for topical application and rinses when porcelain restorations or glass-filled composites are present. (As an alternative, see the following discussion of fluoride varnish.)

Some city and state health departments have instituted "brush-ins" and fluoride rinse programs in grammar schools.[9] Supervised by dental hygienists and teachers who have received special instruction, the students are taught oral hygiene, including brushing and flossing. Then, *en masse*, they are given small amounts of concentrated fluoride to swish inside the mouth for one minute and then spit back into paper cups. Weekly classroom fluoride rinsing is more effective and much less expensive than occasional dental office topical fluoride treatment. It is far more efficient not only for the individual but for the population as a whole because it reaches all of the kids, rich and poor alike.

ANTIMICROBIAL RINSES

If you are developing a large number of cavities on a continual basis, you are probably harboring a high number of mutans streptococci and lactobacilli bacteria, which are believed to be the main cause of dental decay. While it is impossible to eliminate these bacteria completely, it is possible to reduce their numbers and thus the number of new cavities.

Chlorhexidine rinse or gel, available by prescription, is the most effective antimocrobial agent. A daily rinse with chlorhexidine for two weeks will greatly reduce these caries-producing bacteria. Recolonization of the bacteria takes place within three to six months, so that it is then necessary to repeat the chlorexidine rinse for another two weeks every three months.[10]

Chlorhexidine-fluoride rinses are particularly effective in preventing or reducing root caries in individuals who have had radiation therapy for head and neck cancer.[11]

Chlorhexidine rinse may be used alone or in combination with a fluoride. The down side is that chlorhexidine can also stain teeth. However, the stain can be removed easily by a professional cleaning.

In the future it may be possible to accurately assess one's risk of dental caries by laboratory analysis of the saliva. Current methods of testing saliva have yet to be proven sufficiently accurate to justify the cost.

PROFESSIONALLY APPLIED TOPICAL FLUORIDE TREATMENT—GELS AND VARNISH

Topical application of concentrated fluoride solutions has been a dental office procedure, mainly for children, since the mid-1940s. It is the most expensive method of adding fluoride to the enamel surface because it requires individual application by a dental hygienist, a dental assistant, or a dentist. Before self-applied fluorides were made widely available, especially in toothpastes, one had no other choice, since it was believed that the teeth had to be professionally cleaned for the fluoride solution to be effective. Studies have shown that cleaning the teeth (prophylaxis) is not necessary prior to topical fluoride application in the dental office, but it is hard for dentists to discard old habits, particularly when there is an extra fee to be gained.

In the United States, most topical fluoride treatment consists of a gel applied to teeth in a preformed tray. For over 25 years, Canadian, European and Scandinavian dentists have used **fluoride varnish.** The entire procedure takes only a minute and the material cost of the varnish is about 75 cents to $1.50 per application. Fluoride varnishes were introduced in the United States in 1994 but are not yet in widespread use. The advantage of fluoride varnish over fluoride gel is that application is quicker, possibly more effective, and none of the material is swallowed by the child.[12] The teeth are wiped dry with a cotton gauze or blown dry with compressed air, followed immediately by application of the varnish with a brush or pellet of cotton. Unless the teeth are coated with crud, a prophylaxis is not necessary. Because it takes less time, does not require a special tray, and can be done by a dental assistant, the fee charged by the dentist should be less. For best results, this should be done twice a year.

Since infants are seen by pediatricians on a more or less routine basis during the early years of life, simple logististics would have the pediatrician examine the baby's teeth visually. As noted previously, if white, brown or black spots are seen, the child should be referred to a dentist. But pediatric dental supervision should not stop there. The pediatric nurse or assistant can be taught easily how to apply fluoride varnish to the baby's teeth. This should become as routine a part of pediatric care as immunization.

31

Topical fluorides are particularly valuable for children, as well as for adults, who are experiencing dental caries. It has minimal value for caries-free children, particularly in communities with fluoridated water and for families using dietary fluoride supplements, fluoride toothpastes and dilute daily fluoride rinses.

DIET AND DENTAL DECAY

Controlling one's diet as a means of preventing tooth decay has already been discussed in chapter 1. Nonetheless, it warrants repeating that restricting the amount of highly refined carbohydrate foods saturated with sugars that feed bacterial plaque is good for both your dental and your general health. While chewing detergent foods such as fresh fruits and vegetables does not remove plaque, it helps to reduce its formation, as does limiting the frequency of snacking.

PIT AND FISSURE SEALANTS

Deep pits and fissures (grooves) on the occlusal and side surfaces of teeth develop cavities even in fluoridated areas. In fact, 90 percent of the cavities found in school children occurs in these pits and fissures.[13] Although application of composite (plastic) sealants is a treatment procedure, the purpose is to prevent or arrest dental decay in these areas.[14] Not all pits and fissures need to be sealed but only those in which there is a visible defect. Because molars are most likely to develop cavities, many dentists recommend sealing the occlusal or chewing surface whether or not defective; however, this creates an additional expense that may not be necessary. As a general rule, bicuspids do not require sealants as their occlusal pits and fissures are usually well formed.

If pits and fissures have not developed into cavities by the late teens and early twenties, they are very unlikely to decay in the future. That is why sealants are recommended only during the first few years after the eruption of teeth. Since all the permanent teeth except third molars (wisdom teeth) have erupted by age 14 or 15, sealants for these teeth have no value after age 18. Wisdom teeth erupt between ages 16 and 25, sometimes later. They will also benefit from sealants if their pits and fissures are defective.

The procedure is simple, safe, and completely painless. It requires no drilling and no needles for anesthesia. The teeth to be sealed are surrounded by cotton rolls and dried thoroughly. A dilute acid liquid or gel is applied for 60 seconds to the enamel, etching it to a depth of only a few microns. (A micron is a thousandth of a millimeter.) The enamel is not harmed by the acid. A good etch produces a surface that looks dull white to the eye although it still feels smooth to touch. Under an electron microscope the surface is revealed to be incredibly jagged and irregular. A liquid plastic is placed over the etched surface. It seeps into all the jagged peaks and valleys and thus becomes mechanically attached to the enamel when it hardens. Some sealants harden by themselves in less than a minute. Others are hardened in 10 to 20 seconds by a high-intensity fiber-optic ultraviolet light. If the groove is overfilled, normal chewing and biting wears off the excess material quickly.

The seal is so effective that bacteria cannot enter the tooth. Bacteria that have already penetrated through a tiny hole in the fissure will be sealed in and denied the nutrients of the oral fluids, and decay will stop. Although 20 to 30 percent of sealants may be lost after five years, possibly due to poor initial placement, the overall reduction of pit and fissure caries is 70 percent.[15] The only time new sealant needs to be applied is when the groove appears defective at subsequent dental examinations.

More and more dentists are now recommending sealants even over minute cavities. But many dentists who are used to conventional fillings find it difficult to change. Also, there are the charlatans who fill teeth that should be sealed, or even left alone, because fillings pay more—-much more.

From a consumer viewpoint, sealants are-or at least should be-a good buy. Since they can be applied by a dental hygienist or a well-trained assistant, they are less costly than a filling that must be put in by a dentist. Also, it does not take much more time to seal two or four teeth than to seal one. An experienced person can seal all molars (four to eight teeth, depending on the child's age) in 15 or 20 minutes. The cost for sealing a single tooth ranges from $15 to $45. While the cost is low compared to fillings, it rises quickly when many teeth are done at the same time. Since most dentists are realistic about fees, they may charge a **quadrant** fee for sealing multiple adjacent teeth in each side of the jaw. A quadrant charge might range from $30 to $60; at the higher rate about the cost of an occlusal amalgam filling. Sealing all eight first and second molars should cost between $100-150, assuming a further discount for all four quadrants at one visit. But you will not get a reduced fee unless you negotiate for it.

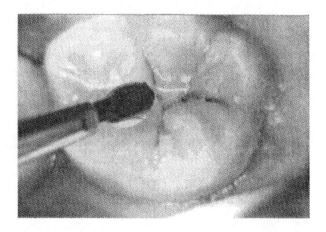

Figure 4-1 Placement of sealant in the defective occlusal groove of a lower molar. After the enamel is etched, a small brush places a drop of sealant into the groove, preventing future decay. The sealant hardens in a minute or less, or may be accelerated by an ultraviolet light.

SCHOOL-BASED CARIES PREVENTIVE PROGRAMS

The ideal place to apply topical fluoride gels or varnishes and sealants is in schools. Public health dentists and hygienists have mobile offices or trailers that can be brought to school grounds or portable equipment that can be set up in an empty classroom or part of a gymnasium. A number of states have demonstrated successful school-based sealant programs in conjunction with topical fluoride programs, all at a fraction of the cost of private dental offices. It is not just a matter of saving money that makes these school-based dental preventive programs so attractive. It is also the only way all the children can be reached. Without school-based programs, less than 25 percent of children in low income areas are likely to see a dentist in any year, and then as often for an extraction as for a preventive service. Fluoridation of community water supplies reaches all children. To match that record for topical flourides and sealants will require school-based programs.

Further, fillings should also be provided in schools if all children are to receive adequate dental care, and not necessarily by dentists. It does not require four years of dental school to learn how to fill a tooth. Over 80 years ago New Zealand pioneered in the two-year training of dental nurses to provide routine prophylaxis, fluoride treatment, and fillings in small clinics located in grammar schools. They eventually cared for over 95 percent of the children and virtually eliminated tooth loss. The New Zealand School Dental Nurse Service established the model for children's dental care that has been adopted in many countries.[16, 17] That the United States has yet to adopt such a system is evidence of the power of the dental profession to prevent development of auxiliaries—similar to nurse practitioners in medicine—that would not only serve the public better but would also allow dentists to expand their own skills.

Remineralization — When Nontreatment Is the Best Treatment

Many incipient or pre-carious lesions are demineralized zones of enamel that have not developed into true cavities. Conservative dentists take note of such areas and then reexamine them a year or two later with subsequent checkup X-rays. If no further change has occurred, treatment is unnecessary even if the area is still observable.

Examination of extracted teeth under a microscope reveals many decalcification zones that are undetectable even in X-rays. Further research has shown that the enamel undergoes constant demineralization and remineralization.[18,19] Saliva contains minerals that have the ability, within limits, to repair these incipient carious lesions. Even early root caries in elderly patients may remineralize and cease to develop further.[20] Because the fluoride ion enhances remineralization, anyone with these early warning signs of cavity formation is well advised to brush daily with fluoride toothpastes and to use a weekly fluoride mouth rinse. Highly susceptible persons should also have fluoride varnish applied every six months to roots exposed by gum recession. The sad fact is that many dentists prescribe an antibiotic-needed or not-at the slightest hint of a gum infection but fail to prescribe fluoride rinses and varnishes that could remineralize incipient carious lesions.

If demineralization proceeds more rapidly than the enamel or root surface can be remineralized and the process extends clearly into the dentin, then it is irreversible. At this stage, the decay almost always must be removed by a dentist before it progresses into the pulp and destroys the tooth. The exception is called **arrested caries**. Some carious lesions, especially in adults, penetrate the enamel and enter the dentin a short distance, and then stop. If periodic checkup X-rays show no further advance, it is not necessary to fill these areas. Your old family dentist may be watching such areas for years, knowing there is no further development. However, if you change dentists, you are at increased risk of getting unnecessary fillings. Every *arrested caries* looks like a new cavity to your new dentist. If you change dentists, the best way to avoid FUN fillings is to take copies of your old X-rays, particularly the bitewing films, for your new dentist to review and compare with his current bitewing films.

There is no great mystery or difficulty in diagnosing caries, although dentists differ as to when to fill or simply "watch" a small cavity. The older and more experienced dentists often watch cavities that younger dentists insist on filling. The most accurate radiograph for the molars and bicuspids is the posterior **bitewing** film that depicts both upper and lower teeth simultaneously. The anterior periapical film that shows the whole tooth is used for diagnosis of the incisors. The X-ray film shows the shell of enamel, the dentin comprising the main body of the tooth, and the pulp chamber in the center of the crown and root. An early **interproximal** cavity-a cavity on the **mesial** (front) or **distal** (back) surfaces-will appear in the film as a thin, dark line partway or all the way through the enamel. When the X-ray shows significant penetration through the enamel into the dentin, there is justification for placement of a filling (Figure 4-2).

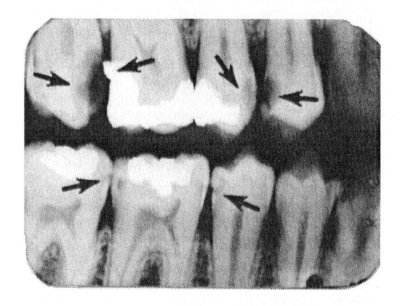

Figure 4-2   Interproximal caries.

Bitewing x-ray showing interproximal caries ranging from early to medium decay in the lower teeth to advanced caries in the upper teeth, with decay penetrating to the nerve in the upper left second molar. Note the "overhang" on the distal of the filling in the upper first molar, which should be removed or the filling replaced. Because this patient is "high risk" for dental decay, even the smaller cavities should be filled.

It takes 1½ to 2 years for a cavity to penetrate the interproximal enamel into dentin. It therefore bears repeating that it is not necessary to have teeth filled that show a thin line of decalcification in the X-rays. Even in adults, as discussed above in regard to arrested caries, areas of small penetration into the dentin can also be "watched" or re-examined in 12 to 18 months on checkup X-rays. If no difference is observed from the last to the current X-rays, no treatment is necessary. If the line has disappeared, remineralization has completely resolved the problem.

REMINERALIZATION OF DEEP CAVITIES

Removal of deep decay in a large cavity risks **pulp exposure**. Sometimes a **pulp cap**—a special cement material—can be placed over the exposed nerve before proceeding with a filling or crown restoration. Pulp caps are more likely to work in baby teeth, which have to last only a few years more. They are not so successful in the permanent teeth. When the nerve degenerates under a pulp cap, a root canal filling is required to save the tooth. Still, be wary of the dentist who wants to perform root canal therapy on every tooth with a deep cavity.

An alternative approach to risking pulp exposure is to remove the gross, soft decay and then to place a therapeutic cement filling over the remaining decay for at least three months. At the end of this period, the temporary filling is removed along with any remaining soft decay. If remineralization is successful, decay will have stopped, the infected dentin will have been sterilized and hardened, and the nerve will remain vital and healthy. The tooth can then receive its final restoration, either a filling or a crown, depending on the size of the cavity.

The problem with remineralization treatment is that it takes patient dentists as well as cooperative patients. Dentists like to get things done immediately, which is the way we are trained. Moreover, many patients simply do not return for follow-up treatment. Sometimes patients think the short-term temporary filling completes the treatment, at least until it falls out. Their funds may be low, or they may simply forget. Of course, the dental office should follow up with reminders to complete treatment, but even with persistent reminders the patient may not return for a year or more instead of in three months. At that time an extraction might be the only recourse because the temporary filling has fallen out and further decay has damaged the tooth beyond salvation.

Anticipating these problems, some dentists decide it is not worth the risk to attempt remineralization when root canal therapy can be done at once, a porcelain crown made to cover the tooth, and the patient sent away with the tooth saved. There is also an economic incentive for the dentist to go directly to root canal therapy. The dentist makes much less money remineralizing teeth. But you have your own economic incentive, and if you have a very deep cavity but there has been no toothache, you should discuss remineralization with your dentist as an alternative to root canal therapy. In year 2002 dollars, the cost of remineralization should be about $75, compared to root canal therapy at $200 to $950, depending on the number of roots.

TO DRILL OR NOT TO DRILL

Dental decay and large fractures of teeth usually require restorations (fillings, onlays, crowns) to prevent further deterioration, restore function, eliminate sensitivities, and maintain a satisfactory appearance. As already noted, incipient caries that have not penetrated the enamel and arrested caries do not require treatment. Small fractures of the tips of teeth can be smoothed for acceptable function and appearance.[21]

When a baby tooth is likely to exfoliate (fall out) before decay causes trouble, it does not have to be filled. To evaluate the need for filling baby teeth, you need to know how long they last and when they are usually replaced by permanent teeth. (See chapter 2, Fig.2-2.)

The first baby molars begin to loosen around 8 or 9 and the second baby molars around 9 or 10 years of age. It is important that these teeth, especially the second baby molars, not be lost prematurely, in order to maintain space for the permanent bicuspid teeth growing underneath that replace them. Small cavities in the first baby molars that are detected around age 8 or 9 do not require filling since these teeth will exfoliate before the decay infects the pulp. Likewise, a cavity in the second baby molar at age 9 or 10 does not usually require restoration. At the ages specified, there should be evidence in the X-ray films that the roots are starting to dissolve as the developing bicuspids erupt. If, as sometimes happens, the permanent tooth is missing, the roots of the baby molar will resorb very slowly over a much longer period of time, often lasting until age 35 and older. In the absence of a permanent tooth to replace it, the deciduous tooth is treated as the permanent tooth it has become.

The same principle of nontreatment applies to cavities in the baby incisors that begin to fall out around age five. Premature loss of deciduous incisors does not affect proper development and eruption of the permanent teeth. Thus, by age four, one can safely ignore small cavities in baby incisors. By age five, even large cavities can be left alone. In the unlikelihood that trouble occurs, these teeth can be removed easily instead of filled, usually at much less cost.

Some dentists argue that all dental decay must be treated to prevent spreading of the "infection" to other teeth, ignoring the fact that bacteria that cause dental decay are always present in the mouth. Removing decay in one area does not prevent, or even make less likely, its occurrence elsewhere. On the other hand, there is evidence, as mentioned previously in the discussion of mouth rinses, that periodic rinsing with the antibacterial chlorhexidine significantly reduces the caries producing bacteria and should be prescribed for those high risk adolescents and adults who never seem to stop developing cavities.

Assuming a tooth must be drilled to fill, the introduction of laser devices has been offered as an alternative to the conventional drill. Laser "drills" are quieter, vibration-free, and generally less painful but they are also limited to simple fillings at your greater expense. Although the whine of the conventional air turbine high speed drill is annoying to some patients, these drills produce minimal vibrations and pain is usually eliminated entirely by a local anesthetic injection. Thus, there is as yet little reason to pay extra for a laser in dentistry.

SPACE MAINTENANCE

If a second baby molar is lost prematurely because of extensive decay and abscessing, the adjacent teeth are likely to "drift" into the space so that the permanent tooth growing underneath will not have room to erupt properly. The unerupted tooth may be totally blocked and remain impacted for life, or it may force its way out sideways. But not always! It depends on how far along the total dentition has developed. Dentists rely on X-rays to determine whether or not a **space maintainer** (spacer) should be placed in the child's mouth. If the bitewing X-ray shows the tip of the underlying permanent bicuspid tooth near the upper level of bone, then it will soon erupt and a spacer is not necessary. If the tip is still covered by bone, space closure is likely to occur and a space maintainer should be placed. When a first baby molar is lost but the child has the first permanent and second baby molars in position, a spacer usually is not necessary since the two back molars will stay in place. But if a second baby molar is lost prematurely, the six-year or first permanent molar will almost always drift forward. That is why it is extremely important always to replace a prematurely lost second deciduous molar with a space maintainer. If space has already been lost, a **space regainer** is necessary; it is similar to a space maintainer but with springs to push the molar back into its correct position.

Space maintainers are not necessary when baby incisors are lost early since there is rarely any space loss. Some dentists recommend spacers for the front teeth, claiming that speech impediments and harmful swallowing habits due to tongue thrusting into the open space will develop. However, all children go through a natural period of tooth loss as baby incisors exfoliate, and there is no evidence that this period results in permanent speech defects or other harmful habits.

When a spacer is needed, a fixed appliance is preferable to a removable one. A **fixed spacer** consists of one or two stainless steel bands or crowns cemented onto the teeth to hold a wire loop or a connecting bar that prevents movement of the teeth into the space. When the permanent tooth erupts into the space, the spacer is easily removed by the dentist. Sometimes a plastic **removable spacer** is used that resembles a little partial denture. The problem with a removable spacer is that it is removable. Many children refuse to wear them all the time, and they are frequently broken and lost, followed by loss of the space they were intended to maintain.

TYPES OF FILLINGS

Having been advised against unnecessary fillings, the reader should nevertheless understand that dental fillings are among the most effective and least expensive methods of preventing tooth loss from decay. Most fillings will last at least five or eight years; many last a lifetime. When fillings fall out within a short time, faulty placement by the dentist is frequently the cause.

The size of a cavity determines whether a tooth can be filled. In the past, and still at present, large fillings may be secured by small pins that are cemented into sound tooth structure for additional retention. Acid-etch bonding has replaced the need for pins in anterior composite fillings and is so routine that there should not be an extra charge for the bonding. More recently, expensive bonding "cements" have come into use that allow the amalgam to be attached (bonded) to the acid-etched surfaces of dentin, in addition to the enamel. Dentists charge extra for bonding amalgam fillings but there is no evidence that it significantly improves retention. Bonding of amalgam is not worth the extra charge.[22]

If the cavity extends over the cusps of the tooth, a cast gold onlay or crown is the best way to restore the tooth. However, "gold" shows and patients may be talked into hi-tech and very expensive porcelain onlays that, while prettier, can still fracture and need replacement.

The advantages of a filling over an onlay or crown are less trauma to the tooth, lower cost, and convenience. A filling preserves more of the natural tooth, lowering the risk of injury to the nerve. A filling is a fraction of the cost of an onlay or crown and can be done in one visit. An onlay or crown requires an interim laboratory step for fabrication so that at least two visits are required to complete the restoration. In addition to taking more time and visits, a laboratory charge of $35 to $100 must be figured into the fee.

Amalgam Fillings

Silver amalgam is still the best filling material for the chewing surfaces of posterior teeth and lingual (tongue) surfaces of any tooth.[23, 24] Unfortunately, opposition to amalgam is on the rise, spurred by a level of hysteria that matches the antifluoridationists. Many of the extremists who oppose fluorides, despite all the evidence of its safety, are leading the fight against amalgam. They ignore all the studies over the last fifty years that have documented the safety of amalgam as a filling material. They ignore the continual endorsement of amalgam as a filling material by the American Dental Association, state dental associations and all recognized scientific and public health organizations, including the U.S. Department of Health and Human Services' National Institute of Dental and Craniofacial Research.

Amalgam is an alloy composed of four basic metals: silver, copper, tin, and zinc, with two-thirds of the alloy silver. When combined with mercury, the alloy sets into a strong metallic filling that is strong enough for chewing in a few hours. The strength of amalgam depends on its bulk. The filling must be large enough to withstand the 150 to 200 pounds of pressure per square inch that is exerted on it during chewing. If fillings fracture or come loose frequently, it is usually because of poor technique, and you would be wise to find another dentist. Remember, though, any amalgam filling that extends over the chewing surfaces and along the sides of the tooth is subject to fracture. Don't blame your dentist unless the fillings fail repeatedly.

The fact that amalgam requires bulk to avoid fracturing does not mean that every amalgam filling should be large. Quite the contrary, the cavity preparation should match the decay. If the decay is small, then a small cavity preparation is appropriate and the filling should not take up half the tooth. However, if the decay is large, then a large amalgam filling is unavoidable.

Composite Fillings

Anterior (front) teeth are usually filled with a composite plastic material that matches natural tooth color and translucency. Composites are the basis for esthetic dentistry because the material can be used to restore small fractures and to bond plastic and porcelain veneers that completely change the shape and color of teeth. Composites are an excellent filling material for the front teeth and for visible gum line fillings. If the gum line cavity is not visible, amalgam makes a more durable filling.

Many dentists are now placing composites in posterior teeth for both occlusal and interproximal fillings in response to patients' demands for fillings that look just like the natural tooth. Or, your dentist may suggest that all old fillings be replaced, not only to improve appearance but to eliminate the mercury in amalgam. Unless an amalgam filling is truly visible to others when you talk or smile, it makes no sense to replace it with a composite. Mercury in amalgam fillings is completely harmless and it is unethical for a dentist to use scare tactics to entice patients into paying for more expensive composites. It is strongly recommended that a patient reject such a suggestion and consult another dentist. Moreover, responsible dentists should make clear to their patients that composites in posterior teeth do not last as long as amalgam because they wear away quickly and must be resurfaced or replaced every few years.[25] The 5-year failure rate in one study was over 27 percent.[26]

Composites in posterior teeth are inferior to amalgam fillings in every respect except esthetics. They are more difficult to do and take more time, which is why they are more costly. Unlike amalgam, composite material cannot be placed into the cavity with pressure, and adaptation to the side or proximal surfaces of the tooth is often faulty. The material must be cured layer by layer, usually by an ultraviolet light. Thus, it is much more *technique sensitive*, which means more care and attention to details must be applied by the dentist. In addition, while amalgam appears white in the X-ray and contrasts sharply with the tooth image, composite material is more radiolucent, appearing gray or dark just like a cavity. Therefore, recurrent decay around the margin of a composite filling cannot be seen in an X-ray film. This is not a problem with anterior and gum line fillings that are visible to the dentist and hygienist and can be probed easily for detection of defects. The best and safest choice for filling a posterior tooth remains silver amalgam.

Intermediate Temporary Fillings

What if you have many *large* cavities and cannot afford permanent fillings in all the teeth at the same time? To prevent further decay, nerve infection, and loss of teeth, all the decay should be removed and temporary fillings placed. A temporary filling material called IRM (Intermediate Restorative Material) combines a resin with a sedative material, zinc oxide and eugenol, which you may have experienced already as a white paste filling with the pungent but not unpleasant taste of oil of cloves. Once set, it can last up to two years, which is one of the reasons it is also used to stimulate remineralization. Individual teeth can then be restored a few at a time with more permanent fillings, spreading the cost over a more affordable time period.

Where cost is a limiting factor, IRM can also be used for large cavities in baby teeth. Since these teeth exfoliate, it may never be necessary to have a more durable and expensive amalgam filling.

An alternative technique called ART—Atraumatic Restorative Treatment—was developed for use in underdeveloped countries, particularly in areas lacking dental facilities and, often electricity or compressed air to power the dental drill.[27] The enamel around the cavity in the tooth is chipped away with small chisels. The soft decay is then removed with spoon-shaped curettes and the enlarged cavity is filled with a glass ionomer filling material. The procedure is virtually painless. For many teeth, particularly baby teeth, the glass ionomer lasts for many years. Though designed for poor countries, there is no reason why ART could not be used in underfinanced public health facilities and school-based services in areas where our own domestic Third World populations are otherwise denied dental treatment.

Gold Inlays and Onlays

Traditionally, an inlay is a solid casting that is cemented into the tooth. Because inlays are used primarily on chewing surfaces, the material must be harder than pure gold. Small amounts of harder metals are alloyed with gold to make inlays, onlays, and three-quarter and full gold crowns. Jewelers understand this limitation of gold. Rings made of pure gold (24K) would easily bend out of shape. Inlays and crowns, like jewelry, are made in 12K to 16K gold.

An inlay fits into a box-shaped cavity within the tooth. An onlay is the same as an inlay except that it extends over the entire chewing surface and the cusps or peaks of the tooth, providing greater protection against biting pressure and possible fracture. Since a cast restoration is necessary only in a tooth that has an extremely large cavity or where the cusps are already chipped or fractured, an onlay is preferred over an inlay. However, an inlay, which is smaller than an onlay and the same basic size as an amalgam filling, is an excellent restoration when properly done, as long as the patient is willing to pay the additional cost. Inlays and onlays require two dental appointments, the first to prepare the tooth and take the impressions and the second to fit and cement the casting. Most castings are done by a laboratory technician who may be employed by the dentist but most often works in an independent laboratory.

The key to a successful casting is the accuracy of the dentist's impression and the careful handling by the technician of the models of the teeth. A poor-fitting inlay or onlay is a greater hazard than a less-than-ideal amalgam filling. In the case of amalgam, the material is pushed into the box preparation and pressed against the tooth and the stainless steel retaining band. Since the amalgam is still pliable at this stage, it will squeeze under pressure into irregularities and seal the tooth. Not so with a solid casting. If it is short of the margin, a hole will develop within a few years as the exposed cement dissolves. In other words, you will have a cavity at the edge of the inlay. If the cavity is not detected and corrected by another restoration, rapid decay, possible destruction of the nerve, and loss of the tooth will result.

Sometimes patients are told to have old amalgam fillings replaced with gold restorations. While it is true that a really good inlay or onlay will last decades, so will many amalgam fillings. The amalgam may not look as pretty, but who else besides the dentist and the hygienist looks that closely at the back teeth? A patient may also be told that the tooth should have an onlay or crown because its enamel cusps or peaks have been undermined by decay or large fillings. While in theory this may be a valid reason for using a cast restoration rather than an amalgam filling, it is widely abused in practice. Administrators of dental insurance plans have observed dentists diagnosing "undermined enamel" to justify the more expensive inlays and crowns while doing amalgam and composite fillings for the same condition when the patient has to pay out-of-pocket.

How can you decide if your dentist is not what may politely be called "overutilizing" the insurance benefit? If you are told that a few teeth need amalgam fillings but one in particular would best be done in gold, then the dentist is being selective and exercising experienced judgment. If you are told all your amalgam fillings should be redone in gold or composite, get a second opinion from another dentist. If this is your first visit to the dental office, you might not tell the receptionist or dentist that you have dental insurance until after the examination and treatment plan have been completed. You would be surprised at how often the factor of insurance is decisive in determining dental as well as medical diagnosis and treatment.

Porcelain Inlays/Onlays

Advances in technology and bonding allow construction of inlays and onlays in porcelain that are quite strong and closely match the natural color of the tooth.[28] Like composites, porcelain is virtually invisible as a filling. No matter how strong the newer porcelains, however, they cannot match the durability of a metal restoration. It makes little sense to consider these expensive tooth colored restorations unless another kind of restoration would be visible and unesthetic to others when you talk or smile.

Gold and Porcelain-metal Crowns

When enamel is damaged by decay or fractured beyond the point that it can be restored successfully with a filling or onlay, a crown or cap must be placed, not unlike a thimble over your finger (See chapter 10, Fig. 2.) If the crown is for a posterior tooth that is not ordinarily visible, such as a lower first molar or any second molar, a solid precious (high noble) or semiprecious (noble) gold alloy casting is the best choice.

The trend today is for dentists to put full crowns on any tooth with a large filling or fractured cusp even where the visible face of the tooth, the facial or buccal surface, can be preserved by a three-quarter gold crown or an onlay. Onlays and three-quarter gold crowns require more skill than a full crown. Although only a small edge of gold might be visible, and then only on close inspection, patients are quick to accept porcelain-metal crowns even on back molars.

Porcelain-fused-to-metal crowns were introduced in the late 1940s, replacing pure porcelain crowns, which were quite beautiful but also very fragile. They have dominated esthetic dentistry until recently challenged by the newer materials such as composites and all-ceramic crowns. The porcelain is fused to a thin metal thimble at a very high temperature, making it strong enough to withstand chewing pressure although never as strong as an unbreakable full gold crown. But the hardness and abrasiveness of porcelain can rapidly wear away enamel on the opposing tooth. Fracture of the porcelain and abrasion can be prevented by designing these crowns with metal on the chewing surface. The trouble is that many people do not want any metal to show even if others would have to peer into the mouth with a flashlight and a dental mirror to see it.

Risk of Metal Allergy

Approximately 75 percent of porcelain-metal crowns are based on non-precious metal cores containing 70 to 80 percent nickel. Too many dentists are unaware that 10 percent of women and 1 percent of men are allergic to nickel and that these crowns can cause severe gingival inflammation and periodontal bone loss around the teeth of nickel-sensitive persons.[29, 30] This risk is easily avoided by using noble semiprecious metal (60 to 80 percent palladium) or high noble precious metal (50 to 80 percent gold) alloys containing no nickel.

Nonprecious metals are very inexpensive, adding little to the cost of fabricating a porcelain metal or full metal crown. Until recently, semiprecious metal was also relatively inexpensive but now the price matches that of gold. Crowns constructed of these metals can cost $30 to $75 more but they are superior to nonprecious metal crowns simply because there is less risk of metal sensitivity. The dentist should always discuss the advantages and disadvantages of the different materials and allow the patient the choice of paying the additional cost. Anyone who has experienced hypersensitivity to metals used in jewelry should avoid nonprecious crowns regardless of cost.

Ceramic (Porcelain) Crowns

An all-ceramic crown may be even more lifelike than porcelain-metal crowns. While more durable than porcelain crowns of the past, ceramic crowns are not as strong as porcelain fused to metal. Porcelain-metal crowns can be quite pleasing in appearance, and they are of proven durability, particularly on anterior teeth, some in the author's experience lasting over thirty years. The all-ceramic crown is a reasonable alternative for special esthetic problems on the upper front teeth but should be avoided on lower front teeth, as well as posterior teeth, where there is a greater chance of fracture.

Risk of Crowns

As in all castings, the secret of crown success is proper tooth preparation and an accurate impression. With modern high-speed dental drills, preparation of the tooth is easy but so is the possibility for abuse. A crown must fit over the tooth. All the bulges and irregularities of the natural tooth must be reduced with the drill. Too much reduction damages the nerve, causing degeneration and abscessing. Or the tooth may be tapered so much that the crown falls off after only a few months or years. The dimensions of a tooth are small, and a drilling error of a millimeter or less can destroy a nerve.

How to recognize a poor crown. A patient cannot tell if the dentist's impression of the tooth preparation is accurate. Inaccuracy usually results in a space between the edge of the finished crown and the surface of the tooth beneath the gum, inviting recurrent decay. But there are symptoms of poor crowns that can be recognized. For example, the casting may be short of the intended margin on the tooth, resulting in an area that is sensitive to touch, sweets, and hot and cold temperatures. The crown may be bulky and stick out into the gum tissue, trapping plaque and causing irritation, inflammation, and bleeding gums. Or there may be a space between the cast crown and the adjacent teeth, resulting in food impaction, annoyance, irritation of the gum tissue, and periodontal breakdown. All these problems can be avoided by a return to the dentist who should remake the improperly fitting crown at no additional charge.

Remakes do not make money, however, and all too often dentists ignore defective crowns. Patients are told the sensitivity will disappear, or years may pass before the defect causes trouble, at which time the patient can be blamed for poor oral hygiene. A good rule of thumb is that if a crown or an onlay comes loose or is sensitive to touch or an open margin or "decay" is detected along the edges within a few years of placement, more than likely the fault lies with the dentist and not the patient. In fact, one should be suspicious of any crown that fails in less than 5 years, particularly if it cannot be fixed with a simple gum line filling. Good crowns last 10 or more years, and 15 to 25 years is not unusual.

Sensitive Fillings and Crowns

Hot and cold temperature sensitivity. Teeth with new fillings or crowns frequently are sensitive to cold and hot temperatures. The discomfort is usually mild and disappears in a few weeks. If it persists and is severe, it may be necessary to remove the restoration and place a temporary sedative filling or crown that provides immediate relief, though it may take weeks or months before all symptoms disappear. Then the permanent restoration can be replaced. The important point to remember is that a healthy nerve responds to both hot and cold temperatures, with the sensitivity disappearing a few seconds afterward. Therefore, you should not be rushed into root canal therapy without giving the nerve a chance to recuperate under a sedative material such as a zinc oxide and eugenol or IRM. On the other hand, if heat is applied to the tooth and the pain intensifies, but is then relieved by swishing with cold water, nerve damage is irreversible and root canal therapy will be necessary to avoid losing the tooth.

High spots. Another cause of sensitive teeth following restoration is high spots. If the filling or crown is not carved properly to the natural contours of the tooth so that the opposing tooth hits it on closure before the other teeth come into contact, the nerve becomes irritated. You may then experience slight pain on chewing or tapping your teeth together, or the tooth may become sensitive to thermal changes. It may also loosen. This condition, hyperocclusion, is easily corrected by returning to the dentist, who will grind down the high spot.

Electrical shocks. Occasionally, following a new amalgam filling, patients experience a tiny electrical shock whenever the jaws are opened and closed. This shock is due to a galvanic current between fillings in the upper and lower jaws as they make and break contact, especially if the tooth opposite the amalgam filling has a gold inlay or crown. The condition is almost always corrected by polishing the amalgam filling. Some dentists recommend replacement of all amalgam fillings with gold to keep the same type of metal throughout the mouth. However, there is no scientific basis for avoiding dissimilar metals in the same or the opposite jaw or for replacing functional fillings.

Fillings Don't Need Polishing

Fillings should be smooth and carved to the contours of the natural tooth surfaces. Polishing fillings to a high luster is not necessary except in the rare occurrence of galvanic shock. Examination of fillings under an electron microscope reveals that even the most highly polished surfaces are not totally smooth. Sufficient smoothness can be obtained by burnishing amalgam fillings just after placement in the tooth. Composite fillings are more likely to require trimming and polishing to remove excess material at their margins.

Over the years amalgam fillings may darken, likewise causing a slight darkening of enamel. Amalgam fillings also become a little uneven at the edges, often forming a small crevice at the junction with the tooth surface that can be detected by a needle-tip dental explorer. At the same time, corrosion of the metal fills in the crevice and actually improves the seal of amalgam against bacterial penetration. If the seal is good enough and the explorer does not actually stick between the filling and the tooth, the filling should not be replaced. Some dentists recommend polishing amalgam periodically to smooth the edges. The procedure is called remargination. If the defect is slight, as described above, nothing is gained. If it is large, polishing will not solve the problem, and the filling should be replaced.

Cracked Tooth Syndrome

How times change! When the first edition of this book was published in 1991, there was a veritable epidemic of cracked tooth syndrome, especially among patients with dental insurance. Ten years later, the condition has diminished to realistic proportions, occurring at a much lower rate as insurance consultants, including the author, started to ask for proof instead of paying on demand.

Considering that the average adult can exert 150 to 200 pounds of biting pressure per square inch, it is surprising how few teeth actually crack or split. One of the reasons is that teeth barely touch in normal chewing. Just as contact is made, a reflex reaction terminates the closing force and separates the teeth. Also, food is usually soft and cushions chewing. However, an accidental hard chomp on a bone or shell or any hard material can fracture, crack, or split a tooth. Some people crack ice with their teeth; occasionally the ice cracks the tooth!

An obvious cracked tooth needs no special diagnosis by a dentist. Sometimes the crack is not obvious at all except that the tooth has become very sensitive to temperature changes and to biting pressure. Examination of the tooth reveals nothing except pain when pressure is applied to a cusp of the tooth in a splitting direction rather than up and down. What this means is that a hairline fracture or splitting of a cusp has occurred. If the split is so slight that the central pulp chamber has not been opened up to bacteria and the nerve is still healthy, root canal treatment is not necessary. The solution is to cap the cusps. If the tooth is otherwise sound, with small or no fillings, a gold onlay or three-quarter crown is the best type of capping restoration because the smallest amount of natural tooth is removed. If a large filling is present, a full crown will be required.

The symptoms of a cracked tooth are very similar to the symptoms previously described for sensitive fillings. They are also the symptoms experienced by patients who clench and grind their teeth excessively or who are heavy gum chewers. Instead of treating the sensitivity conservatively, some dentists immediately recommend root canal therapy and placement of full crowns. A suspected cracked tooth should be treated first by adjusting the occlusion (grinding off a very slight layer of enamel on the chewing surface) to relieve the bite so that excessive pressure cannot be applied. The patient must make a conscious attempt to stop clenching and grinding and to eliminate chewing gum. If the sensitivity persists or worsens despite these conservative measures, then it is reasonable to conclude the presence of a cracked tooth.

Excessive clenchers and grinders (bruxers) can experience sensitivity in a number of teeth, not always the same ones at the same time. The fact that several teeth hurt over time usually rules out a specific cracked tooth. What one needs to relieve this type of discomfort is a plastic occlusal guard, also called an occlusal night guard or splint, similar to an athletic tooth protector that can be obtained from an athletic supply store for under $10 or from your dentist for $75 to $250. The professionally made guard is more esthetic because less of it shows and may be more comfortable since it is likely to be smaller, but it is not necessarily better than a prefabricated one.

Enamel Line Fracture

Another diagnosis linked to the proliferation of dental insurance is enamel line fracture. As with cracked tooth syndrome, diagnosis of enamel line fracture was much abused, serving as an opportunity for charlatan dentists to fleece the insurance company or your pocketbook. But this does not mean that enamel line fractures don't occur. Indeed, they are not uncommon as we age.

Although the tooth shows nothing wrong with it in the X-ray film, the dentist will write on the insurance form that it needs a porcelain-metal crown because of enamel fracture lines. The implied prognosis is that if the tooth is not capped, it will inevitably fracture. True, the enamel of the tooth will likely show minute fracture lines on close inspection, but a fracture line is not a fracture.

Many dentists have intra-oral cameras that project monumental images of your teeth on a television screen to point out dark amalgam fillings with ragged edges or tiny fracture lines that don't look so tiny in the enlarged image. More often than not, the camera is used to pitch FUN treatment-replacement of functional fillings or putting crowns on sound teeth with otherwise insignificant defects. These lines mostly result from rapid temperature changes applied to the crystalline structure of the enamel. If we did not drink hot coffee while eating cold ice cream or crack ice with our teeth, we might have fewer enamel fracture lines. As long as there is no actual fracture of a tooth, the best treatment is no treatment.

Crown Buildups and Dowel Posts

Crowns are fabricated to restore badly damaged teeth. Sometimes it is necessary to build up the remainder of the natural tooth or to place a post in the root so that the crown will have adequate support. The buildup thus becomes part of the tooth preparation. It consists of a cement or composite base much like a filling that is placed in the tooth. Prior to dental insurance, cement bases were included in the price of the crown. Now the procedure is an add-on. When buildups are extensive, involving 50 percent of the crown, an additional charge is warranted, but surely not for most teeth. Some dentists charge for buildups on every tooth to be crowned, adding $50 to $100 to the price of the crown.

Many dentists also place posts in the canal of every tooth that has had endodontic treatment regardless of necessity. The additional charge for a prefabricated metal post ranges from $65 to $150, even though the dentist's cost for the post is at most a few dollars and takes only 10 or 15 minutes to insert. Many dentists use laboratory cast dowel posts that cost more but actually are not as good as a properly fitted prefabricated post. Because the post also transfers biting forces to the root, increasing the risk of root fracture and complete loss of the tooth, a post should be used only when the natural tooth has fractured or decayed so badly that a crown restoration would be unstable without one.[31]

Fee Buildups—Upgrades and Add-ons

As long as dentistry is merchandised on the basis of a separate charge for every procedure, the consumer is at risk of overcharges, but it is not only fee-for-service dentistry that is exploiting the consumer and adding to the nation's dental bill. Excess charges-known as *upgrades and add-ons*-are being pushed on patients in prepaid or "managed" dental plans, with the knowledge if not the approval of the insurance companies and the state agencies regulating them (see chapter 15). Dental practice management courses, for which dentists earn continuing education credit required for renewal of their licenses, teach them how to "sell dentistry." More and more dentists list "Cosmetic Dentistry" on their office signs, which are nearly as big as billboards. The commercial insurance companies often pay so little to the dentists on their capitated managed care plans that they actively encourage dentists to *upgrade* and *add-on*.

One way to protect yourself is to negotiate with the dentist prior to treatment. The treatment plan should be reviewed item by item, and if the dentist charges for gum irrigation, buildups or other add-ons such as pulp caps on every tooth, or wants to replace your amalgam fillings with composites, or convert every large filling or enamel line fracture into a porcelain crown, or recommends you bleach or whiten your teeth until they shine in the dark, you should be prepared to defend yourself. He or she may be a first-rate technician but running an office is expensive and every dentist wants to maximize his or her income.

Many of these extra charges such as for pulp caps or cement bases (build-ups) should be included in the fee for the restoration unless the doctor can demonstrate to you that the cavity is very large and the decay is very deep. Other charges such as for gum irrigation while scaling your teeth are worthless. Many dentists call polishing your teeth to remove stains a prophylaxis and add on charges for scaling to remove calculus at or just beneath the gum level that should be included in the fee for the prophylaxis. Unless you have a true periodontal disease problem, you should not pay extra for *scaling and root planing* (SRP).

If the dentist refuses to discuss these issues with you and provide you with satisfactory evidence to convince you that these extra charges for upgrades and add-ons are justified, you must then decide whether to pay the added freight or take your business elsewhere.

RECOMMENDATIONS

1. Brush and floss thoroughly at least once a day, preferably twice, morning and night.
2. Use fluoride toothpastes and include fluoride supplements in the diets of infants and children where the water does not contain an adequate fluoride level.
3. Avoid the expense of professionally applied topical fluoride if your children are essentially caries-free, use fluoridated toothpaste, and reside in a fluoridated community. If you decide on professionally applied topical fluorides, ask your dentist about fluoride varnish.
4. If you or your children have lots of cavities, ask your dentist about fluoride and antimicrobial (chlorhexidine) mouth rinses.
5. Don't let the dentist charge you extra for gum irrigation when your teeth are cleaned.
6. The dental prophylaxis includes scaling and removal of subgingival calculus. Don't let the dentist charge extra for scaling and root planing unless you have diagnosed periodontal disease.
7. Under age 19, have sealants applied but only to defective pits and grooves especially of the permanent molars.
8. Do not have interproximal fillings unless the dentist documents caries through the enamel into the dentin in the X-ray film.
9. Discuss remineralization or pulp capping of very large cavities with your dentist before consenting to root canal therapy.
7. Don't ask for or accept composite fillings on chewing surfaces of posterior teeth. Stick with amalgam.
8. Don't let your dentist replace large fillings with crowns unless
   (a) there is something demonstrably wrong with the filling and
   (b) the tooth cannot be refilled.
9. If a new filling or crown is hypersensitive to heat or cold more than two or three weeks, do not rush into root canal treatment. Ask your dentist to consider removing the new restoration in order to treat the nerve with a temporary sedative filling or crown.
10. If a new crown is sensitive to touch along the gum line and your dentist refuses to replace it, obtain a second opinion.
11. Don't accept a crown on a tooth with nonsymptomatic cracks and minor fractures.

12. Don't accept charges for pulp caps, buildups, and dowel posts in conjunction with a crown unless at least 50 percent of the tooth is decayed or has fractured. This is best discussed before the procedure, not afterwards.
13. Be wary of *upgrades* and *add-ons*, which are more likely to benefit the dentist than yourself.
14. Don't be taken in by televised images of your teeth, which magnify supposed defects to "sell" dentistry.
15. Cosmetic Dentistry is an appeal to your vanity. Only you can protect yourself.

5

Common Diseases of the Gum and Soft Tissues of the Mouth

Many diseases and abnormal conditions that occur in the mouth are limited to the gum, lips, tongue, or mucosal lining of the oral cavity, as distinct from pyorrhea, which involves soft tissue but also the bone surrounding teeth. Periodontal diseases are covered in the following three chapters. This chapter reviews the more common gum and soft tissue diseases.[1-3] Halitosis, though not a disease *per se,* is included as a common concern. It is important to remember that there are other conditions beyond the scope of this book. Any abnormal condition of the mouth, tongue, or lips that persists over two weeks should be examined by a dentist.

Dentists have always speculated about the effect of oral diseases and conditions on one's general health. In the 1920s and 1930s many dentists and physicians espoused a "theory of focal infection," claiming non-vital teeth, even if treated successfully with root canal fillings, were the cause of just about anything that ailed someone. Countless teeth were extracted to no avail until the theory was finally abandoned, only to be replaced by other quack theories espoused by those who oppose fluorides in your drinking water and silver amalgam fillings in your teeth.

We must also be concerned with research reports that can be misconstrued to assign *causation* to *association,* such as a statistical link between the severity of periodontal disease and hardening of the arteries, heart attack and stroke, as well as preterm low birth weight.[4] There is sufficient reason to take periodontal disease seriously as it effects your oral health, function and sense of well-being, without scaring you with a statistical association to other diseases that is not proof of a cause and effect.

GUM DISEASES

Gingivitis

Description Gingivitis is the most common gum disease. Characterized by red or inflamed gum (gingival) tissue, it is experienced by just about everyone with teeth from time to time and in varying degrees. Sometimes the inflammation appears as a thin red or bluish red line-**marginal gingivitis**-around all or a few teeth, depending on whether the condition is generalized or localized.

Cause. The most common cause of gingivitis is poor oral hygiene. If teeth are not brushed, gingivitis develops within a week as bacteria-infested plaque deposits form around and just beneath the gum.

Some systemic diseases induce or exaggerate gingivitis. Spontaneous hemorrhaging may indicate a serious disease such as leukemia. In fact, any disease that interferes with the blood's normal clotting mechanism, including hemophilia, uremia, and liver disease, is likely to cause **hemorrhagic gingivitis**.

Drugs such as heparin sodium (heparin is a component of normal blood), dicumarol, and coumadin inhibit coagulation of blood and reduce the risk of heart attack or stroke from clots forming in blood vessels narrowed by cholesterol deposits (a completely different type of plaque). They can also cause bleeding gums.

Many people with no heart disease take low dosage aspirin for its blood-thinning quality, which reduces the risk of heart attack. Millions of arthritis victims are on high doses of aspirin, which can also contribute to bleeding gums.

Symptoms. Gums bleed easily to touch and pressure with little or no pain, although some patients complain of slight soreness. In more severe cases, gums bleed when eating as food presses against the tissue. The toothbrush and dental floss turn pink, and saliva and rinse water are red with blood as one spits out after brushing.

Treatment and prevention. Early gingivitis can be cured by self-treatment-thorough daily brushing and flossing to remove irritating food debris and soft plaque deposits. A soft nylon brush should be directed at a 45-degree angle and jiggled in a massaging motion directly on the gum. Special rubber cup massagers are also available. If gums are not firm or appear puffy, the rubber tip attached to a brush should be inserted between the teeth to massage the gum tissue called the interdental papilla. Stimudents or toothpicks are also effective. Oral irrigators remove gross debris but are ineffective against plaque deposits. Irrigation is a supplement, not a substitute, for brushing and flossing. If inflammation and bleeding do not clear up after one or two weeks of conscientious oral hygiene, a dental consultation is in order. Once plaque and tartar are firmly established on the teeth and beneath the gum, professional prophylaxis, including subgingival scaling, is necessary to remove these deposits.

Pregnancy and Menstrual Gingivitis

Description. Around the third month of pregnancy and during menstruation, some women experience minor gum inflammation, including swelling and enlargement of the interdental papilla. Occasionally, a large overgrowth of the gums takes place at the border of a few teeth. This so-called pregnancy tumor is not a neoplasm but rather a response of the gum to local irritation.

Cause. Hormonal changes associated with pregnancy and menstruation, particularly in the presence of poor oral hygiene, are the cause of this gingivitis.

Symptoms. The condition is painless and notable mainly for an increase in the size of the gum papilla and minor bleeding on brushing. The gums also appear bluish or bright red.

Treatment and prevention. Careful brushing and flossing reduce inflammation and swelling. Hard calculus must be removed by a dental prophylaxis. If a growth on the gum becomes annoyingly large, it can be removed surgically. However, most symptoms disappear after pregnancy and the cessation of menstruation.

Inflammatory Gum Hyperplasia (Enlargement)

Description. This generic condition is differentiated from gingivitis by the extent of the enlargement. The gingiva appear red or bluish red (magenta) and swollen. The surface is usually glossy. Depending on the degree of inflammation and overgrowth, the tissue may be painful to touch and may bleed easily.

Cause. Some frequently encountered conditions that irritate and cause inflammatory gum enlargement are gross tartar, fillings with rough, overhanging margins, artificial crowns (caps) that are poorly constructed and fit improperly at the gum line, and hypersensitivity to the materials used. Bonded veneers and poor-fitting crowns that are bulky or have overhangs or openings like cavities at the gum line are common culprits, but unsightly swollen gums and bluish red or dark discoloration rimming the gum line can occur even with the best of crowns and veneers. That is why cosmetic caps and veneers occasionally create a poorer appearance than the condition they were intended to correct

Nutritional deficiencies are frequently blamed for gum problems when the real cause is poor oral hygiene. Nonetheless, severe vitamin C deficiency decreases collagen, a protein essential to the structure of the underlying connective tissue, resulting in enlargement and hemorrhaging of the gums. Called **scurvy**, it was the scourge of ancient sailors and others whose diets lacked fresh fruits and vegetables. Today, with improved nutrition, scurvy is rarely encountered in Western civilization.

Symptom. Unsightly, tender gums that bleed easily.

Treatment and prevention. If defective restorations are the cause, they must be replaced. Tartar must be removed by a dentist or hygienist before the tissue can regain full health. When the source of the inflammation is eliminated, the gum usually shrinks back to normal size and shape, often taking as long as six months to do so. However, if the gum remains enlarged and unsightly after six months of good oral hygiene, surgical intervention-gingivectomy or gingivoplasty-may be necessary to restore normal tissue contours.

Minor vitamin deficiencies are not likely to affect the gums. Vitamin supplements are no substitute for personal oral hygiene and adequate dental care. Vitamin C is frequently advocated as a cure for inflamed gums but has no value unless there is a real deficiency due to an inadequate diet or digestive problems.

Noninflammatory Gum Hyperplasia

Description. The terms hyperplasia and hypertrophy are used interchangeably to describe enlargement of the gingiva. Strictly speaking, they are not synonymous. Hypertrophy refers to a nontumorous increase in the size or bulk of an organ, not to an increase in the number of cells. Hyperplasia is an abnormal increase in the number of cells in an organ or a tissue with consequent enlargement-for example, the amount of fibrous connective tissue within the gums. In noninflammatory hyperplasia, the gums are usually firm and a healthy pink, though bulbous and, because they cover part or all of the crowns of teeth, very unsightly.

Cause. Noninflammatory hyperplasia or overgrowth of the gum tissues is a frequent side effect of phenytoin (Dilantin, Epanutin), a drug that prevents convulsions and is used most frequently by epileptics and others with seizure disorders. Also, cyclosporin used in organ-transplant patients can cause hyperplasia. Mechanical irritation from orthodontic bands, ill-fitting crowns, bridges, and dentures may stimulate overgrowth of gum or palatal tissue. Hypersensitivity or allergic reactions to metals and plastics in these restorations may also induce hyperplasia.

Symptoms. Gingival hyperplasia is painless. Initially, the problem is esthetic, but gross overgrowth can cause movement of teeth, interference in chewing, and difficulty in wearing prosthetic appliances.

Treatment and prevention. When mechanical irritation or sensitivity to dental materials is the cause, the obvious solution is elimination of the irritant. When orthodontic bands are removed, the gums usually return to normal. The greater the enlargement, the longer it will take. When the irritant is a restoration, the excess tissue often must be removed to make replacement of the restoration possible.

Drug-induced gingival hyperplasia is a tolerable side effect of essential drug therapy. The enlargement can be minimized but not totally prevented by maintaining meticulous oral hygiene and having frequent dental prophylaxis. Periodically, the hyperplastic tissue has to be removed surgically. Gingivectomy is relatively simple and can be done painlessly with local anesthetics.

Infections and Ulcerations of the Gums, Lips, and Mouth

Oral infections vary in severity according to a person's susceptibility and resistance. Generally, the healthier you are, the more resistant you are likely to be, but even where general health is good, the health of the gums may be poor. Not infrequently a balance is reached between the host—you—and the invading organisms, in which case a standoff occurs. The condition becomes chronic, ever present but in a rather mild form. Also, many dental infections are due not to the introduction of new organisms but to an increase in the virulence of the viruses and bacteria normally present in the mouth, particularly as your resistance decreases. Because we are all likely to have the same organisms in our mouths, the more common dental infections are not contagious. It is lowered resistance to our own bugs rather than invasion by others that causes most diseases of the mouth.

Trench Mouth

Description. Trench mouth, Vincent's infection, and ANUG are interchangeable names for acute necrotizing ulcerative gingivostomatitis.[5] Marginal gingivitis is frequently a precursor of the ulceration and degeneration (or necrosis) of the gums that characterizes ANUG. The interdental papilla between each tooth looks "punched out," and the surrounding gum cuff is loose and raw.

If untreated or if superimposed on a more serious illness that affects gum tissue, such as anemia or leukemia, ANUG becomes progressively worse, destroying the underlying periodontal bone and extending to other tissues. Such extensive infection is rare today since the disease responds well to therapy.

Cause. Microscopic examination of the infected tissues reveals an unusually large number of fusiforms and spirochetes, bacteria that are always present in our mouth, though normally in lesser numbers. ANUG is associated with lowered resistance, stress, poor nutrition, and poor oral hygiene. It is more common among young persons, especially during adolescence and the early twenties. In World War I it cropped up in epidemic numbers among the troops in trenches, giving rise to the term "trench mouth." Epidemic outbreaks also occur among students during examination week. However, the epidemic is not caused by the communication of the fusospirochetes to others but by the shared stress, fatigue, and neglected oral hygiene that lower the resistance of many members of the group simultaneously.

Symptoms. The tissue is covered by a gray pseudomembrane that peels off, leaving a red, raw surface that bleeds easily and is extremely painful to touch. There is usually a foul smell, and the patient frequently has a fever and feels listless.

Treatment and prevention. The infection is not contagious. It responds quickly to antibiotics, usually penicillin. Simpler remedies such as frequent rinsing with a dilute solution of hydrogen peroxide are also effective. Scaling of the teeth to remove subgingival calculus and plaque is also necessary to reduce the infection and prevent recurrence. Without dental prophylaxis and adequate oral hygiene, the condition settles in as a subacute or chronic infection, with acute flare-ups during periods of stress.

Apthous Ulcer (Canker Sore)

Description. Canker sores usually occur in the soft fold of mucosal tissue at the junction of the inside of the cheeks and the gums and the inside of the cheeks and the lips. They also occur on the soft palate, the side of the tongue, and the floor of the mouth.[6] They seldom occur on the gingiva and the hard palate, common sites for herpes simplex ulcers described below.

Minor apthous ulcers measure from a few millimeters to a centimeter (nearly half an inch) in diameter, whereas major apthous ulcers can be as large as two centimeters. Beginning as small red areas, the center portion sloughs to create a crater that is yellow or grayish white in color. Although these ulcers usually occur as a single sore, multiple lesions may be present.

Cause. The exact cause of canker sores is unknown. Stress may bring on attacks in susceptible persons. Biting the inside of the cheek or lip may incite an ulcer. The tissue may be traumatized by the bristle of a toothbrush or the prick of a bone fragment while eating. Some patients develop a canker sore following a dental appointment, no matter how gentle the treatment. Nutritional deficiencies may account for recurrent lesions in some people. But the underlying cause is more likely related to an immunologic dysfunction in which antibody-producing cells attack rather than protect the healthy oral tissues.[6]

Symptoms. The ulcer is particularly painful if located on highly mobile surfaces such as the tongue or the mucobuccal folds on the inside of the cheeks. Eating, careless toothbrushing, and even speaking may be acutely painful. Spicy and acidic foods also irritate the ulcers.

Treatment. Small canker sores are not too painful and they usually do not require treatment. They disappear in a week or two. Large ulcers, however, can be extremely painful. Temporary relief may be obtained by applying topical anesthetic ointments, which are available in drug stores without prescription.

Topical steroids have been used with limited success because the ointments do not adhere for very long to the ulcer. Moreover, the ulcer itself cannot be kept dry because of saliva. An oral suspension combining tetracycline and nystatin has been used with some success, possibly because it eliminates secondary bacterial infection. Overall, however, there is no treatment that is consistently reliable. This is not of critical importance since the disease is self-limiting and recurs less often with age.

Herpes Simplex Ulcers (Cold Sores)

Description. Most of us have small cold sores in or around our mouth from time to time. They usually recur on the lips, the hard palate, and the gingiva. The lesion begins as multiple vesicular eruptions that soon disintegrate to form ulcers varying in size from a few millimeters to a centimeter in width. When large numbers crop up simultaneously and spread throughout the mouth, the condition is called **acute herpetic gingivostomatitis.** These profuse attacks occur more frequently in infants and in children under six years of age.

When the lesion occurs on the lips, it is called a **cold sore** or **herpes labialis**. Small transparent blisters (vesicles) form that soon coalesce and rupture, yielding a yellowish fluid that then hardens to form a crust that eventually heals.

Herpes simplex lesions are distinguished from apthous ulcers, which are more likely to occur singly and are not preceded by vesicular eruptions.

Cause. Cold sores are caused by the herpes simplex virus that takes up permanent residence in our mouths shortly after birth. It is most likely passed on to us by our mothers. Thus, the ulcers result not from a new invasion but from some trauma or change in the tissue that lowers resistance. Cold sores are so-called because the common cold is often the agent that lowers resistance and brings on the acute attack. Sunburn of the lips is also a frequent precursor to herpes labialis.

Symptoms. Herpes simplex ulcers on the lips are usually preceded by an itching, tingling, or burning sensation. Once formed, they are particularly painful because of the constant movement of the cheeks and lips containing the sores against the teeth. Even smiling stretches the lips and, likewise, the sore. Eating and toothbrushing hurt, the more so with greater numbers or larger size of the lesions inside the mouth.

Treatment and prevention. Regardless of the extent of the disease, the lesions become less painful after a few days, and complete healing takes place within two weeks, leaving no residual scarring. Topical anesthetics in an adhesive base can be applied to the ulcer for temporary relief, but it is difficult to treat any lesions inside the mouth because of the diluting and washing action of saliva. Spicy and irritating foods and beverages should be avoided. Soft foods and careful toothbrushing will prevent injury to the healing sores. At present there are no preventive measures.

Teething

Description. The emergence of teeth through the gums is called teething. Teething begins at about 6 months of age, when the baby incisors erupt, and continues until all the permanent teeth have taken their normal place in the mouth, usually by age 25 or so.

Symptoms. The pain and discomfort of teething is caused not by infection but by teeth pushing through the gums. Indeed, the gum becomes inflamed and extremely irritated not only during infancy teething but even when teeth erupt later in life, such as during the eruption of wisdom teeth. (See *Pericoronitis* below.)

Treatment. Infants can chew on teething rings and biscuits to help relieve symptoms. Baby "gum drops," available in the local pharmacy, may provide some relief, but all that is usually required is time and patience for the teeth to erupt fully.

Thrush

Description. Thrush or **candidiasis** or **moniliasis** is more likely to occur in infants under six months old and the elderly but will occur in anyone with lowered resistance. White or grayish white patches appear on the mucous membranes of the entire mouth—the tongue, lips, cheeks, gums, and throat.

Cause. Thrush is caused by an overgrowth of the fungus (yeast) *Candida albicans*, which is normally present in the mouth. Infant thrush may derive from improperly sterilized bottle nipples or infected breast nipples. It may be a side effect of antibiotics or corticosteroids (oral or nasal/oral inhalants) taken at any age that destroy normal oral bacteria, which feed on the fungus, allowing its proliferation.

Symptoms. Multiple white patches, appearing as curdled milk throughout the mouth, easily identify thrush. If they are scraped off, the raw surface bleeds and is painful. Infants may develop fever and cough and have difficulty feeding.

Treatment and prevention. Mild cases of thrush are likely to disappear without treatment. The pediatrician or family physician should be consulted for infant thrush because he or she has more experience treating the disease than most dentists. Severe cases may require topical application of nystatin, an antibiotic that destroys fungi. If thrush occurs as a consequence of a systemic antibiotic, it usually disappears on cessation of the drug as the oral flora and fauna return to their normal, symbiotic balance. More resistant cases require treatment with nystatin or other topical antifungicides. People suffering from xerostomia (dry mouth) are also at greater risk of candidiasis.

Pericoronitis

Description. Pericoronitis is an inflammation and infection of the gum tissue around a partially erupted tooth, most commonly the mandibular third molar (wisdom tooth), as it emerges in late adolescence. It should not be confused with normal teething, which, as stated above, is simply the irritability and minor inflammation to be expected as a tooth pushes its way through the gum.

Cause. Accumulation of food debris and proliferation of bacteria beneath the loose gum tissue as well as traumatic biting of the tissue by an opposing tooth produce an acute infection.

Symptoms. Pericoronitis is characterized by swelling of the gum over the tooth and the surrounding soft tissue. If the opposing tooth has erupted, it will traumatize the swollen gum on each bite, making it difficult to close the teeth. Once bacterial infection sets in, there will be constant pain and fever. If neglected. the infection spreads into the surrounding tissues and can be dangerous.

Treatment and prevention. The infected area should be kept clean. The gum flap can be irrigated with warm salt water, peroxide, or glyoxide solutions by placing the small nozzle of a dental irrigator or a rubber syringe (such as a baby enema purchased in the pharmacy) under the loose tissue. Antibiotics, usually penicillin, cure the infection quickly, but the infection will recur unless the underlying problem is eliminated. If there is sufficient space in the jaw for the tooth to erupt fully, reinfection is prevented by cutting away the loose tissue and fully exposing the crown. Surgical intervention is indicated only if the condition becomes chronic or recurs. When there is insufficient room in the jaw for the fully erupted tooth and it continues to be a problem, the tooth has to be removed.

BENIGN TUMORS AND TISSUE CHANGES

Fibroma and Papilloma

Description. Most tumors of the gums and tongue are benign. The most common growth is an irritation fibroma, which appears as a smooth-surfaced, pink mushroom suspended by a small stalk attached to the lip, tongue, or inner cheek. The papilloma is also mushroom-shaped but with an irregular, white surface.

Cause. Irritation fibromas are caused by lip, tongue, and cheek biting or sucking. Frequently the growth occurs opposite a small space between the teeth where the tissue can be sucked in. The papilloma is a benign growth that occurs of its own accord.

Symptoms. The patient first becomes aware of the fibroma or papilloma by feeling or observing the irregularity or by frequent, accidental biting of the outgrowth of tissue.

Treatment and prevention. Simple excision is the usual cure. Since the diagnosis is obvious and the entire growth is removed without difficulty, biopsy is not necessary. Avoidance of lip or tongue "doodling" usually prevents recurrence. If recurrence is due to a space between the teeth, then closure of the space with a small fixed bridge may be indicated. However, once the growth is removed it seldom recurs, and no further treatment is necessary.

Tori

Description. These are bony growths, not uncommon in adults, in the middle of the palate (**torus palatinus**) or on the inside lateral or tongue side of the lower jaw (**torus mandibularis**). They consist of normal bone substance that in the palate appears as an irregular oval protuberance and in the mandible more or less as small single or multiple marbles beneath the mucosa.

Cause. Unknown.

Symptoms. These growths are completely symptomless. Occasionally, they grow so large as to be traumatized by chewing or interfere with the wearing of dentures. Most people are unaware of their presence until a dentist or hygienist points them out.

Treatment and prevention. Unless tori cause a problem, there is no reason to have them removed. If their size becomes annoying or interferes with the placement of a denture, they are removed by simple surgery. Once removed, tori usually do not recur.

Hairy Tongue

Description. Hairy tongue is a harmless elongation of the hairlike filiform papillae on the top surface of the tongue. The surface usually appears white but may be stained brown or black by tobacco or pigments in food. The condition occurs only in adults.

Cause. A white-coated tongue is not unusual during a dehydrating illness, but what causes hairy tongue in the absence of systemic illness is unknown.

Symptoms. The condition is painless and noted only for its abnormal color. Since food debris can collect in the hairy filaments, the tongue may emit an unpleasant odor.

Treatment and prevention. Both treatment and prevention consist of daily brushing of the tongue to keep its surface clean.

Leukoplakia

Description. Leukoplakia is observed more frequently among older males, and in persons using smokeless tobacco. Although most lesions remain benign, the condition should be viewed as precancerous. Lesions vary in size from a few millimeters to many centimeters (an inch or more) across. It may be flat, fissured, or ulcerated with a somewhat rough and scaly surface, and whitish yellow, pearly white, or grayish white in color. Leukoplakia is usually found behind and to the outside of the lower molars, on the inside of the cheeks, and on the floor of the mouth or the side of the tongue.

Cause. Leukoplakia occurs spontaneously or may be caused by irritation from heavy smoking, chewing tobacco, jagged teeth, ill-fitting prosthetic appliances, and poor oral hygiene.

Symptoms. Leukoplakia develops very slowly and painlessly. Patients are seldom aware of its presence until the lesions are observed by a dentist or hygienist.

Treatment and prevention. Leukoplakia of the tongue and floor of the mouth has a very high risk of developing into invasive cancer. It is recommended, therefore, that all such lesions be excised completely. When located on the inner surface of the cheek or gums, the lesion is less likely to become malignant. Biopsy should be performed in the event of cracking or fissuring. It may diminish with removal of irritants or, more likely, remain unchanged. Because the condition is chronic, noticeable improvement after the removal of irritants is not likely for months. All such lesions should be examined every three or four months and removed if there is any indication of deleterious change, with microscopic examination of the tissue for signs of malignancy.

MALIGNANT ORAL AND PHARYNGEAL (THROAT) TUMORS

Squamous Cell Carcinomas

Description. Malignant tumors or carcinomas occur on the lip, the cheek, the tongue, the floor of the mouth, within the jaw bones, occasionally on the gums and in the throat. About 30,000 (3%) of the 1.2 million new cancer cases each year in the United States are located in the oral cavity or throat, resulting in 7,800 annual deaths. Over 90 percent of these cancers are attributed to use and abuse of tobacco![7]

There are many kinds of oral cancers, but the most common is squamous cell carcinoma, so named because it involves cells within the skin (squamous means scaly). The lesion may begin as a small white area that develops into an ulcer with raised, inwardly folding or invaginated edges.

Cause. Irritants such as smoking, chewing tobacco, excessive alcohol consumption, fractured or jagged teeth, ill-fitting dentures, and overexposure to sunlight are contributing factors, with tobacco being the major culprit, as noted above.

Symptoms. In the beginning, and sometimes even in a fairly advanced stage, the lesion is completely painless although it may bleed easily. An unusual growth or color change may be a signal that something is wrong. Cancers on the floor of the mouth and under the tongue are the most insidious because they are painless and grow unobserved until well advanced. Patients will not be aware of the cancer until it is quite large, by which time it may be too late.

Treatment and prevention. Whenever a lesion of any size within or around the mouth or the throat does not heal within two weeks, one should consult a dentist. A prudent dentist does not rush into radical treatment. He will quickly recognize a nonmalignant fibroma or a typical herpes ulcer. If even a "typical" condition does not resolve in a few weeks, however, a consultation with an oral surgeon or oral pathologist who has experience with carcinomas is indicated. This is all the more important when the lesion is on the lips, where initially it resembles a cold sore, or on the undersurface of the tongue and the floor of the mouth where it looks like an ulcer. If the lesion is small and carcinoma is suspected, it will be totally excised under a local anesthetic and then biopsied. If the area is large, a small section will be removed for biopsy and more extensive surgery scheduled if the diagnosis is a malignancy.

It is worth remembering that excessive smoking and drinking are bad for all parts of the body. Irritating teeth and prosthetic appliances should be corrected by a dentist. If a removable partial or full denture is eroding the tissue, it should be kept out of the mouth pending a dental examination. One should as a matter of course avoid sunbathing or exposure of the face and arms to sunlight during work or play. Protective "sun-screens" prevent many skin and lip cancers.

Because oral malignancies are not rare, a good dentist or dental hygienist examines not only your teeth and gums at each examination but also the lips, tongue, floor of the mouth, hard and soft palate, the back of the throat, and insides of the cheeks. This kind of thorough examination is extremely important because oral cancers, especially beneath the tongue and on the floor of the mouth, are so easily overlooked in early stages when therapy is most effective.

Leukemia

Description. The term leukemia covers a number of diseases characterized by massive proliferation of white blood cells. Diagnosis is made by bone marrow biopsy and blood count.

Symptoms. Leukemia may be acute or chronic. The more acute, the greater the fever, malaise, and weakness experienced by patients. Lymph glands in the lower jaw and neck are swollen. Oral symptoms are common. There is usually enlargement of the gingiva, sometimes covering most of the teeth. Gums have a bluish color and bleed spontaneously. Lip sores can be extensive. The oral mucosa bruises easily and becomes discolored. In more extreme cases, the mucosa sloughs and the breath has a fetid odor.

Treatment. Chemotherapy cures between 20 and 80 percent of all leukemias, depending on the type. It is now particularly effective in children, for whom the prognosis following a diagnosis of leukemia was always dismal. Because of the high risk of excessive bleeding, extractions and routine dental treatment should be delayed until acute symptoms subside. Prophylactic antibiotics should be administered if surgery cannot be avoided. Assuming successful medical chemotherapy, dental treatment can be done when the blood count has returned to normal.

AIDS— Acquired Immunodeficiency Syndrome

Description. Certain oral diseases precede the first manifestation of systemic AIDS or may be concurrent with diagnosed AIDS. The more common ones are candidiasis, herpes simplex ulcerations, necrotizing gingivitis (ANUG), and rapid loss of periodontal bone, all of which are described elsewhere in this chapter. Also common in AIDS patients are hairy leukoplakia and Kaposi's sarcoma. Hairy leukoplakia appears as a raised white patch with long, hairy filaments along the lateral border of the tongue. It should not be confused with a white hairy tongue, which consists of enlarged hair-like papillae on the top of the tongue. Kaposi's sarcoma, relatively rare before the AIDS epidemic that was first recognized in 1981, appears in the mouth as blue, brown, or black lesions.[8]

Cause. AIDS is an infection caused by the human immunodeficieny virus (HIV). It is most commonly transmitted sexually, through the use of contaminated injection needles, and through transfusion of contaminated blood. The disease may be dormant for years or may manifest itself soon after exposure by breaking down the victim's immunologic defense systems. Since its inception, AIDS has taken the lives of nearly 12 million people and there are currently over 30 million HIV/AIDS infected persons throughout the world. It is estimated that in 1997 there were 820,000 people living with HIV/AIDS in the United States, almost all adults 15 to 49 years of age. Most infected persons have no outward symptoms and, with current treatment, the death rate is decreasing. Nonetheless, there are about 28,000 deaths annually from AIDS.[9] There is no one specific AIDS disease. Rather, it is a series of "opportunistic" diseases that ravage the body when normal immunological defense mechanisms have been destroyed.

Symptoms. Candidiasis or thrush, a fungal infection, is often the first sign of AIDS, resulting in a thick, whitish coating of the mouth and tongue. Red or purplish sores may appear on the face or mucous membranes of the mouth, signaling the beginning of Kaposi's sarcoma.

Treatment and prevention. HIV can be suppressed for many years by current chemotherapy. When specific symptoms occur, treatment consists of whatever is appropriate for the specific disease. Oral diseases may be treated by bacterial antibiotics, topical or systemic antifungal agents, and corticosteroids. Kaposi's sarcoma and other cancers receive radiation and chemotherapy.

Prevention requires avoiding contamination of your blood with the HIV virus by using condoms or other "safe sex" techniques and by never sharing needles with any other person. It is also possible to acquire the virus through blood transfusions, but since the development of a blood- screening test in 1984, risk of infection through this means has been very nearly eliminated. With the adoption of more conscientious sterilization and antiseptic protocols in the dental office, there is virtually no chance of picking up the disease from a previously treated HIV/AIDS patient.

A COMMON CONCERN

Halitosis

Description. Halitosis, also called *bad breath* or *oral malodor,* is a condition that is episodic for everyone and chronic for some. It is estimated that 1 in 20 people are seriously affected. Self-diagnosis doesn't work because you can't really smell your own breath and there are no reliable tests that you can do on yourself. If you suspect you have bad breath, your best source for positive or negative confirmation is to ask someone you can trust for an honest opinion.[10]

Cause. Early morning bad breath is not uncommon if the mouth dries due to mouth breathing during sleep or a decrease in salivary flow. Bad breath also stems from excessive smoking, excessive alcohol consumption, food retention around the teeth, chronic gum infections, tonsilitis, chronic nasal and sinus secretions, diseased lungs and indigestion. Diabetes produces an acetone or sweet breath, and certain foods such as onions and garlic are particularly noted for their effect on mouth odors. Other causes include: poor fitting bridges and dentures that are not cleaned properly so that food debris collects and putrefies; gross dental decay; untreated periodontal disease; xerostomia or *dry mouth,* which becomes more prevalent with age due to a decrease in saliva; prolonged use of antibiotics, which upset the mouth's ecosystem; systemic diseases such as cirrhosis of the liver and oral cancers.[11]

But far and away the most common source of oral malodor is the action of bacteria on debris and plaque embedded on the back surface of the tongue that produce volatile sulfur compounds such as hydrogen sulfide, which, simply put, smell bad.[12]

Treatment and prevention. Many people have an almost morbid fear of bad breath. They constantly chew (hopefully sugar-free) gum, suck on mint wafers and swish with a variety of proprietary mouthrinses, all of which provide only temporary sweet breath. Excessive chewing, sucking and swishing with commercial rinses can have deleterious effects as well, such as sore jaw joints and irritated gums and tongue.[13] On the other hand, chewing gum will increase salivary flow and therefore may be helpful if one suffers from chronic dry mouth, and judicious use of mouthrinses may reduce the activity of odor-producing bacteria.

Elimination of halitosis requires identification of the source. In the absence of conditions that can only be resolved by medical or dental treatment, halitosis can be reduced or eliminated by diligent tooth brushing, flossing and cleaning of the surface of the tongue as far back as your gagging reflex will allow. Plastic or metal scrapers are also available that can be used daily, along with tongue brushing, to remove the yellow or white coating on the tongue until it appears clean and pink.

RECOMMENDATIONS

A multitude of diseases and abnormalities can affect the gums and soft tissues of the mouth. Except for the more simple and obvious conditions that have been described, you should not attempt self-diagnosis, but neither should you automatically agree to whatever treatment is suggested to you, because some of it may be unnecessary. The following recommendations should help you decide when to seek prompt professional help and how to evaluate the dentist's recommendations.

1. Consult your dentist if local gingivitis does not respond to improved toothbrushing, flossing, and gum massage.
2. Enlargement of the gums usually can be minimized by meticulous daily oral hygiene and frequent dental prophylaxis.
3. Gingivectomy (cutting away excess gum tissue) should be avoided unless gum tissue is significantly enlarged and unsightly and does not respond to prophylaxis and good oral hygiene.
4. Canker and cold sores usually require no professional treatment and disappear within two weeks. Short-term relief may be obtained by

applying topical anesthetics in an adhesive base and avoidance of spicy foods and mechanical irritation.

5. Infant teething discomfort is natural to tooth eruption and can be relieved by topical anesthetics, teething rings, and biscuits designed for the purpose.

6. Infections around wisdom teeth require prompt treatment but not necessarily removal of the teeth if there is room for full eruption or the symptoms disappear and never reappear.

7. Any unnatural swelling, growth, or tissue change that persists over two weeks should be examined by a dentist.

8. Spontaneous gum bleeding, white patches along the border of the tongue, tissue changes and ulcerations on the underside of the tongue and on the floor of the mouth may be a sign of more serious local or systemic disease and should receive prompt professional diagnosis.

9. Halitosis can be minimized or prevented by avoiding odor-producing foods and thorough tooth brushing, flossing and cleansing of the tongue. If the condition persists, see your dentist.

6

Chronic Destructive Periodontal Disease

Periodontal disease, or pyorrhea, as it is commonly called, is usually thought of as bad, soft, or bleeding gums and loose teeth. While it may be all of that, pyorrhea does not inevitably lead to loss of teeth, at least not all or even most teeth. Periodontal disease is treatable, but a major part and the most important part of that treatment is how you-the patient and the person-take care of your teeth and gums.[1, 2]

Periodontitis

Description. Periodontitis is the technical name for the most common form of periodontal disease. The suffix *-itis* means inflammation, in this case inflammation of the tissues around (perio) the teeth (dontium). In this disease the inflammation comes from infection as bacteria invade the periodontal tissues, but the disease cannot be transmitted from one person to another since it is not caused by a specific microorganism. We are all hosts to the many organisms associated with periodontal disease. It is the susceptibility of the individual that determines if the attachment of the gum to the tooth will be destroyed, exposing the ligaments and bone holding the teeth in the jaws to the destructive disease process.

It is estimated that 35 percent of the population over age 30 has periodontitis.[3] Not all of these persons have serious disease and are at risk of losing teeth. It is only as the disease progresses over the years through neglect of oral hygiene and periodic dental treatment, as well as susceptibility, that tooth loss occurs.

There have been some recent concerns that periodontitis might increase the risk of coronary heart disease. However, there are too many confounding factors to allow such an assumption. One of the largest epidemiological studies to date concludes that there is no convincing evidence to support this concern.[4]

Advanced periodontal disease is easy to recognize by the dentist and the patient. The teeth appear elongated because of gum recession. Large spaces develop as teeth loosen and spread apart. Dark brown or black tartar encircles the exposed roots, which may also be stained by coffee and tobacco. What dentists and patients do not see, however, is the beginning stages of periodontitis because most often there are no symptoms and no pain, and the chronic gingivitis is so long-standing and so mild that the gums appear relatively normal. That is why most people do not know they have serious periodontal disease until it is quite advanced and an abscess develops or a tooth becomes loose and painful.

Cause. Bacterial plaque and tartar have the potential to damage the epithelial attachment and ultimately destroy the underlying supporting bone. Tartar, also called calculus, is plaque that has been calcified. Initially soft, white, and chalky, it gradually hardens, turning yellow and brown as it remains on the teeth over time. Some people accumulate tartar very rapidly on the tongue side of the lower front teeth and on the cheek side of the upper molars where the larger salivary ducts pour saliva into the mouth. Continued accumulation of tartar can impact on the gum tissue mechanically as it creeps down beneath the gingival cuff, opening up pathways for bacterial invasion. But it is usually creeping bacterial plaque rather than the tartar itself that produces the inflammation and bacterial infection of chronic destructive periodontal disease.

Thus, the beginning of periodontal disease is the breakdown of the attachment of the gum to the tooth surface, permitting extension of bacterial plaque into the gingival pocket and the further deepening of the pocket. Bacteria produce toxic chemicals and enzymes that destroy the **epithelial attachment,** opening up the underlying tissue to colonization by microorganisms. Once in this protected environment beneath the gums, the population of bacteria grows into the millions. Not only is the tissue irritated by the toxic by-products of bacterial metabolism but some bacteria invade beyond the epithelial attachment into the connective tissue and, in some instances, even the alveolar bone.[5, 6] Cells that defend the body are mobilized early in the disease. The function of defense cells is to digest the bacteria and remove toxins. Unfortunately, these cells also digest some of the supporting tissues. Overreaction of the body's defense mechanisms to continued bacterial irritation may be the primary cause of tissue loss in periodontal disease.[7]

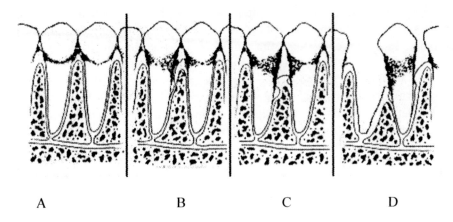

A   B   C   D

Figure 6-1   Progress of periodontal disease.

A. Food and calcareous deposits irritate the gingiva, causing it to withdraw from the teeth.
B. Further destruction, including the beginning of a periodontal pocket between the teeth.
C. The infection has destroyed most of the gum tissue and some of the bone between the teeth, causing them to loosen in their sockets.
D. One tooth has been lost, the other weakened.

The process is not one-way. At the same time that tissue-destroying defense cells are at work, others are producing new collagen and bone to restore the periodontal tissue.[8] If this was not the case, if bone and gum tissue were not also being repaired and regenerated, all teeth would loosen and fall out at an early age. Furthermore, studies indicate that periodontal disease does not progress steadily throughout the dentition but rather is episodic over many decades. A few teeth are attacked in one part of the mouth, with destruction of some of the supporting bone, and then the area goes into remission. It may be years before the same or another area is attacked again.[9]

Other less common causes of periodontal tissue disease are destructive gum infections such as **ANUG** (trench mouth) and severe nutritional deficiencies. Occasionally rapid bone loss occurs around a few teeth, usually the lower front teeth and first molars in young people, though it may also affect the entire dentition at any age. Termed **localized juvenile periodontitis**, it is often associated with Down's syndrome, diabetes, and other systemic diseases, and the cause appears related to certain bacteria, although the disease process is not fully understood. Clenching of the teeth or bruxism does not ordinarily cause periodontal disease, although in extreme cases some teeth may loosen.[10]

Symptoms. Although it is often an acute flare-up such as a periodontal abscess that first brings the patient to the dentist, most periodontal disease is chronic. In the chronic stage, the gums are deep red or bluish red in color and slightly swollen or puffy, consequences of an increased blood supply to the irritated and infected tissue. They also appear smoother and glossier than normal gums, which have a pink, stippled appearance. Because the inner wall of the unattached gingiva is eroded, the gums bleed easily on touch and pressure, sometimes spontaneously. If inflammation and tissue breakdown is more severe, pus will exude from the periodontal pocket with pressure.

Discomfort, pain, or observed changes in the gums including gingival bleeding are not definitive indicators of periodontal disease. For that, we must rely on competent dental examination and diagnosis.

Diagnosing Periodontal Disease

Many dentists ignore the disease out of ignorance or frustration or both. Even though it is common for dentists to take X-ray films of the teeth, dental diagnosis is often limited to a search for dental decay rather than a review of periodontal status. Dental X-rays are useful for periodontal diagnosis, but because they are two-dimensional, major areas of bone destruction may not be visible in the films. Part of the dental profession's periodontal lethargy stems from inadequate attention to the disease during dental school training. Some dentists get discouraged because treatment requires more cooperation and participation than many patients are willing to give. Unless the gum tissue around the teeth is examined physically and radiographically, as described below, one can have periodic dental visits over many years without recognition of existing periodontal disease until it is quite advanced.

The Periodontal Pocket

In the early stages, appearance is not the key to diagnosing the common form of chronic destructive periodontal disease we call periodontitis. Rather, it is the depth of the sulcus or pocket formed by the fold of oral skin, the gingival cuff, that is designed to seal off the root of the tooth at the gum line. The normal depth of the sulcus is from one to three millimeters. When the attachment of the gum to the tooth at the depth of the sulcus is damaged and the sulcus extends beyond three millimeters along the side of the root, a pathological periodontal pocket may have formed.

There is nothing magical about three millimeters. A shallower pocket may also be eroded and infected by bacteria. A deeper pocket could be due to edematous or swollen gingiva as well as to the inflammation of gingivitis or it may be due to slight hypertrophy or overgrowth of gingiva without attachment damage. In some areas, such as behind the last molars, measurement of five to six millimeters is normal because of natural gum contours. In general, pocket depths less than four millimeters are considered normal as long as probing does not induce bleeding of the gums. It is bleeding that indicates the pocket is inflamed and unhealthy.

True periodontal pockets must be distinguished from pseudopockets that result from enlargement of the gum tissue on the crown of the tooth. Here one can have a normal attachment of the gum to the tooth but with excessive gum tissue. The problem then becomes primarily esthetic, with treatment geared to reduction or surgical removal of the excess tissue (gingivectomy).

Red, bleeding, puffy, or swollen gums may alert the individual to a problem, but the diagnosis of periodontitis requires clinical measurement of the gingival sulci throughout the mouth to determine if true periodontal pocketing is present.

Where there has been long-standing periodontal disease or rapid destruction of bone in certain areas, pocket depths of 6 or 7 millimeters may be recorded without necessarily indicating that any teeth will be lost. When the pocket approaches the entire length of the root, which may be 8 to 10 millimeters, or extends between the roots of a molar crown, eventual loss of the tooth is highly likely. Treatment has so improved that many of these previously "hopeless" teeth may be saved, at least for a few years, provided the patient has the money and the dedication to attempt it. But some teeth are beyond the redemption of dentistry's best effort.

Loss of a few teeth from advanced disease does not mean that all the teeth will be lost, even without professional periodontal treatment. Many people have had all their teeth removed even though only a few required extraction, in the mistaken belief by both patient and dentist that periodontitis would inevitably destroy the remaining teeth anyway.

The Periodontal Examination

Measuring pockets. Probing all the surfaces of all the teeth must be done periodically to assess periodontal health. At first this would seem to be an extremely difficult task, considering that each tooth has 6 areas that must be probed-168 pocket measures for a full set of 28 permanent teeth. The probe can be passed around each tooth quickly, however, with measurements recorded of only those areas that exceed 3 millimeters. The entire measurement of periodontal pockets seldom takes more than 5 minutes.

A narrow instrument, the **periodontal probe**, is inserted between the gum and the tooth, more or less parallel to the long axis of the root. The probe is a calibrated ruler with depth lines marked off in millimeters. There are also electronic probes linked to computers but they are no more accurate than mechanical probes. When connected to a computer, they provide beautiful printouts that are very impressive and can be used to promote excessive treatment, much like intraoral cameras that project enlarged images of teeth on TV screens. Used correctly, both modalities can be very educational for the patient.

As with any instrument, dentists and hygienists must use the probe properly. If too little pressure is exerted on the probe as it is extended into the sulcus, a false "negative" or undermeasurement results. Excess pressure is usually inhibited by the patient's pain response, but some patients overreact to any discomfort, leading to misdiagnosis. If the probe is inserted at the wrong angle, an overmeasurement results in a false "positive," incorrectly indicating a deep pocket when the pocket may be normal.

Bleeding points. Notation should also be made of bleeding points during probing because it is not only the depth of the pocket that is important but also the presence of inflammation. Bleeding points become more significant after initial treatment since the primary goal of periodontal therapy is to reduce inflammation whether or not pockets are eliminated.[11] Bleeding points that persist or recur are indicative of an inflamed and eroded epithelial attachment, probably with bacterial infection. Unfortunately, many dentists and hygienists ignore bleeding points, relying solely on pocket depth for diagnosis and determination of treatment needs.

Baseline data. The periodontal examination should also include observation of the color and texture of the gum tissue, areas of gum recession, evidence of traumatic occlusion including grinding and clenching of teeth, and measurement of tooth mobility. All this information should be recorded on a special periodontal examination form to provide a baseline for future reference. Baseline data is particularly important because once periodontal bone loss has occurred, it usually does not regenerate. The objective of periodontal care is to prevent further bone loss, which can be monitored only by comparing present measurements with past measurements.

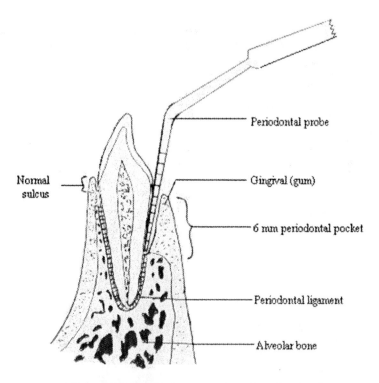

Normal sulcus

Periodontal probe

Gingival (gum)

6 mm periodontal pocket

Periodontal ligament

Alveolar bone

Figure 6-2 Measuring periodontal pocket depth

Probing measurements are not precise. Different dentists and hygienists get different measurements of the same pockets as well as variations in their own measurements from one day to the next. However, there is sufficient standardization for accuracy to within one millimeter. It is when the dentist or hygienist refers to bone regeneration or pocket depth reduction in tenths or even half-millimeters that one should raise a skeptical eyebrow or two. There simply is not that much accuracy in probing, nor is it required for a general assessment of periodontal disease and health.

When to probe. Not infrequently, a patient with gross tartar and puffy, bleeding gums may have pocket measurements of four to five millimeters throughout the mouth. After a good dental prophylaxis including subgingival scaling to remove the tartar and good home care with brushing and flossing, the pockets may shrink to a healthy two to three millimeters. In this case the four to five-millimeter measurements were of pseudopockets. While there is no harm in recording pseudopockets, a more meaningful periodontal evaluation takes place after the initial treatment to eliminate marginal gingivitis. Reevaluation of pocket measurements should be done three to six months following the last scaling, depending on the extent of the original condition. Reexamination before three months does not allow sufficient time for healing and home care to remedy the condition and often leads to premature or unnecessary periodontal surgery.

Radiographic (X-Ray) Diagnosis

Types of X-rays. Dental X-rays are an additional tool for diagnosing periodontal disease. Since many dentists do not perform routine probing examinations, it is often the radiographs that first reveal periodontal bone loss.

The most useful X-rays for this purpose are **bitewing** films (Figure 6-3), so named because they are taken of the upper and lower bicuspids and molars simultaneously in a biting position. The bitewing films show the level of bone between the posterior teeth.

Figure 6-3   *Bitewing X-rays-Normal bone, interproximal calculus and periodontal bone loss*

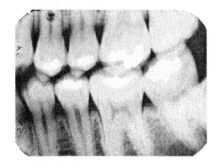

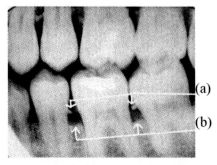

A. Bitewing X-ray showing normal level of interproximal bone.

B. Calculus deposits (a) are visible on the side or interproximal surfaces of the teeth; (b) Early interproximal bone loss.

C. Advanced periodontal bone loss about the root of the 2nd molar. Prognosis is hopeless and the tooth needs to be extracted.

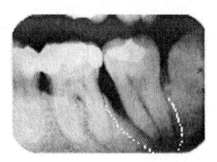

Periapical X-rays are necessary for the anterior teeth; they also show the entire root and surrounding bone of all teeth in close detail. The full-mouth X-ray series shown below includes both periapical and bitewing films, which document the status of the bone between the teeth down along the roots, but the inside and outside root surfaces are blocked out of view by the teeth themselves. That is one of the major reasons probing is a must, since only the probe can discover bone loss along all root surfaces. Figure 6-4 illustrates a normal dentition with no evidence of periodontal bone loss.

Figure 6-4   Full-mouth periapical and bitewing X-ray series.

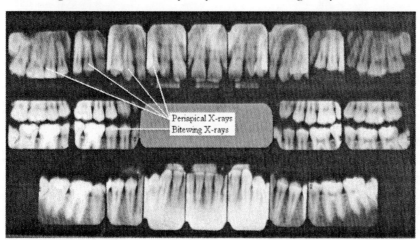

The least useful film is the **panoramic X-ray or panograph,** so named for the sweeping panoramic view of both upper and lower jaws in their entirety (Figure 6-5). While valuable as a screening film for major pathology and abnormalities, panographs are of limited value especially for periodontal diagnosis. Unfortunately, panographs have become popular in dental offices as a substitute for full-mouth periapical radiographs.

The panograph film is taken extraorally, which means the film is placed outside the mouth; therefore, it is much easier and quicker to do. The full-mouth intraoral periapical and bitewing series requires separate exposures for the 14 to 18 small films, which obviously takes longer and is more uncomfortable for the patient than the panograph. Even when the panograph is properly taken, and many are not, the diagnostic detail of the panograph is far inferior to a conventional intraoral series for routine diagnosis.

Figure 6-5   Panoramic X-ray (Panograph)

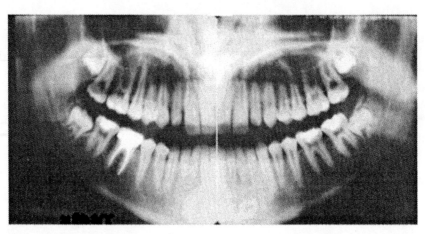

Longitudinal evaluation.   Comparison of X-rays taken over the years provides a longitudinal picture of the progress of the disease.   Therefore, it is important that dentists keep X-ray films mounted in special holders, not stuffed into coin envelopes, so that at subsequent examinations comparisons can be made between the first baseline X-rays and current films.   Without this historical perspective, patients are frequently led to believe that pyorrhea has just occurred when it has been present all along, with little change evident in the X-rays over the years.   There is, or at least there should be, a big difference in the approach to periodontal treatment if the disease process is chronic and slow compared with an acute, rapidly deteriorating condition.   (See chapter 14 for recommended frequency of X-rays.)

Other Diagnostic Indicators

Mobility   Tooth mobility may be the cause or the result of periodontal breakdown.   Minor mobility is not of itself a problem.   It may result from bruxing (grinding), clenching, biting on toothpicks, hairpins, pencils, and pipe stems, and from "doodling" one tooth against another.   Individual teeth may be loosened by traumatic occlusion.   If the bite is incorrect, if one tooth hits another with sufficient force, mobility of one or both teeth can occur.   Poor dentistry can also be the cause.   If, for example, a crown or a bridge hits the opposing tooth before the rest of the teeth meet, the striking teeth may loosen.   Removable bridges (partial dentures) are held in place by clasps on natural teeth.   If the clasps are too tight or the partial denture puts too much pressure on the supporting teeth, breakdown of the periodontal structure results and the teeth become loose.

Mobility from mechanical or traumatic forces disappears once the cause is removed, provided there has not been associated bone loss. But mobility from 50 percent or more bone loss due to periodontal disease is much more serious and may not be reversible.

Every normal tooth has slight movement that can barely be felt or observed. Because the difference between normal and abnormal or pathologic movement is so small, the measurement of mobility is hardly precise. It may be described as slight, moderate, or extreme, with notations on the dental chart such as +, + +, + + +, respectively. Suffice it to say that if the tooth moves more than one-quarter (.25) of a millimeter, it is mobile! Minor movement is not a serious problem, but if a tooth moves one-half to one millimeter, it may be too late to avoid an extraction.

Attrition. Abnormal wear facets on the surface of the enamel indicate grinding and clenching. The bone support of the root is so strong that instead of the tooth becoming loose, part of the chewing surface of the crown is worn away, leaving a flat surface. Unless the tooth becomes hypersensitive to touch and temperature change, most of this wear, or attrition, is not harmful except to the appearance of the teeth. In fact, as we age the sharp cusps of our teeth gradually wear down and flatten out. When the teeth are both worn flat and loose, with loss of periodontal bone, both the cause and the effect are observed simultaneously.

Gum recession. Receding gums may be caused by excessive, overly vigorous, toothbrushing and traumatic occlusion including bruxing, grinding or restorations that interfere with the normal bite. Recession sometimes follows orthodontic treatment, but more often the cause is idiopathic-unknown. Instead of recession, small **clefts** and **fissures** sometimes develop on the outside gum tissue covering the root. These conditions do not indicate inflammatory periodontal disease. The cause may be traumatic occlusion or bad habits-again, horizontal toothbrushing, clenching, and grinding. The dentist or hygienist should record as accurately as possible the extent of the recession or clefts. This measurement can then be compared over the years for change. More often than not it remains the same, and nothing need be done. But if the recession progresses to three millimeters or more, if the cleft lengthens, a **gingival graft** may be in order to restore the defect.

RECOMMENDATIONS

Most patients know that a dental examination consists of inspection for dental decay, defective restorations, and granulomas or abscesses around the roots of teeth. But it is not a complete examination unless it includes careful examination of the periodontal tissues—the gums and alveolar bone support.

1. Whether or not gums appear normal, adults should receive a complete periodontal examination at the initial visit and annually thereafter.
2. Make sure your dentist or hygienist probes around all your teeth.
3. Do not accept a panographic X-ray for periodontal diagnosis. If a problem is present, full-mouth periapical and bitewing films provide more accurate diagnosis and a baseline for future comparison. (A good dentist keeps baseline X-rays in special mounts for ready comparison with current films.)
4. If periodontal disease is diagnosed, ask your dentist to obtain the original or duplicated X-ray films from your previous dentists to provide a longitudinal perspective of the progression of the condition.
5. Most periodontal disease is chronic and responds to conservative treatment. Do not be rushed into surgery.

7

Primary Prevention of Periodontal Disease

The primary objective of periodontal disease prevention is to remove plaque from the teeth and to keep it off once removed. Because plaque re-forms within 24 hours, only personal hygiene can keep it from reestablishing itself. Some people are more susceptible than others. Therefore, not everyone must practice prevention with the same diligence.

Anyone with recognized periodontal disease, even in the early stages, is well advised not only to brush but also to floss the teeth thoroughly at least once a day, preferably twice a day. By the same token, excessive brushing and flossing can be harmful. A woman with an immaculately clean mouth complained that her teeth were very sensitive to cold water and brushing, even to breathing through her mouth. When she reported that she brushed five or six times a day, she was advised to brush no more than twice a day and to avoid scrubbing the necks of the teeth in a straight back-and-forth stroke. Within a few weeks the sensitivity to cold and brushing disappeared.

Similarly, there was a young man who never had a cavity. His gums were healthy, but the tissue between the teeth was "punched out." He had been advised to use dental floss. Figuring if a little floss was good, a lot was better, he tied knots in the string and pulled them through the teeth, destroying the interdental papilla, the triangular-shaped gum tissue that normally fills the space between teeth. On cessation of this destructive flossing, the gum tissue gradually grew back to its normal shape.

Professional treatment for diagnosed periodontal disease is generally divided into nonsurgical and surgical phases. Antibiotics and antimicrobial chemicals are used for acute infections and for supportive therapy. Brushing, flossing, and gum massage are forms of physical therapy. Mechanical protective devices such as plastic occlusal guards relieve problems caused by compulsive grinding. Orthodontic realignment of teeth corrects severe and traumatic occlusion. Prosthetic appliances-fixed and removable bridges and splints-may be necessary to restore and stabilize the teeth. And, of course, there is no substitute for personal effort.

PERSONAL PRIMARY PREVENTION

Basic Oral Hygiene

There are two major motivations for a person to practice good oral hygiene. They are to have sparkling clean teeth and wholesome breath, just like the chewing gum twins of the TV ads. Preventing periodontal disease, which requires an understanding and perhaps fear of its cause, is seldom foremost in the avid tooth brusher's mind.

Primary prevention of periodontal disease requires good personal home care with particular emphasis on diligent daily toothbrushing and flossing.[1] Once the disease has occurred, the same methods, supplemented by professional treatment and special devices and rinses, prevent further extension of the disease. Over the years various brushing and flossing methods have been advocated: this shape, that shape, soft bristles, hard bristles, waxed floss, unwaxed floss, and so on. Whenever we find such inconsistency among the authorities, we can reasonably conclude that there is no one best way, but rather a number of modalities that work well.

How to brush. As long as one brushes without abrading, puncturing, or otherwise irritating the gums, one technique is probably as good as another, provided plaque is effectively removed. One should not scrub the teeth with a straight back-and-forth stroke because of the danger of wearing grooves along the necks of the teeth, the area at the gum line where the crown joins the root. Brushing from the gums to the tips of the teeth or with a circular motion removes most plaque without damaging the surfaces of teeth. However, plaque also forms beneath the gingival cuff. If the bristles are placed at a 45-degree angle at the neck of the tooth so that the tips slip under the cuff and the brush is then jiggled back and forth, newly formed plaque can be removed from this covered area.

The average person takes less than a minutes to brush his or her teeth and fails to remove nearly two-thirds of plaque.[2] One two-minute episode of really thorough brushing and flossing would be sufficient to remove most plaque. Since few people are that patient or diligent at one brushing, twice-daily brushing is recommended. Brushing more than twice a day is no more effective and, indeed, may actually be harmful.

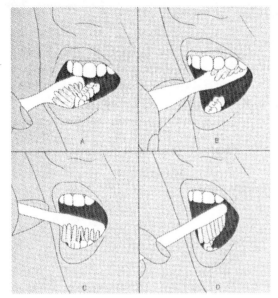

Figure 7-1. Acceptable Tooth Brushing Method.

(A-B) Place the bristles at a 45-degree angle toward the gums. Jiggle the brush so that the tips of the bristles slip beneath the gums and then rotate the brush toward the tops of the teeth. Repeat 10 times on all inside and outside surfaces. Do not scrub back and forth. (C) Brush the lower front teeth with an upward stroke. (D) Brush chewing surfaces and the tongue. Rinse with water.

While emphasizing the importance of tooth and gum care in oral health, one should not ignore the tongue. A healthy tongue is smooth and pink. Excessive smoking and coffee consumption can cause stains and irritate the top surface. Mouth breathing, particularly during sleep, dries out the mouth, preventing adequate lubrication by saliva. A dry mouth may leave the tongue with an unpleasant white coating of dead surface tissue cells that are normally washed away by saliva. As some people age, their tongues becomes fissured and the taste buds and other papillae on the top of the tongue grow longer, giving the appearance of a hairy surface. To eliminate stains and mouth odors emanating from the tongue, it should be cleaned daily with a soft nylon toothbrush. (*See also* the section on Halitosis in chapter 5.)

Choosing a toothbrush. Many dentists recommend a rectangular-shaped soft nylon brush without fancy curves and tufts. Others prefer a harder brush that softens a little after some use. The advantage of a soft brush is that it can be used on the gum as well as the teeth and tongue with less risk of abrasion. That is why a soft nylon brush is better for young children. However, a medium-hard brush with nylon or natural bristles cleans the hard surfaces of teeth better. One way for you to evaluate which brush is best for you is to run your tongue over your teeth after brushing. If the teeth do not feel smooth and clean, you may want to switch to a harder toothbrush. You can have the best of both worlds by using a soft brush at a 45-degree angle against the gums and a medium hard brush for the enamel surfaces.

Plaque **disclosing tablets** (wafers), available in the local pharmacy, contain a vegetable dye that stains red any plaque that remains on the teeth after brushing and flossing. The wafer is chewed and mixed with saliva and then swished to bathe all the teeth with the solution. By disclosing the residual plaque to view, you can learn where better brushing and flossing are needed. Disclosing tablets are not recommended for daily use but only as an occasional checkup on brushing efficiency. Since most brushing is deficient anyway, the best advise is to take a little more time and work conscientiously at being more thorough.

The toothbrush should be replaced when it has lost its original shape and the bristles are bent and frayed. If you brush more than once a day, it is a good idea to have two brushes. By alternating, the bristles have time to dry out and become firm again for reuse.

Rechargeable battery operated toothbrushes are recommended for handicapped persons who lack the manual dexterity required for hand brushing. Electric toothbrushes, though quite expensive, remove plaque effectively from exposed tooth surfaces, though the same results can be obtained from a hand brush if you brush long enough. Individuals who are too impatient for thorough manual brushing would benefit from one of the newer electric toothbrushes with programmed timers that tell you when to shift from one side of the mouth to another over a period of two minutes.

Following treatment for moderate to advanced periodontal disease, an electric toothbrush, with its high speed oscillation, may be nearly as effective as brushing with both a conventional toothbrush and a small interproximal brush.[3-5] However, the electric brush cannot completely remove plaque from the proximal surfaces, especially if the spaces between the teeth are filled with gum tissue. Interproximal plaque can be removed from these surfaces only by use of dental floss.

For a person with average dexterity and no special dental problems, an electric brush may be just one more superfluous gadget.

Choosing a toothpaste. Brushing with a toothpaste that combines a very mild abrasive and a safe detergent is the most effective way to clean teeth. You should not use so much paste that you foam at the mouth when you brush. A half-inch dollop of paste is more than sufficient. The addition of fluorides reduces dental decay and gum line sensitivity. The fluoride can also repair early caries by promoting remineralization of enamel. Some toothpastes, described as tooth whiteners, may contain harsher abrasives to remove tobacco stains. They are not intended for daily use since the abrasive may wear away the tooth surface, especially at the gum line, and produce areas of hypersensitivity. Do not brush with table salt, which is excessively abrasive. Baking soda, popular in the past, is not as effective as modern toothpastes. Unless one forms a great deal of tartar, tartar-reducing toothpastes have little advantage over regular pastes. The best guide is to choose a fluoride toothpaste that has the approval of the American Dental Association and suits your personal taste.[6]

How to floss. (See Figure 7-2) The function of dental floss is to clean the side surfaces of incisors and cuspids and the front and back surfaces of the bicuspids and molars that cannot be reached by the toothbrush—what dentists call the *proximal* surfaces, meaning the sides next to each other. The floss is stretched taut between fingers, which are placed inside and outside the teeth. The floss is then gently slipped between the teeth. Excessive pressure that snaps the floss through the contact points of the teeth can injure the gum tissue, so it is important to ease rather than force the floss through. The floss should then be worked three or four times up and down in a scraping motion against the front and back tooth surfaces without rubbing against the gum as it passes from side to side. The floss should not be pulled back and forth like a shoeshine cloth. This "sawing" action can wear grooves into the roots.

Flossing is a skill that does not come easily. It must be practiced until one's fingers get a "feel" for where they are and what they are doing. Floss holders can be purchased to make it easier, but they are not necessary for anyone with normal dexterity. As long as you can hold a string taut between two fingers you can learn to floss. But even a skilled flosser has difficulty where contacts between the teeth are very tight or there are rough or sharp edges on fillings and tartar deposits that tear or fray the nylon. A trip to the dentist will be necessary to eliminate these problems by smoothing or replacing defective fillings and scaling the teeth.

Flossing should be completely painless. Too much pressure is being applied the wrong way if the gums hurt. Bleeding when one begins to floss usually indicates that more regular flossing is necessary. The reason is the ubiquitous bacterial plaque that irritates and inflames the tissue. As plaque is removed by the floss and prevented from re-forming by repeated flossing, the tissue regains its health and bleeding ceases. Instead of stopping, as some people do when they see blood on the dental floss, continuing to floss will help end the bleeding by eliminating the inflammation that causes it.

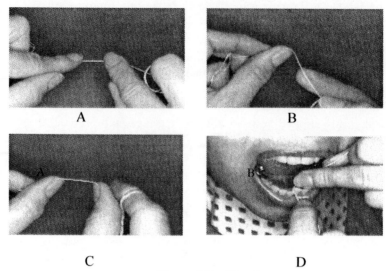

Figure 7-2   Flossing

A. *Wrap the ends of a 12-inch piece of lightly waxed dental floss around the middle fingers or forefingers. Stretch the floss taut between the thumbs to reach front and back teeth.*
B. *Or stretch between a thumb and forefinger.*
C. *Or stretch between both thumbs.*
D. *Gently slip the floss between the teeth and firmly rub each interproximal surface (front and back sides) **up and down**. Do not "saw" back and forth and avoid excess pressure on the gums.*

Flossing may also elicit an unpleasant taste and smell as decomposed food debris that has accumulated between the teeth is removed. No matter how thoroughly one brushes, only floss (or little interproximal brushes for large spaces) can clean these otherwise inaccessible proximal surfaces and further reduce some unpleasant mouth odors. Since bacteria thrive on the same food we eat, removal of bacterial plaque prevents not only gingivitis and periodontal disease but also dental decay.

Choosing a dental floss. Dental floss is a string of nylon or other fibers that come thick and thin, round and flat, waxed and unwaxed, flavored and unflavored. Each type has its advocates. Originally, all floss was waxed to permit easy passage between the teeth, but advocates of unwaxed floss claim that waxed floss glides over the tooth surface without removing plaque. In fact, it makes no difference. Waxed floss cleans as well as unwaxed, and both can be beneficial if used properly, and useless or harmful if abused.[7]

A waxed dental floss has the advantage of slipping between the teeth more easily. It is also less likely to fray and tear. Nothing is more exasperating than floss stuck between the teeth, an event much more frequent with unwaxed floss. If your choice is unwaxed, always be sure to have a waxed floss on hand in case an unwaxed piece gets stuck. If you cannot get it out at once, try again in a few hours with the waxed floss. Sooner or later you will succeed.

Other Devices

Many toothbrushes have **rubber tips** on the end of the handle to stimulate or massage the gum tissue between the teeth. Special gum massagers are also available with similar tips and little suction cups at the opposite end to be rubbed over the gums. The pointed tips slip between the teeth and massage the interdental papillae by a rotary or jiggling action. If the gums are puffy or enlarged, the stimulation provided by these devices can return them to normal once the underlying cause, such as tartar deposits, is removed. **Toothpicks** have been used throughout the ages to pick food out from between the teeth. They come round and flat, narrow and thick, hard and soft and mostly pointed but some blunt, and some made out of ivory with gold handles. Toothpicks push large food particles from the teeth, but they are not as effective as dental floss. Care must be exercised not to damage the gum by excessive pressure. Specially designed toothpicks made out of soft orangewood are available to massage the gum papillae as well as to clean the side surfaces of the teeth. Chewing on toothpicks can traumatize and loosen teeth. Excessive pressure on the gums worsens the condition. A good rule is that if it hurts, stop doing it.

Tiny **interproximal brushes** are also available. They look like little bottle brushes and are small enough to slip between the teeth when the spaces have been opened up by periodontal disease or periodontal surgery. The bristles of these brushes clean the crevices and concavities of the roots, areas likely to be missed by floss and other interdental stimulators. But they should only be used where there is adequate space to slip between the teeth without force.

Water irrigators direct pressurized water in a steady stream or pulsating jets against the teeth and gums.[8] A reservoir holds water or a solution that is forced through a narrow nozzle by a small electric pump. Water irrigators are of little value for a manually dextrous person with healthy teeth and gums since their cleansing ability is limited to removal of debris that can also be removed by brushing and flossing. But they are effective for those with limited dexterity who have large spaces between their teeth or who have orthodontic braces that retain food in areas the brush cannot reach.

Irrigators are frequently recommended for home use for persons with periodontal disease. Solutions containing antibacterials like chlorhexidine or tetracycline, available through a dentist's prescription, can be added to the reservoir and pumped directly into periodontal pockets through special tips, supposedly to reduce bacterial inflammation and infection.[9] However, water irrigators, whether applied at home or in the dental office, can not conduct these antibacterials into the depth of the periodontal pocket, without which there is little if any benefit. The only way antimicrobials can effectively reduce bacteria in the pocket is to have a dentist place the substance directly into the pocket in the form of small chips or impregnated fibers, the latter having to be removed at the end of two weeks. Even though this therapy has a short-term effect, it requires repeated application, and studies have yet to prove its long-term value. It is not a substitute for periodic scaling and root planing and conscientious home care, and can lead to development of microbial resistance.[10, 11] If you do use an irrigator, avoid excessive water force to avoid further damage to the already damaged tissue. If pain or discomfort is felt, reduce the pressure.

The smart dental consumer will be wary of dentists who offer antibacterial gum irrigation in the dental office at an additional $50 to $200 following "deep scaling," for which another couple of hundred dollars is charged. Patient's with no significant periodontal disease but heavy calculus deposits on many teeth may require deep, or rather, thorough subgingival scaling. If the calculus is really heavy, two visits may be required to remove it all. It is the removal of the calculus that eliminates gingivitis. Dental office "irrigation" after a scaling is a worthless procedure that is no more effective than rinsing out your mouth.

For the average person, a home water irrigator is a questionable luxury. Contented users like the sense of freshness, but the same result is achieved with thorough brushing and flossing followed by swishing with clean water.

Commercial mouth rinses also have little value for the dentally healthy person. Because they contain a large amount of alcohol, excessive use irritates the oral mucosa. They are not even effective in reducing halitosis—bad breath—except momentarily (*See* chapter 5). Unless you have a special problem, the best mouth rinse is half a teaspoon of table salt dissolved in a glass of warm water, or just plain water. Persons with hypersensitive roots or with dry mouth due to decreased saliva will benefit from the caries-inhibiting effects of concentrated fluoride rinses. Antiseptic mouth rinses are no substitute for thorough toothbrushing and flossing to reduce gingivitis, but they can serve as a supplement if mechanical procedures are not adequate. Prolonged used of antiseptic rinses should be avoided. If an abnormal condition does not clear up in a few days, a trip to the dentist is recommended.

PROFESSIONAL PREVENTION

Dental Prophylaxis

Some types of primary prevention require professional intervention. Poliomyelitis, smallpox, and diphtheria can be prevented by vaccines that stimulate formation of antibodies in the blood to combat the invading organism when we are exposed to it later on. As yet there are no effective vaccines to fight the multitude of bacteria and viruses that cause the common oral diseases. Instead, we rely on preventive measures such as personal oral hygiene and periodic dental prophylaxis.

Prophylaxis means "to prevent." In dentistry the term refers to professional **cleaning and scaling** of the teeth by a dentist or dental hygienist. The purpose of the prophylaxis is the prevention of gingivitis, pyorrhea and dental decay, but it should be clear by now that an occasional professional prophylaxis cannot substitute for adequate daily personal oral hygiene.

Elements of a dental prophylaxis. The purpose of a prophylaxis is to eliminate deposits on the teeth that cannot be removed by diligent brushing and flossing. It consists of **scaling** the teeth to remove tartar and **coronal polishing** to remove stains. Stains themselves present no significant problem other than that they may detract from your appearance. It is the tartar and plaque on the crowns and roots above and below the gum—supragingival and subgingival deposits—that present a health risk unless they are removed.

Plaque begins to form almost immediately after a prophylaxis, but it takes about three months for toxic products in retained deposits to mature to the point where tissue damage begins to occur. In a healthy mouth, this time is extended by daily brushing and flossing. Nonetheless, plaque creeps down along the sides of the teeth into the gingival sulcus. Since plaque cannot be removed completely from the sulcus by personal effort, periodic professional treatment, as frequently as every three months for patients with periodontal disease, is necessary to remove the remaining deposits. Thus, removal of soft and hard subgingival plaque, not stain removal, is the significant function of a prophylaxis. Thorough tooth brushing and flossing every day removes food debris and newly formed plaque and minimizes tartar formation. But once plaque and tartar are firmly established beneath the gum tissue, professional scaling and root planing are necessary to remove it and to maintain periodontal health.

Coronal polishing is usually performed with a rubber cup mounted on the dental handpiece, what most people refer to as the "drill." A small amount of polishing paste, similar to toothpaste but more abrasive, is placed in the rubber cup, which is then rotated against the exposed surfaces of the teeth to remove the stains. Stains within the recesses of tiny cracks, pits, and fissures have to be scraped off with picks and scalers or blown away with a mildly abrasive air jet. Coronal polishing of all the teeth can be accomplished in a few minutes.

A device called a Prophy-Jet removes difficult stains easily by "sand blasting" with baking soda.[12] Baking soda is a very mild abrasive, sufficient to blast away the stains without damaging enamel.

Stains come in a variety of colors, from green to brown to black. Green stains are usually found on the upper front teeth of young children-the incisors.

When these teeth first come into the mouth, they are covered by a thin cuticle, a remnant of the surrounding sac in which the teeth develop This cuticle, which is stained by bacteria and fungi normally present in the mouth, usually wears off in a few years, but sometimes professional coronal polishing is necessary to remove it. Some black and brown stains are the result of pigments produced by bacteria. Most stains in adults come from tobacco, coffee, and tea, and can usually be removed easily.

Not all stains can be removed by coronal polishing. Tobacco stains can permanently discolor teeth in heavy users. Teeth of miners exposed to copper and iron dusts may be permanently discolored green or brown. Drugs containing similar metal salts have the same effect. But by far the worst medically induced discoloration results from the improper prescription of tetracycline, an otherwise exceptionally safe antibiotic. **Tetracycline staining** occurs when the drug is administered during the last half of pregnancy and the first eight years of childhood. During this period the crowns of the permanent teeth are developing, and tetracycline produces a gray, yellow, or brown discoloration that ranges from mild to severe. Because most physicians and dentists are now aware of this danger and substitute other antibiotics, tetracycline staining in children is no longer as common as it used to be. The condition is not damaging to the teeth other than to their appearance. In many cases the teeth can be bleached by a dentist to a natural light yellow-white hue. If repeated bleaching fails, then the teeth can be resurfaced with composite or laboratory-fabricated veneers.

Mottled enamel or fluorosis is another type of permanent stain that comes about through ingestion of excessive amounts of a chemical, in this case fluorine. Fluorides-the salts of fluorine-are found in natural water supplies throughout the world. A concentration not exceeding two parts of fluoride per million parts of water may cause a small amount of discoloration, which is not necessarily unsightly. Small areas of light yellow or light brown spots or patches-mottling-may be noticed on close inspection but not from a normal speaking distance. As the concentration of fluoride increases, mottling becomes more pronounced and more unsightly. When the concentration reaches six or seven parts per million, the enamel may not only be unevenly discolored yellow-brown but also pitted and altogether unsightly. Except for the effect on the color of the enamel, there is no known bad effect on general or dental health from ingesting fluorides in these amounts, either from naturally or artificially fluoridated water or dietary supplements. In fact, all the research demonstrates that the combined effect of water fluoridation and topical fluorides reduce tooth decay by as much as 70 percent with no adverse effect on general health. Further, fluoride supplements can also strengthen bones and are used in the treatment of osteoporosis, although its effectiveness in alleviating this disease has not been proved.[13]

Coronal polishing cannot change the appearance of mottling or pitting that has become an integral part of the enamel. Mild cases can be bleached under a dentist's supervision, and more severe discoloration and pitting are easily corrected by applying composite filling material and bonded plastic and porcelain veneers.

Most children require only coronal polishing for their prophylaxes, whereas most adults need to have their teeth scaled as well as polished. Because coronal polishing is confined to the exposed surfaces of teeth, the procedure is uncomplicated and does not require the sophisticated training that dentists and dental hygienists undergo. A trained dental assistant can polish the teeth as well as anyone else. Some states, notably California, Oregon, and Washington, permit registered dental assistants (RDAs) who have been trained in this extended function to perform coronal polishing after the dentist or hygienist has done the necessary scaling.

You may wonder why most state regulatory agencies prohibit dental assistants from polishing teeth. It has less to do with quality control than the insecurity of dentists who fear that expanding the role of auxiliaries might reduce their income. In this regard, dentistry lags far behind medicine. Physicians have a large array of specially trained auxiliaries and technicians to assist them, which not only allows them to treat more patients better but also to maintain or improve their income. Dentists as well as patients would benefit from allowing auxiliaries to perform, under supervision, such functions as coronal polishing, applying sealants, and even placing fillings. The tragedy is that restriction of auxiliaries not only denies the public needed services at a more reasonable cost but causes dentists to become bored and frustrated doing again and again, over many years, tasks that auxiliaries could do as well. Policies governing public services should be based on what is best for the public. In the long run, what is best for the public will also be best for those who serve it.

Supragingival and Subgingival Scaling

The hard, calcified plaque—**tartar, plaque, or scale**—that forms on both the exposed crown near the gum line and below the gum can be removed only by chipping or scraping it off. The procedure is called supragingival scaling when the tartar is above the gum line and subgingival scaling when below.

Because scaling is more complicated than coronal polishing, it requires special training and must be done by a dentist or dental hygienist. Dental hygienists receive two years of intensive clinical training, more supervised training in scaling than is taught general dentists in dental schools. Most scaling can be done without anesthesia, but some patients are particularly sensitive and prefer the minor discomfort of the needle and the numbness of the anesthetic to the discomfort or pain of scaling. In some states the hygienist is permitted to administer local anesthetics, that is, to give injections. Many dental offices provide nitrous oxide (N_2O) analgesia. This allays anxiety and reduces apprehension, permitting extensive scaling of the hyper-reactive patient without local anesthetics. Analgesia is not quite an anesthetic. It numbs the sense of pain, rendering it more tolerable even though it may still be felt, but it is no substitute for anesthesia when the pain, real or anticipated, threatens to be unacceptable. (See chapter 13 for a discussion of the pros and cons of nitrous oxide analgesia.)

Supragingival calculus is easy to remove because it is visible. Subgingival calculus sometimes can be seen as a dark line beneath the tip of the gingival cuff. More often it is not visible and therefore must be detected manually to be removed. Detection of calculus requires a highly developed tactile sense, consisting of a light touch with a fine metal instrument—a scaler or dental explorer—that transmits the rough surface or "catch" to the fingertips, telling the dentist or hygienist that calculus is present. Every moviegoer has seen the safecracker, sometimes with sandpapered fingertips for increased sensitivity, feeling his way on the lock's dial to detect the clicks of the combination. So it is with the hygienist and dentist. They must have that light touch, that highly developed tactile sense, to detect the tartar on the root surface. Then it takes firm pressure to remove the scale. But the diagnostic touch to find the calculus and the post-scaling touch to make sure it is all gone must be safecracker-light.

How Teeth Are Scaled. The most commonly used instruments are hand scalers, which are shaped like sickles, curved spoons, hoes, or files, depending on the teeth to be scaled and the preferences of the dentist or hygienist. The scaler is placed on the tooth and gently inserted beneath the gum and beyond the calculus. Once the edge of the scaler is just beyond the calculus, firm pressure is applied toward the crown or top of the tooth to dislodge it. The scale does not always come off conveniently in one piece, so the process may have to be repeated a few times. Then it may be necessary to scrape and plane the surface of the tooth smooth. Most supragingival and subgingival scaling does not hurt at all because it is against enamel, which has no sensitivity. However, if the instrument is too large for the task or is used in the wrong place or at the wrong angle, discomfort is unavoidable. Even in the hands of the best operator, there will always be some discomfort, some pain, when the instrument presses against the gum tissue. For most people it is not sufficient to require an anesthetic.

If a dentist or hygienist causes more than minimal pain or discomfort during a routine prophylactic scaling, it is usually due to a heavy hand, an insensitive operator, or what the profession refers to as poor technique. Tolerance for pain is very subjective, and you should not hesitate to tell the dentist or hygienist when you feel it is excessive. To relieve minor pain, a topical anesthetic can be applied to the gum tissue in the form of a gel. It numbs the tissue enough to make the procedure tolerable. If a routine prophylaxis still hurts quite a bit, you should consider changing to another dentist or hygienist. But if it does not hurt at all, you may not be receiving necessary subgingival scaling.

Ultrasonic scalers are devices that cause very rapid vibration of the tips of the instrument. When placed against or beneath the tartar, the ultrasonic vibrations dislodge heavy deposits. Since rapid vibrations against the tooth surface also produce heat and pain, the tips are bathed in a cool water spray. The ultrasonic scaler is a favorite instrument of some hygienists and dentists because it relieves the tedium and strain of hand scaling. Many patients also prefer the ultrasonic scaler because for them it may be less painful. However, some patients react just the opposite, feeling that the ultrasonic device is as bad as the dental drill.

Previously considered an adjunct to rather than a substitute for hand scaling, the newly designed ultrasonic scaler tips allow access to periodontal pockets and removal of calculus as effectively as manual scaling.[14] Manual or ultrasonic scaling can damage the roots of teeth if done with excessive force or improper angulation of the scaler. Even when done properly, the root surfaces may become sensitive over time as the protective layer of cementum is thinned or removed.

The ultrasonic scaler does not permit the same fine tactile sense of a manual scaler. Therefore, after the heavy, gross, hard deposits are removed by the ultrasonic scaler, the dentist or hygienist should carefully go over all the surfaces of the teeth with an explorer or small hand scaler to feel for any remnants of calculus beneath the gum. A good operator will remove these smaller deposits with the hand scaler to finish the job.

Rotary scalers are used by some dentists to remove calculus. Shaped like a drill and placed in the dental handpiece that dentists use for drilling teeth, they rotate at high speed to shake loose and dislodge the calculus. But they are more prone to damage the tooth surface, especially if placed on the root that lacks the protective hard shell of enamel. You would be wise to decline the use of drill-operated rotary scalers. Hand and ultrasonic scalers are much safer.

How Often Is a Dental Prophylaxis Necessary?

Coronal polishing is essentially a cosmetic service to remove stains on teeth that are not removed by ordinary toothbrushing. Unless stains are particularly heavy and persistent, there is no reason to have a professional cleaning at all. Yet it is customary for dentists to recommend that you and your children have your teeth cleaned twice a year even though dentists rarely have it done to themselves that often. If you practice good oral hygiene, you can save your teeth and your money by having a professional polishing no more than every year or two.

Scaling is another matter. Even though one practices good oral hygiene and is effective in keeping supragingival tartar off the teeth, tartar eventually accumulates beneath the gum, with but few exceptions. The frequency of scaling depends on how rapidly this occurs. In young children, most calculus is supragingival—above the gums. Subgingival calculus usually is not a problem until middle or late adolescence. Even then, an annual scaling is sufficient. Unless there is a special problem, children who brush do not require a professional prophylaxis more frequently than every 12 to 18 months.

The same frequency applies to adults unless there is a recognizable need for higher frequency. If you have diagnosed periodontal disease, professional scaling may be appropriate as often as every 3 months.[15] Remember, though, that what you do for yourself every day is much more important than what the dentist or hygienist does every 3 or 4 or 6 or 12 months. You are the only one who can, by maintaining adequate oral hygiene, keep daily plaque from hardening into calculus.[16]

RECOMMENDATIONS

1. Brush and floss daily to prevent periodontal disease.
2. One carefully done two-minute session is more effective than frequent haphazard brushings throughout the day.
3. Jiggle a soft nylon brush at a 45-degree angle against the gingival cuff to remove subgingival plaque. A medium-hard brush cleans the exposed surfaces of teeth more effectively.
4. Check your technique occasionally with disclosing tablets.
5. Electric toothbrushes are effective for individuals with limited manual dexterity, but otherwise have no special advantage over a regular toothbrush.
6. Use a lightly waxed dental floss and move the floss up and down against the sides of the teeth in a scraping, not "sawing," motion.
7. Unless you have a special problem, the best mouth rinse is half a teaspoon of table salt dissolved in a glass of warm water, or just plain water.
8. If you do have periodontal disease, ask your dentist about chlorhexidine rinses and home or self-irrigation of the pockets.
9. Most people should have a semiannual or annual prophylaxis by a dentist or dental hygienist to remove tartar and plaque deposits beneath the gingival cuff. Don't let the dentist talk you into paying extra for gum irrigation as part of a routine prophylaxis.
10. The most important element of a prophylaxis is subgingival scaling, and periodic root planing if you have periodontal disease.

8

Treatment of
Periodontal Disease

SECONDARY PREVENTION —
NONSURGICAL TREATMENT

Unlike many diseases that, once treated, are effectively cured, periodontal disease is a concomitant of aging, affecting at least 35 percent of the population with teeth aged 30 years and older.[1] If good oral hygiene is practiced, as described in the preceding chapter, most of us can avoid serious periodontal disease. But some periodontal pockets and bone loss will occur around at least a few teeth as we age, so that more intensive professional treatment may be required to slow down the process. Thus, if primary prevention cannot prevent the disease entirely, secondary prevention or treatment is necessary to minimize the damage.

By now you know that the loss of supporting tissues around the teeth is caused by toxins produced by bacteria that grow in the plaque and that these toxic products may invade the gingival tissue. Bacterial toxins also permeate the thin layer of cementum that covers the surfaces of roots and contains the fibers of the periodontal ligament, which attaches the roots to their bony sockets. The body's natural defense mechanism brings specialized cells into the infected area to destroy the bacteria and eliminate the toxins. Overreaction of these defensive mechanisms causes loss of connective tissue and partial or complete destruction of the periodontal ligament and alveolar bone, with loosening and loss of teeth.

Root Planing

As a general rule, once the bone encasing a tooth has been lost, it cannot be restored; therefore, the goal is to prevent further bone loss, abscess formation, loosening of teeth, and eventual tooth loss. Basic nonsurgical therapy consists of periodic root planing. Frequency depends on the severity of the condition. In moderate to severe periodontitis, periodontal therapy is recommended every three to four months since that is about how long it takes for bacterial plaque to become firmly reestablished in the depths of the pockets.[2]

Root planing removes plaque, calculus, and infected cementum and smoothes root surfaces by means of manually applied sharp scalers and curettes or power-driven ultrasonic scalers, both of which have been shown to be equally effective when properly done.[3] The goal is to remove the hard plaque deposits (calculus) and smooth the rough surfaces of the roots. Although described separately, gingival curettage is a concomitant of root planing.

Gingival Curettage

Gingival curettage removes the epithelial or outer lining and inflamed tissue inside periodontal pockets. Whether inadvertent or intentional, curettage is a natural consequence of root planing. The space between the gum and the teeth is so small that the outer edge of the scaler/curette opposite the tooth rubs against and curettes the tissue surface of the sulcus. This is why gums bleed during scaling and root planing.

Gingival curettage is sometimes employed as a separate procedure to control chronic inflammation and to attempt reattachment of the epithelial lining of the pocket to the root. The epithelial lining is the "skin" covering the inside of the gum tissue. It is this lining that attaches to the root and to the bottom of the gingival cuff or sulcus. When it becomes inflamed and eroded, a pathway is opened for the invasion of bacteria between the gum tissue and the root, down into the bone. The hope is that after curettage removes inflamed and infected tissue, a new epithelial attachment will grow back, sealing the pocket and preventing future bacterial invasion. It is not certain that the epithelium ever fully reattaches itself to the tooth root, but at least the pocket closes sufficiently to minimize reinfection.

In contrast to nonsurgical scaling and root planing, gingival curettage is a surgical procedure. The distinction is specious, however, since one cannot scale and root plane without also curetting the adjacent gum tissue. On the other hand, there are times when gingival curettage alone is needed, as when inflammation is present in the absence of calculus and roughened root surfaces.

Correcting Defective Restorations

Any rough or irregular surface becomes an area for the accumulation and protection of plaque. Not infrequently, fillings and artificial crowns have rough or defective margins extending into the periodontal pocket. Although the role of defective restorations in producing periodontal disease has been exaggerated, all such defects should be smoothed by the dentist with files or rotary drills to minimize irritation of the gum and accumulation of plaque.

Indication for Scaling and Root Planing (SRP)

If the regular scaling provided by your dentist or hygienist, coupled with conscientious brushing and flossing, still leaves your gums spongy and bleeding, you probably have more than gingivitis. If the dental examination reveals numerous periodontal pocket depths exceeding four millimeters, you most likely also have periodontal bone loss and therefore some degree of periodontitis or pyorrhea.

Phase I therapy-*SRP*, oral hygiene and home care instruction-is the *sine qua non* for the treatment of periodontitis. No one should contemplate Phase II or surgical treatment until the effects of Phase I therapy have been evaluated over a minimum 3 to 6 month period. As noted above, the indication for SRP is the presence of inflammatory (bleeding) periodontal pockets 4 mm or more in depth.

Repeated scaling and root planing does not cause significant damage to the tooth or its attachment. The outer layer of cementum removed is too small to be of any consequence. Over years of intensive scaling, however, enough cementum may be removed to result in root sensitivity to toothbrushing, hot and cold temperatures, certain types of foods, and subsequent scalings.[4]

Although pocket depths are literally the measure of the disease, the condition is more important than the depth. For example, if there is little or no bleeding when pockets are probed by the dentist or hygienist, the condition is not as serious as when bleeding or hemorrhaging occurs. It is more important to eliminate inflammation than pockets. If pocket depth is so great that it becomes difficult to maintain adequate cleanliness, however, it may be necessary to lower the depth by surgery. (See the following section on surgical therapy.)

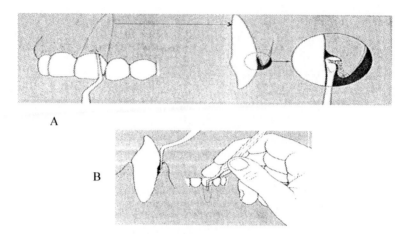

Figure 8-1 Manual gingival curettage and root planing

A. *Gingival curettage-debridement of the soft tissue wall of a gingival pocket, removing the inflammatory granulation tissue.*

B. *Root planing—removal of calcified plaque (tartar) and softened or rough cementum from the surface of the tooth root.*

Avoid Overcharges: Count Your Pockets

Following an initial diagnosis of periodontitis, some dentists will prescribe four quadrants of root planing, regardless of the number of deep pockets found. To understand what is meant by a quadrant, visualize your mouth divided into four parts-the two jaws each divided in half. Each quadrant will include the teeth from the central incisor (the upper and lower front teeth at the midline of your face) to the back molars on each side. If the dentist suggests four quadrants of scaling, the implication is that all of the teeth in each quadrant have pocket depths exceeding three millimeters. But this may not be the case. Only one, two, or three teeth in each quadrant, not six or seven, may have significant periodontal pockets. Only these teeth require root planing. In fact, root planing teeth with normal pocket (sulcus) depths of two to three millimeters damages the epithelial attachment, producing rather than eliminating a periodontal disease condition.[5]

You or your dental insurance plan should not be charged for four quadrants of treatment when the sum total of all the teeth with periodontal pocketing is the equivalent of only one or two quadrants. Since it is standard procedure for dentists to charge for all four quadrants even if only a few teeth in each quadrant need treatment, it is up to you to insist that the treatment as well as the charges be consistent with real need. One hour of scaling and root planing may be all that is necessary, and the charge should be for the equivalent of one quadrant if only six or seven teeth throughout the mouth have significant pocket depths. The only way you can find out how many pockets are to be treated is to ask to see the periodontal pocket measure chart. A good compromise would be to ask that the charge be based on time, in which case be prepared to spend $150 to $200 an hour. If only an hour is required to root plan a few teeth in each quadrant, you will have saved more than double that amount compared to being charged by the quadrant.

If you are taking good care of your mouth and have only a few periodontal pockets exceeding four millimeters, you do not need a professional scaling more than twice a year, especially if there is no evidence of bleeding gums on flossing. Remember that gums tend to bleed when you do not floss. A little bleeding when you resume flossing is to be expected, as long as it stops shortly thereafter. If bleeding remains fairly constant, a thorough periodontal examination should be arranged. If you have a number of teeth in each quadrant with deep pockets, then it is advisable to have a session of root planing—a periodontal prophylaxis—very three or four months.

Setting Aside the Time

Initial periodontal therapy generally takes from 1 to 4 hours, sometimes longer, depending on the number of teeth needing treatment. For moderate to advanced periodontal disease, 45 to 60 minutes is necessary to scale and root plane each quadrant of 7 or 8 teeth. If all or almost all your teeth have diseased pockets, 3 to 4 hours of intensive root planing with local anesthesia is the standard of good initial treatment. Since this is more than most people can tolerate at one session, four 45 to 60 minute appointments are usually scheduled. Some patients have 2 quadrants done at one appointment, requiring only about an hour and a half. When appointments run shorter than 45 minutes, you have cause to be concerned. As a rule, proper root planing requires a separate appointment that is at least 45 minutes long.

Avoiding Pain with Local Anesthetics and Analgesia

Though some people never require numbing for root planing, it is becoming the rule rather than the exception to have local anesthesia for the procedure. If there is only minor sensitivity, a topical anesthetic gel is sufficient to numb the gums. Deeper and more effective anesthesia is obtained by relatively painless injection of a few drops of solution directly into the interdental papilla, the triangular gum tissue between the teeth. But if the roots—or the patient connected to the roots—are hypersensitive, then both the teeth and the gums must be anesthetized by traditional injection of a nerve-blocking drug—what people call a *shot*. The dentist or hygienist will do a better job if he or she knows the patient is comfortable.

In the past, only dentists were allowed to inject local anesthetics. Some enlightened states now permit dental hygienists to administer the anesthetic. There is no rational reason why dental hygienists in all states should not be permitted to give dental anesthetic injections. The irrational reason is the dental profession's obsession with limiting the role of auxiliaries, which is injurious to both the public and itself

Nitrous oxide, also known as "laughing gas," may enliven the dental experience, but routine use is not advisable; patients should take it only if they are so anxious that they are afraid they will not be able to tolerate an impending procedure without it. Because nitrous oxide analgesia reduces but does not entirely eliminate pain, many offices offer it in combination with local anesthesia. This is redundant and does not represent good practice. If anxiety is the main problem or the discomfort of root planning is minor, analgesia is often sufficient, and the injection can be avoided. Many people really do need a local anesthetic after repeated root planings, but the necessity for nitrous oxide is exaggerated and not without hazard, particularly to dental personnel who may be exposed to it over the years.

You should not be intimidated by all this. Occasional exposure of patients to properly administered nitrous oxide does not have any significant physical side effects, even to pregnant women.[6] Still, it is a mind-altering drug and should be treated with respect.

There is one important concern here. Because analgesia, unlike local anesthesia, affects your reflexes and judgment long after treatment is completed, you should arrange to have someone else drive you home.

Root Planing by Appointment

Some dentists do root planing and curettage while the patient is numb from an injection administered to do fillings. It warrants emphasis that while there is nothing wrong with this in principle, it may suggest a once-over-lightly attitude toward periodontal therapy on the part of the office. Unless you have a very minor condition, root planing done in 15 minutes or less cannot do justice to the job required. For you to be assured that your dentist takes periodontal disease as seriously as he or she ought to, root planing and curettage should not be an add-on to other procedures but should have a separate appointment dedicated to that purpose. Certainly, if the procedure is done in so short a time, you should make sure you are charged only for the time spent.

The Cost of Root Planing

Dental charges have increased greatly in recent years, much beyond the inflation rate and with no end in sight. Knowing that the bill will be paid in part by insurance coverage and not entirely by the patient allows some dentists to justify charging more than they once did. Where the patient has insurance, many dentists will define a prophylaxis as restricted to polishing the exposed crowns of the teeth with a pumice paste, a procedure previously defined as *coronal polishing*. Subgingival scaling (removal of calculus just beneath the gum tissue) is then charged additionally as root planing or curettage. Some unethical dentists do this even with adolescent and young adult patients who have no periodontal pockets, no periodontal bone loss, and no exposed roots to plane. The total charge for what is no more than a routine prophylaxis may therefore be 400 percent higher than it should be.

Legitimate charges are based on the time the procedure actually takes. The cost of a 30 to 45 minute prophylaxis appointment varies in different geographic areas, ranging from $50 to $85. Periodontal scaling and root planing costs more, from $80 to $250 per session. Thus, initial full-mouth root planing is likely to cost from $320 to $1000, sometimes more, to which are often added charges for examination, consultation, and oral hygiene instruction, in the range of $40 to $150, and X-rays at about $75.

Periodontists (specialists in periodontal disease) charge more than general practitioners for a three-month periodontal prophylaxis, usually performed by a dental hygienist, with the cost ranging from $75 to $125. If this seems high, remember that many people do not think twice about spending that much or more on haircuts, facials, manicures, and pedicures.

SPT—Supportive Periodontal Therapy or Maintenance Care

After the first phase of treatment is completed, patients with generalized periodontal disease are usually recalled in three months for evaluation of the effectiveness of root planing and the diligence of their home care, and for supportive periodontal therapy.[7] At that time, pocket depths are measured again and bleeding points noted. Many of the pockets will have shrunk to a more manageable size with good home care following the root planing. Thus, a five-millimeter pocket may become four or three millimeters, which indicates a positive response to both the initial root planing and personal efforts. **Bleeding points**, indicators of active periodontal inflammation, are the specific pockets that bleed when the periodontal probe is inserted for measurement.[8] These areas need improved flossing and possibly other measures, such as gum massagers and interdental stimulators, or additional professional treatment.

Many dentists and periodontists depend on the three-month reevaluation to determine if and where periodontal surgery would be beneficial. If pockets are very deep and little improvement has been noted, it is assumed that the initial scaling did not obtain the desired result and that the pockets are not "manageable" with surgical intervention. But unless pockets are six or seven millimeters, it is questionable if surgery should be done so soon. There is no harm in having three-month scalings over the next year. If the condition stabilizes, more extensive surgical treatment may not be necessary. Caution should be exercised when periodontal surgery is recommended without a first attempt at root planing. The diagnosis could possibly be based on the higher fee rather than current concepts of competent care.

Surgery should not be undertaken immediately following root planing; a minimum three-month interval is necessary before the results of the procedure can be reliably assessed. Reevaluation done only a few weeks after completion of root planing is worthless since the tissues have not had an opportunity to respond, and the diligence and efficacy of home care cannot be evaluated in such a short time. While some periodontal conditions will not be resolved without surgery, the average case should be observed for at least three months to see how the tissue responds to maintenance therapy and your home care. But there is nothing magical about a three-month period. Periodontal disease is essentially chronic and seldom is there any harm in waiting a year before deciding if and how much surgery should be done.

Periodontal Prophylaxis

A good dental office recalls most patients on a maintenance schedule at least once a year. Patients with periodontal disease are recalled more frequently, usually every three or four months.

Reinforcement of previous oral hygiene instruction (OHI) is an important part of the recall. The patient should demonstrate before the therapist—the hygienist or dentist—how he or she brushes, flosses, and uses other interproximal (cleaning and massaging) devices. This will allow the therapist to evaluate and reinforce home care techniques that all too often become sloppy and ineffective without periodic correction.

If oral hygiene is not well maintained or if more bleeding points occur, it is advisable to repeat intensive root planing every few years for optimum periodontal therapy. But it is much more valuable to have one periodontal prophylaxis every three or four months than to have three or four root planings in one month and not return for maintenance therapy until a year or two has gone by.

Bear in mind that we are discussing the needs of patients with recognized periodontal disease. People with healthy teeth and gums and good oral hygiene practices at home do not need dental examinations and prophylaxis more than once a year. Continuity of care is really the key to health. What you do at home, how you practice oral hygiene by way of flossing and brushing, will far outweigh what the dentist or hygienist can do in one or two annual visits.

Antimicrobial Periodontal Irrigation

In addition to conventional oral hygiene techniques, some periodontists recommend intersulcus irrigation with antibacterial agents to reduce plaque formation and bacterial infection. The effectiveness of irrigation is promising, but some reports of success appear exaggerated.

Tetracycline and Chlorhexidine. Irrigation with a tetracycline or chlorhexidine solution may be done by the hygienist or dentist in the dental office for advanced cases of periodontal disease. (It may also be done by unscrupulous dentists on patients who have no periodontal disease but a ready credit card.) Chlorhexidine rinses or gels may be recommended for home use, with varying degrees of effectiveness. Over-the-counter antiseptic mouth rinses reduce superficial plaque on the crowns of teeth but not on the roots beneath the gums where it does its harmful work.[9]

Chlorhexidine is available for home use only when prescribed by a dentist, usually as a mouth rinse. Used in irrigators, it is somewhat more effective in reducing plaque formation on root surfaces as well as bacterial inflammation.

Other Types of Antimicrobials

Similar to chlorhexidine, povidine iodine is also used for topical antisepsis in home maintenance therapy. Resorbable antimicrobial impregnated gels and chips can be placed in deep pockets to eliminate inflammation and infection. A low dose tetracycline taken systemically (orally) for three months or longer may retard bone loss and inflammation. And special antimicrobial toothpastes are being developed that look promising. [10] But most studies extend over only a few years. And since every year there is a new product, one can only wonder about what was wrong or ineffective with the last product.

No magic bullets. Even though the short-term effects of antimicrobial rinses, intersulcus irrigation, low dose local and systemic antibiotics, and designer toothpastes show promise, they are not a panacea, much less a substitute for periodic professional periodontal therapy. There are no magic bullets, no quick cures for periodontal disease. Even professional treatment, important as it is, will not be effective if personal oral hygiene is neglected.

SURGICAL THERAPY

Reshaping the Gums and Bone

Teeth with severe periodontal defects can be maintained for many years with nonsurgical treatment and good oral hygiene.[11,12] As previously noted, many patients are subjected to periodontal surgery before the effects of conservative, nonsurgical treatment can be fully evaluated. Some periodontists argue that without surgical intervention the patient cannot achieve adequate oral hygiene and that reliance on root planing and home care without surgery is simply postponing the inevitable. Most, however, maintain that periodontal surgery prior to the establishment of effective home care techniques is a waste of time and money because the periodontium will continue to degenerate without adequate patient cooperation.[13]

Thus, agreement is far from complete on the need and effectiveness of periodontal surgery. Sad to say, much less surgery might be done if surgery were not highly remunerative. To be sure, some conditions eventually require corrective surgery but, like any surgical procedure, periodontal surgery should be approached cautiously and conservatively.

Periodontal surgery has three main objectives: First, to remove calculus more effectively than can be done in some cases by nonsurgical scaling and root planing alone. Second, to reduce pocket depth without excessive and disfiguring exposure of the roots. Third, to reshape the gum (mucosal) and bone (osseous) tissue so that better oral hygiene can be maintained. Called *open flap surgery* and *muco-osseous surgery*, the two terms are often used interchangeably.

Open Flap Surgery

One would think that all surfaces of the teeth would be thoroughly free of calculus after three or four hours of scaling and root planing. Yet when the roots are exposed surgically by lifting the gum tissue away from the bone surrounding the teeth, some residual calculus is usually found. These deposits are removed from the exposed root surfaces, which are planed smooth in the process. The flap is sutured back in place at a slightly lower level, thereby reducing the depths of the periodontal pockets (Figure 8-2).

Because the necks of the teeth—where the crowns of the teeth meet the roots—are no longer protected by gum tissue, sensitivity to brushing, to hot and cold drinks, and to sweets and acidic foods frequently occurs following surgery. This hypersensitivity usually diminishes over time; fluoride mouth rinses and desensitizing toothpastes may help, but it may never disappear completely.[14]

Muco-osseous Surgery

Reshaping of the bone around the teeth is necessary to eliminate deep crevices and irregularities that prevent healing of periodontal pockets, epithelial reattachment, and a return of smooth contours on the gum tissue. At times this surgery is done to expose pockets that have formed between the roots of molars so that the area can be kept clean with special devices such as interproximal brushes, toothpicks, or even pipe cleaners. Osseous surgery is an extension of open flap surgery. After the flap is lifted and all tartar deposits and infected cementum removed, chisels, files, and special drills are used to reshape the bone. Whenever bone is reshaped, some additional resorption (loss) of bone takes place. Some new bone may grow back in the deep crevices, partially eliminating the bony pocket and strengthening the support of the root. It should also be noted that new bone growth sometimes follows nonsurgical curettage and root planing. But at best, regrowth of bone is minimal and will not eliminate underlying bony defects.

Gingivectomy.

Gingivectomy was a common procedure to eliminate periodontal pockets before the introduction of open flap surgery. The gum tissue above the pocket was cut off in the belief that better oral hygiene would be possible and that the gum would reattach to the teeth more securely. In fact, the opposite was the case.

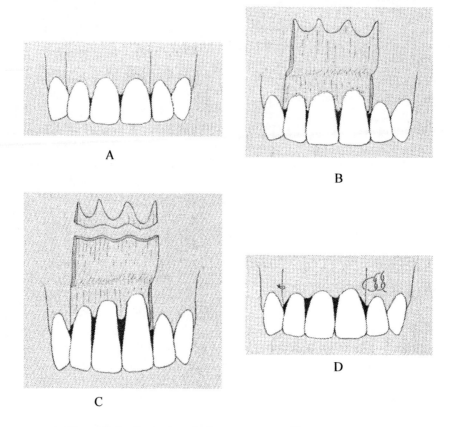

Figure 8-2   Periodontal flap surgery.   This operation permits ready access to the affected portion of the periodontium.

A.   *Vertical incisions are made in the healthy periodontal tissues on both sides of the affected area.*
B.   *The gum tissue is retracted sufficiently to provide easy access.*
C.   *The diseased portion of the bone and soft tissue are removed with curettes and other instruments, the bone is recontoured and the excess flap tissue is cut away.*
D.   *The flap is repositioned and sutured in place.   The sutures are removed after five or six days.*

Food lodged easily in the open spaces created by the removal of the interdental papilla.   Lacking the protective shell of enamel, roots were more likely to decay, and hypersensitivity to hot and cold temperatures and acidic foods could be severe.   Appearance was often grotesque.   When a person smiled, the teeth appeared excessively long. They seemed to grow out of the jaws like teeth on a demonstration skull.

Flap surgery avoids most of the esthetic problems of gingivectomy in the treatment of periodontitis. However, gingivectomy is properly used today not to treat periodontitis but to remove excessive hyperplastic or hypertrophied gum tissue that has overgrown part or even all of the crown of the tooth, producing **pseudopockets**. Such overgrowth is caused by the chronic irritation and inflammation of gross calculus, poorly fitted orthodontic bands, defective crowns and bridges, drugs like Dilantin (phenytoin) and L-dopa for the control of epilepsy and Parkinsonism, hormonal changes, and causes unknown (idiopathic). Overgrowth of the gums can be minimized by good oral hygiene and dental prophylaxis, but in some patients periodic gingivectomy may be necessary to remove excess tissue and restore a natural, esthetically pleasing appearance.[15]

Gingivectomy is also performed when the gum tissue above a periodontal pocket is so thick and fibrous that it does not shrink after curettage and root planing. One should not rush into gingival surgery for this purpose. The gums may shrink over a longer period of time than many dentists, including periodontists, want to wait.

Bone Grafts

Natural and artificial bone may be grafted in areas of extensive bone loss, particularly where deep crevices are present. Natural grafts are obtained by drilling out small cores of bone from the jaw or the hipbone, which are then placed into the crevices around the roots to provide additional support. Sometimes the bone is taken from the area of a tooth that has to be extracted because the periodontal disease is too advanced to save it. Because of the difficulty of obtaining natural bone grafts and the limited success in their use, artificial bone graft materials that are composed of special ceramics and other materials have been developed.

The success rate of the various materials and techniques has not been spectacular, which is why new methods come and go like fads. Many grafts are resorbed or come loose soon after placement. Bone grafts, ceramics, guided tissue regeneration, acellular dermal graft materials—some new and some old procedures—are all highly "technique sensitive." Considerable skill and experience are required to prepare the tissues to receive these materials, whether natural or artificial. Since the cost is high, one should make sure that the dentist or periodontist is well experienced in this particular work. Ask him or to show you pre- and post-surgical X-ray films of cases at least five years old that he or she has treated successfully with grafts.[16]

Gum Grafts

Some teeth will experience gingival recession, exposing roots to oral fluids and toothbrushing. In extreme cases half or more of the root is exposed. More often the condition extends only two or three millimeters, and further recession is very slow. In fact, many of these recessions stabilize without any treatment, remaining unchanged for decades.

The cause is not clear. Some dentists believe recession is due to occlusal trauma from chewing, bruxing, and grinding, but many people with occlusal trauma have no gum recession. Unless the recession is bothersome or particularly unsightly on smiling, the best advice is to have the dentist note it on the dental chart and then observe it over a period of time. If no change occurs, leave it alone. If the condition worsens appreciably, a soft tissue or gum graft can cover the exposed root. Unfortunately, grafts do not always "take," and over time the condition may revert to where it was before surgery.

Soft tissue grafts are also used to thicken gum tissue that is very thin and friable. This condition is not uncommon around the small front teeth in the lower jaw, the central and lateral incisors. If the tissue is too fragile, the epithelial attachment can break down, resulting in recession and pocket formation. The condition is generally self-limiting, however. Again, rather than rush into surgery, you should make sure the condition is noted, photographed and observed for a year or more. If no change occurs, no surgery is needed.

There are a number of gum-grafting methods. The simplest—the sliding graft—is to move tissue from an adjacent tooth by slitting and sliding it over the exposed root and then allowing new tissue to grow in the space created by the surgery. If larger numbers of adjacent teeth are to receive grafts, a strip of tissue is taken from another part of the mouth, frequently the palate, and sutured into position over the exposed roots. If the objective is to thicken gum tissue, then a small piece of palatal tissue is sutured over the existing gum.[17]

This discussion of periodontal surgery by no means covers the full range of procedures employed in the treatment of periodontal disease. One procedure not discussed is extraction. The best if not the only cure for a periodontally diseased tooth with a poor prognosis is extraction. Removal of such diseased teeth eliminates much if not all of the disease and improves the periodontal condition of adjacent teeth. Altogether too much time and money are spent, and pain experienced, by patients in the treatment of hopelessly diseased teeth.

Perhaps the most important point to remember about periodontal disease is not to rush into surgery no matter how extensive the problem. Periodontal disease is predominantly chronic and its progress is erratic. For long periods of time—even years—little change may occur. If root planing is done thoroughly, if good daily oral hygiene and periodic maintenance treatment is continued, periodontal surgery may never be needed.

RECOMMENDATIONS

1. Patients should make sure that charges for root planing are based on time.
2. The number of quadrants billed should be based on the equivalence of seven teeth per quadrant, regardless of their location.
3. Pocket depths less than four millimeters are normal and should not be counted as requiring treatment.
4. A quadrant root planing appointment should last at least 45 minutes.
5. Local anesthetics are advisable for most patients to assure not only painless but more thorough root planing.
6. Avoid routine nitrous oxide analgesia, and do not drive after receiving it.
7. Do not be rushed into periodontal surgery. Supportive periodontal therapy (SPT) consisting of periodontal prophylaxis every three to four months and conscientious home care may be sufficient.
8. Observe the following guidelines for periodontal therapy:

    Gingivitis and early periodontitis: annual or six-month prophylaxis when pocket depth is less than four millimeters.

    Moderate periodontitis: more intensive scaling and root planing where pocket depths range from four to six millimeters. Initial treatment may require as much as four quadrants of root planing, with supportive periodontal therapy every three or four months.

    Advanced periodontitis: pocket depths exceed six millimeters; intensive scaling and root planing, reevaluation of effectiveness of root planing, and oral hygiene at a minimum of three months. Reductive periodontal surgery should be considered for pockets exceeding six millimeters that remain inflamed and bleed on probing. Periodontal prophylaxis recommended every three or four months.

9

Cosmetic Dentistry and Orthodontics

COSMETIC—ESTHETIC—DENTISTRY

Cosmetics or esthetics has always been a major aspect of dental treatment. After all, each of our teeth has its role to play, but never do we rush to the dentist faster than when we have lost a front tooth. Even when crooked teeth don't interfere with function, we want them straightened simply because we think they are unsightly. Cosmetic dentistry becomes particularly important where a dental problem turns into a social disability. Adolescents with severely crooked teeth develop negative attitudes about themselves that can be reflected in school grades and social development. Many people with unsightly front teeth tend to avoid smiling. Because they are then seen as less friendly than those who smile more often, they are at a disadvantage in obtaining jobs, especially those that deal with the public.

Is There a Significant Problem? Risk versus Benefit

We all know people with unattractive teeth who do smile, who are gracious, and who have succeeded in all kinds of occupations, for esthetics is an attitude of mind as well as appearance. Before deciding on a course of cosmetic dentistry, you should ask yourself if your problem is severe enough to affect your behavior and if changes in the appearance of your teeth will make a meaningful difference. You should ask these questions even if money is no object, because there is always a risk that any medical or dental treatment may actually do harm. For example, many people, regardless of age, have their teeth capped with porcelain crowns or veneered to make them whiter and more regular. However, poorly fitted caps often cause teeth to decay or initiate periodontal disease. The nerve may be damaged irreversibly, leading to root canal therapy and sometimes loss of the tooth. Also, the gums do not always take kindly even to well-fitted artificial crowns and veneers, particularly on the front teeth.

So much for the bad news. The good news is that current techniques and materials allow for substantial improvements in cosmetic and restorative dental treatment, and with less damage to the dentition.

Maintaining Appearance—Oral Hygiene

The easiest and most important kind of cosmetic dentistry involves oral hygiene. From the point of view of health, the main purpose of oral hygiene is to prevent dental decay and pyorrhea. Toothpaste advertisements, particularly on television, stress this role of the product in preventing dental disease, but they also appeal to our vanity and our sexuality. To look pretty, to have sweet breath, to be more kissable may be far more compelling reasons for many people to brush and floss than the more abstract notion of dental health.

In addition to home care, periodic cleaning of teeth by a dentist or hygienist is necessary to remove unsightly stains and calculus that survive daily brushing and to help reduce swollen and inflamed gums. Together, you and your dentist can work cosmetic wonders with a previously neglected mouth merely by exercising good dental hygiene. Home and professional cleaning should be the first step in any cosmetic dental program; however, some conditions require additional treatment.

Discolored Teeth

Cause. The main causes of discolored teeth are deep decay, dead nerves, heavy smoking, coffee and tea consumption, excessive ingestion of fluorides from birth to about age 13, and tetracycline prescribed for pregnant women and young children. Some discoloration and pitting of the crowns of permanent teeth result from high fevers experienced during uterine development or in childhood up to age 8. The typical deep gray tetracycline stain is rare today. Most physicians are aware of the problem and prescribe other antibiotics for children and pregnant women.

When naturally fluoridated water exceeds 2 parts of fluoride per million parts of water and is ingested during infancy until about age 13, varying degrees of enamel fluorosis or mottling occurs.[1] Mottling varies with the concentration of fluorides and ranges from barely noticeable small white specks or bands interspersed through the light yellow shade of a healthy tooth to an irregular dark yellow or brown discoloration, sometimes with pitting, over the entire face of the crown. Most mottling is so mild as to be virtually unnoticeable.[2]

Teeth become yellower as we age. The translucent incisal edges characteristic of young teeth are gradually worn away. The pulp grows smaller by forming dentin within its chamber. This makes the teeth more dense, less translucent. Dentin is naturally yellower than enamel, and so the more dentin, the yellower the tooth. Natural yellowing should not be considered unattractive; in fact, it adds character to a maturing face.

Large amalgam fillings sometimes turn black with corrosion and darken the enamel. Since amalgam fillings are restricted to posterior teeth, such discoloration usually does not show. Unless there is a serious esthetic problem, replacement of functional fillings is not recommended.

Treatment of Discolored Teeth

Removal of decay. If deep decay has discolored a front tooth, removal of the decay and restoration with a composite filling are usually sufficient to restore the tooth's natural color. But if the nerve tissue within the center of the tooth degenerates, some of the infecting bacteria may produce a gray or black stain that penetrates into the enamel. Much of the stain can be drilled away as root canal therapy is performed. Bleaching may also be required to lighten the enamel.

Bleaching. Individual teeth that have darkened due to pulp degeneration can be bleached following root canal treatment by means of a "walking bleach." A potent hydrogen peroxide solution can be sealed inside the crown of the tooth to bleach out the discoloration and lighten its shade.[3] The treatment may have to be repeated a few times.

Bleaching of healthy teeth simply to make them whiter has become a big money-maker for the dental profession. It doesn't require any special skills and is often administered by dental assistants. Dentists are taught in practice management courses to prey on your vanity. They will whiten their office staff's teeth so they glisten like a flashing advertisement when they smile at you, inciting, so they hope, your envy and loosening your pocketbook or credit card to the tune of $300 to $600. There are free-standing bleaching centers that will lighten your teeth with a special bleach activated by a high powered ultra-violet light. Just one visit to change your entire personality!

A good part of this promotion is directed towards the vanity of attractive young people who are deluded into thinking anything less than white chalk-colored teeth will render them social outcasts. But there are people, both young and older who have a legitimate concern. For them, office or home bleaching can be effective in reducing unsightly discoloration to a point where a more acceptable appearance is achieved.[4]

The shade of teeth naturally yellowed with age or severely discolored during their formation by tetracycline or excessive fluorides or turned dark due to the death of the nerve may be lightened by bleaching in the dental office. The teeth are isolated, preferably by punching small holes in a sheet of latex called a **rubber dam** through which the crowns protrude while the rest of the mouth is covered. The dentist or dental assistant applies the concentrated tooth whitener to each tooth and then exposes the tooth to a high-intensity ultraviolet light or heat lamp for about five minutes. A fluoride gel may be applied afterward to reduce post-treatment sensitivity. Multiple treatments a few weeks apart are often necessary before the desired lightening is achieved. Not all severe stains lighten to complete satisfaction. Nonetheless, bleaching of these unsightly discolorations is worth trying before subjecting your teeth to the more drastic procedures and expense of bonded veneers or porcelain caps.

In 1989, a home-use bleach technique was introduced to lighten the shade of all one's teeth simultaneously. A special tray like an athletic mouth guard is constructed in the dental office to hold the low concentration bleach gel against the teeth. Continuous tray bleaching is most effective in lightening teeth that have yellowed with age, but the results can be uneven or spotty. Two or three drops of solution or gel are placed in the tray for each tooth to be bleached. The tray is worn 4 to 10 hours a day, usually at night, over a period of two weeks with the solution changed every two hours. Since the bleach contacts the gums and is swallowed as it leaks into the mouth, tissue irritation and gastric upset may occur. One should immediately discontinue use at the first sign of irritation or discomfort.[5]

Purely *vanity* or cosmetic bleaching that does not involve a severe, unsightly discoloration can be attempted by yourself without the direct supervision of a dentist. Fabrication of simple, inexpensive clear plastic trays, one for the upper and one for the lower teeth, is necessary. If the dentist makes the tray, the fee including time and material should not be more than $150. Bleaching kits that allow you to construct your own trays can be purchased in drugstores and groceries. A newer product that does not require trays consists of strips of material impregnated with hydrogen peroxide for self-application over the front teeth.[6] Unless you have a severe discoloration, it makes little sense to pay high fees to a dentist for light bleaching that you can probably do as well yourself. Whatever you do, don't use household hydrogen peroxide or hair bleaches, which will corrode the gums. And don't be surprised if the results are less than hoped for or if the color of the teeth comes out uneven.

Most people are pleased with their bleaching, even those whose teeth have turned so white that they look like a stack of Chiclets or a glossy picket fence. Re-bleaching may be necessary every year or two to maintain the desired lightening but there is no guarantee that all the teeth will turn out the same. After all, manufacturers have had lot more experience developing and marketing hair bleach products for home use, and still the results are not always as uniform as the user would like. Bleaching can be uneven or disappointing, particularly since, contrary to expectations, it won't improve your social or sex life.

Bonded Veneers. The method used in applying bonded veneers is based on the etching technique developed for applying sealants to prevent dental decay. (See chapter 4.) In the past, an incisal edge fracture of a front tooth could be fixed only by constructing a gold inlay to replace the broken part or by covering the entire tooth with a porcelain crown. Gold in front teeth is no longer popular, and though the porcelain crown is still used frequently, it is very expensive. Composite resins can be used at much lower cost not only to repair fractured edges but also to cover the entire visible surfaces of teeth. Severely damaged and discolored teeth can be restored satisfactorily by veneering, with minimal grinding away of the natural tooth and as good or better esthetic results.[7]

The terms *bonding* and *veneering* are often used interchangeably. Properly used, bonding means attachment of two materials through the use of a connecting substance such as glue or cement. Veneering is the placement of a thin layer of material over an entire surface, to provide a new, more attractive surface. An example is the covering of inexpensive wood with a thin sheet of mahogany or oak to provide a more pleasing appearance. In a similar way a mixture of composite resin can be layered over a tooth's surface to present a more attractive surface. In this application the bonding material is also the veneering material, similar to fingernail polish but more durable. More often the two materials are used together, a bonding composite overlaid by a veneer of composite, plastic, or porcelain.

Indications for veneering. Veneers are used to resurface stained, pitted, and worn enamel, to close natural spaces (diastemas), and to correct minor irregularities and crookedness of the front teeth. Veneers can be applied to any nonchewing surface. Custom-made veneers are made in the dental laboratory. They are more durable than composite resin veneers that are applied directly to the tooth and are particularly suitable for extensive resurfacing. Custom-made veneers are usually constructed of porcelain, which has the advantage of inherent color stability and resistance to abrasion. On the other hand, porcelain is more susceptible to fracture than plastic or composite.

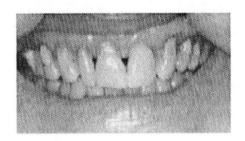

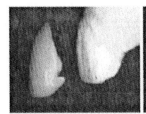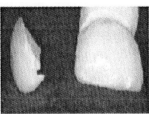

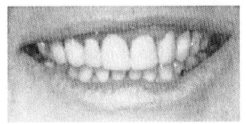

Figure 9-1 Porcelain veneers-cosmetic facings

Top - Before
Middle - Laboratory fabrication of a veneer
Bottom - Veneers bonded to upper anterior teeth

When Permanence Is Not Permanent

Although dentists speak of permanent fillings, crowns, and bridges, it must be remembered that the only really permanent thing we do is extract teeth. When you consider that teeth are subjected to great chewing forces, to acids in foods and drinks, to rapid temperature changes, to brushing abrasion, to attrition and erosion, and to attack by bacteria it is a wonder that any restoration lasts more than a few months. Yet most of the composite or plastic fillings applied by a good dentist will last more than 5 years, amalgam fillings will last over 10 years, and crowns and bridges that are properly made will last 15 years or longer.[8]

Bonding and veneering will also last many years, but they are more subject to wear and fracture that a well-constructed crown.

Veneers are least harmful. The big advantage of veneering over crowning is based on the Hippocratic mandate for a doctor to *do the least possible harm.* Veneering requires very little alteration of the natural tooth. Sometimes a composite veneer requires only etching prior to application. More often a small amount of enamel is removed to reshape the tooth. Although etching sometimes makes teeth sensitive, the risk of irreversible nerve damage is small, and reveneering can be done with minimal additional trauma. Not so with a porcelain crown. If the nerve is damaged by overgrinding or if the crown is done poorly and gum line decay penetrates to the nerve, root canal therapy becomes necessary; if that fails, the tooth is lost. Also, each time a tooth is recrowned, it is subjected to more grinding and new potential nerve injury and degeneration.

Disadvantages. The disadvantages of veneering relate to color stability, physical strength, and irritation of the gum. Composites and plastic tend to discolor when exposed to sunlight. The outer surface will inevitably wear, and as it does, it becomes dull. But as noted above, the veneers can be redone easily. Porcelain veneers are color stable because the color is fused into the ceramic material, but porcelain is more fragile than composites and plastics and can fracture under a heavy bite.

Composite resins are best used to restore fractured and worn incisal edges of upper front teeth but are prone to failure when used on the lower front teeth. The reason is that the upper incisal edges overlap the lower teeth and are not subjected to excessive pressure. The incisal edges of the lower teeth jut up, into, and against the hard inner surface of the upper teeth on swallowing, chewing, grinding, and clenching. Restoration of these surfaces with composite resins cannot be expected to last long.

No matter how good the veneer, it is a foreign substance, and when it contacts the gum tissue, the body treats it as such. Even if thin, it is still likely to thicken the tooth slightly since a certain amount of material bulk is essential for strength and color. When the tooth is thus thickened, the gums often become red, puffy, and bleed easily—marginal gingivitis—or the tissue may actually be stimulated to overgrowth—hyperplasia. Thus, an attempt at improved appearance may result in impaired and unsightly gingival tissue. The cure for minor irregularity or discoloration of teeth may not be worth the disfigurement it may create. Before deciding on any of these esthetic procedures, be sure you are dealing with a problem serious enough to warrant a dentist's intervention.

Veneers are not cheap. Considering the relative simplicity of veneering compared to a porcelain-metal crown, one might expect the cost to be considerably less. For the most part it is, but it is still expensive. The charge for a composite veneer may range from $200 to $400, not necessarily high since it may take an hour or an hour and a half to complete. A bonded custom porcelain veneer is likely to cost $500 or more because a laboratory charge has to be included. This fee can be compared to the $375 to $800 charged for porcelain-metal crowns. At the low end of the scale, a veneer may represent a substantial saving. However, if it has to be replaced a few times during the next 10 to 20 years, the veneer will prove to be more costly than a well-made porcelain crown, which can be expected to last that long.

Unwritten Guarantees—a Goodwill Policy

As a rule, dentists do not guarantee their work. Guarantees are both unethical and impractical since success is dependent not only on the dentist's skill but also on the patient's response to treatment. Nonetheless, most dentists back up their work with an unwritten guarantee of sorts. If, for example, a filling falls out within a few weeks or months of placement, a dentist usually replaces it free of charge. This should happen only rarely in a good dental practice. If a more costly service such as a porcelain bridge fails in a short time, many dentists adjust the fee for replacement even if the failure had nothing to do with the quality of the original work. As an act of goodwill, the fee may be reduced significantly or the laboratory cost alone passed on to the patient.

Since veneering is so expensive, you should ask about your own dentist's policy regarding early failure. Some dentists redo the veneers at 50 percent of the original cost if the need arises within a couple of years. Or you might be charged only the laboratory fabrication cost. Though dentists are not obligated to guarantee the results of their work, and should not be expected to, most have a goodwill policy in the event of early treatment failure. Just what this policy is may be a factor in choosing between one dentist and another.

ORTHODONTIC TREATMENT

Malocclusion Is Not a Disease

Many years ago, kids tried hard to avoid orthodontic appliances. So did their parents once they knew the high cost of orthodontic treatment. Now it is virtually a status symbol for middle- and upper-class children to have metal bands and wires on their teeth for a couple of years to emerge with perfect smiles. Television advertisements show pert teenagers speaking to each other with closed mouths, only to break into broad grins as each recognizes the other has braces. There are jokes about kids calling out the emergency squads to separate braces entangled during a kiss. Even adults who have long suffered unsightly crooked front teeth now undergo years of orthodontic treatment.

Given the popular concern over crooked teeth, one cannot overemphasize that malocclusion is not a disease. There is no convincing evidence linking crooked teeth to decay and periodontal disease.[9,10] Dental caries and periodontal disease are bacterial plaque diseases. Even though the uneven surface presented by crooked teeth requires a little more diligence in brushing and flossing, people with malocclusion do not necessarily experience more decay or gum problems.

There are exceptions to most generalizations. The lower front teeth may hit the palate rather than coming to rest on the inside of the upper front teeth. The palate and gum may then be periodically, sometimes continuously, traumatized. Correction of this type of malocclusion is the best way to eliminate discomfort and prevent further injury.

Dentists also recommend correction of malocclusion to improve mastication, the chewing of food. But unless the condition is so severe as to prevent the opposing teeth from coming together, virtually any bite— "good" or "bad" from the dentist's viewpoint—functions adequately. In fact, teeth barely meet in chewing. The mouth senses contact of opposing teeth as they shear and grind food, immediately reversing the movement of the lower jaw so that the teeth are not gnashed together. It is sort of like touch football. You do not have to tackle the ball carrier to stop the action. A slight touch of tooth contact is all that is necessary to have the play whistled dead. If it were not for this protective **proprioceptive** mechanism, the teeth would be ground down to the gum line in the first two or three decades of life.

Nonetheless, many people develop pernicious habits such as clenching and grinding—**bruxism**—of teeth, which wears the enamel flat and may even penetrate into dentin, causing hypersensitivity and pain. Night grinding is also quite common even among children and can be damaging to the teeth and supporting bone. But these habits have nothing to do with normal chewing. Correction of malocclusion does not cure bruxism. In fact, bruxism may not be curable, particularly when it is done during sleep. In that event, the patient needs a protective plastic **occlusal night guard**, much like a football or basketball player's mouthpiece to prevent tooth-on-tooth contact during sleep or even during the daytime.

Malocclusion Does Not Cause MPD and TMJ/TMD

Other conditions frequently attributed to malocclusion are **myofacial pain dysfunction** (MPD) and **temporomandibular joint disorder** (TMJ/TMD), in which the individual suffers mild to extreme pain in the facial muscles and joints of the jaws. For unknown reasons, MPD and TMD problems occur much more frequently among women in their late twenties and early thirties, after which the pain frequently disappears whether or not treated.[11,12]

Despite the lack of controlled studies to link MPD and TMD pain with malocclusion, orthodontic treatment is often recommended for present or anticipated problems. Rather than malocclusion, the common causes of MPD or TMJ discomfort are tension, clenching. and muscle spasms or injury to the attachment ligaments of the joints, which makes opening and closing painful. The injury may follow a large yawn or third molar surgery or, occasionally, orthodontic treatment. Quite often the condition is alleviated by physiotherapy, including dry or moist heat packs and ultrasonic treatment, muscle relaxants, antidepressant drugs for chronic pain, special muscle stretching and relaxation therapy, the avoidance of extreme jaw movements such as yawning and biting whole apples, and simply outliving the symptoms. In a small number of TMJ cases the cartilaginous articulating disc has been damaged by trauma or osteoarthritic degeneration of the bony ball and socket that comprise the joint. In such extreme cases surgery may be necessary to replace the disc with a plastic insert or to reconstruct the jaw joint. This procedure is far from reliable and is notorious for its failures. It should be considered only when there is no other recourse. Too often premature and unnecessary surgery is performed, at times leaving the patient much worse off than if nothing had been done.[13]

TMJ/MPD diagnosis and treatment should be viewed with caution and skepticism. Most X-rays taken for TMJ diagnosis are not worth the price of the film. X-ray films of the joints purportedly demonstrating displaced discs or osteoarthritis often are of such poor quality as to require a great deal of imagination in diagnosis. Even with good films, X-ray diagnosis of the jaw joints is notably inaccurate.[14] Before subjecting yourself to head X-rays, which radiate the brain as well as the joints, rely on symptomatic diagnosis to identify the location of the pain and restriction of movement. Initial treatment should be limited to alleviation of the symptoms. Only when significant pain persists for a long time and is not relieved by symptomatic treatment should one consider TMJ X-rays, and then only by a qualified TMJ X-ray technician.

Social Disability: When Malocclusion Is a Problem

If malocclusion does not cause these functional problems, it is nonetheless the source of much misery, albeit mainly emotional. Straight teeth are prettier than crooked teeth, though slight irregularity looks quite natural. If the irregularity is severe, if one has "buck" teeth that really stand out or a chin that recedes into one's throat, there may be equally severe emotional problems, especially in a culture that constantly emphasizes eternal youth and beauty. Boys and girls, men and women may be afraid to smile. They may become notably shy. They also may be excluded from professions and jobs that "face" the public. When the cause of these social disabilities is crooked teeth, the cure is orthodontic treatment.

Negative Outcomes

Most malocclusions are not related to significant functional problems, much less social disabilities. People of all ages with minor malocclusions are seeking treatment because it is fashionable. As long as the cost does not work a hardship on the family, no harm is done—assuming that good orthodontic treatment is received.

But orthodontics is not always successful and sometimes it is harmful. One of the most common failures is a relapse to pretreatment irregularity, particularly of the lower incisors. The anterior teeth, so nicely straight at the termination of treatment, revert back to previous crookedness because the arch of the underlying jaw bone is too small for them to remain straight.[15,16] Relapse also occurs if the patient does not wear the post-treatment retainer long enough. But too often the patient is blamed for neglect when the cause of relapse is faulty diagnosis and inadequate treatment.

Sometimes perfectly good back teeth—the four bicuspids—are extracted to create space for retruding the protruding incisors, the so-called buck teeth, or even for correcting minor anterior irregularities. While the result may be straight front teeth, many of these people end up with very flat, nearly concave or quartermoon-shaped profiles and weak or flaccid lips. Not infrequently, too much extra space is created, leaving annoying spaces between the teeth.

Moving teeth risks root resorption, leaving the teeth weakened in their bony sockets. As many as one out of eight orthodontic patients have some root resorption.[17,18] Gingival recession can be caused by tooth movement or poorly fitted bands.[19] Excessive or too rapid movement can also kill the dental nerve. Perhaps the most common side effect is decay under poorly fitted bands, or even properly fitted bands if the teeth are not kept meticulously clean by the patient.

How frequently these bad outcomes occur is not known. The health professions are sometimes long on treatment and very short on end-result studies. Nonetheless, orthodontic treatment generally proves satisfactory to patients whose appearance has been improved. Yet every orthodontist has some failures, and you should not hesitate to discuss potential problems at the beginning of treatment. Treatment of any kind should be done only when probable good outweighs potential harm.

Cause and Correction of Malocclusion

Space is the problem, either too much or too little. Either the teeth are too large for the size of the jaws or the jaws are too large for the size of the teeth. You may have inherited a large upper jaw from one parent and a small lower jaw from the other, or vice versa. Some teeth may be forced out of occlusion, growing inside or outside the arch, or rotating and overlapping adjacent teeth. Overlapping occurs most frequently with the front incisors. Orthodontic correction of even a minor irregularity usually involves attachment of bands and brackets to all teeth so that slowly, over a minimum of 18 to 24 months, they are moved into position along an arch wire or brace.

In really severe cases, where the problem is over- or undersized jaws, major **orthognathic surgery** is performed prior to orthodontic treatment. The jawbones are reduced in size or made larger by moving entire segments of the teeth and bone into better position. Reducing jutting jaws corrects extreme buck teeth. Increasing jaw length, with implantation of cartilage or synthetic bone in extreme cases, can change a severely receding chin into a classic profile. Even though orthognathic surgery risks permanent damage, such as injury to nerves and the lifelong numbness of the lips, tongue, or chin, it is understandable that many individuals with gross deformities of the jaws and corresponding personality problems are willing to take their chances.[20]

Third Molars Are Innocent

Third molars or **wisdom teeth** are often blamed for causing initial crookedness or post-treatment relapse. Many general dentists, many if not most orthodontists, and virtually all oral surgeons in private practice recommend the removal of all four wisdom teeth whether or not there is evidence of abnormality, impaction, or the likelihood of impaction.

Wisdom teeth that cause problems justify removal. Some grow at an angle against a second molar, causing root resorption or decay. Occasionally a cyst forms from the developmental sac. Quite often an adolescent experiences the pain of teething as the crown of a wisdom tooth penetrates the gum. Teething should not dictate extraction, but extraction may be the best solution if the overlying gum tissue becomes infected repeatedly.

Thus, there are good reasons for removing some wisdom teeth. To prevent crowding of front teeth or post-treatment relapse is not a good reason, because wisdom teeth do not cause such problems. Yet these teeth are removed as though they were agents of an epidemic disease, and at considerable expense and no small amount of postsurgical misery.

The irrationality of extracting third molars to prevent orthodontic malocclusion is staggering. Many dentists argue that third molars exert tremendous pressure against second molars and that this pressure is transmitted forward from one tooth to another until the front teeth shift, twist, and overlap. You do not have to be an engineer to understand the fallacy of this argument. Each dental arch has 14 permanent teeth, not counting third molars, encased vertically in bone, each in contact with the adjacent tooth forming a horseshoe arrangement. It is like having a picket fence with each picket a post buried in hard-packed earth, each one connected to the next picket, and so on. In addition, the lower teeth are contained within the outer ring of the upper teeth, which are in turn kept in place by intercuspation, or interlocking with the lower teeth when the jaws are closed, and by the strong musculature of the lips and cheek. In order to exert sufficient force to move these teeth, the wisdom teeth would require, in the least, a firm foothold, but there is none. The developing wisdom teeth are contained within soft, cancellous bone filled with bone marrow. The roots lack a strong buttress against which to push all the other teeth forward and out of position. The proposition that third molars cause either initial crowding or relapse of the front teeth is absurd on its face.[21-23]

Crowding Due to a Natural Cause

If there are no wisdom teeth to blame, orthodontists attribute post- treatment relapse to continued growth of the lower jaw so that the anterior teeth crunch together and overlap to relieve the strain. But there is also a natural tendency for a tooth to move forward, to remain in contact with the tooth in front of it, each side meeting at the midline where the forces on one side are countered and neutralized by the opposite forces. This phenomenon is called the **anterior component of force**. The teeth are not set in the bone absolutely vertically but are tilted slightly toward the front or midline of the jaw. As the teeth come together in chewing and swallowing, forces are applied in a forward moving direction. This action is usually sufficient to keep the teeth in fairly tight contact with each other, preventing separation and food impaction. Without it, everyone's teeth would likely separate. Of course, no system is perfect, and if there is disharmony or imbalance in these structures and forces, if the anterior segment of the arch, especially the lower arch, is too narrow or small, the incisors slip past each other, resulting in the minor overlapping that so many people complain about. The movement is self-limiting and harmless. Minor crowding and overlapping of teeth do not warrant intervention or correction.

Orthodontic Extractions

As already noted, in addition to the 4 third molars, orthodontists frequently prescribe removal of the 4 first bicuspids, 1 in each quadrant of the mouth, when the problem is protruding front teeth.[24] Few people realize that these 8 extractions represent 25 percent of their 32 natural adult teeth. It is even more disturbing that dentists who place such emphasis on preserving the natural dentition are so willing to sacrifice one-fourth of it for the sake of appearance.

In fact, enough but not too much additional space to push back the anterior teeth (dentists call this process *retrusion*) can be obtained by removal of only 4 teeth, the second permanent molars. For this alternative, the child must be 13 or

14 years of age, with normally developing third molars. This approach has the advantage not only of providing enough space for repositioning all the teeth but of permitting adequate room for the eruption of the third molars, thereby reducing the risk of impactions. It also eliminates the open contact spaces behind the cuspids that often remain after bicuspid extractions. Retention of all the bicuspids maintains a natural appearance to the smiling mouth and prevents that flattening of the profile that often happens when bicuspids are removed.[25-28] Before subjecting your child or yourself to the sacrifice of one-fourth of the natural teeth, the orthodontist should be requested to consider the alternative of second molar extractions.

When to Begin Orthodontic Treatment

Most orthodontic treatment begins in early adolescence, when all the permanent teeth have erupted except the third molars. However, some minor malocclusions can be treated at age eight or so, often with a removable headgear appliance consisting of a strap around the back of the neck connected to a stainless steel bow that puts pressure against the teeth to retrude them. It is therefore advisable to obtain an orthodontic consultation as soon as you suspect a problem.

Some orthodontists contend that early or Phase I treatment simplifies regular Phase II treatment. Others believe that little is gained unless full-banded orthodontic treatment can be avoided by less complex early treatment. Without such assurance, one might just as well wait until age 12 or 13 to avoid the additional cost of Phase I.

Orthodontic treatment has no age limits. Many adults in their thirties, forties, and older have successful treatment. Since appearance during treatment can be as important as after treatment, particularly for working people, barely visible ceramic brackets can be substituted for the traditional metal brackets that are cemented to the outside surfaces of teeth. However, the thin metal arch wires will still be visible. Brackets can also be placed on the inside surfaces of teeth next to the tongue where neither the brackets nor the metal arch wire can be seen.[29]

Ceramic brackets are bonded to enamel. Sometimes the enamel is fractured in the process of removal so that a veneer is necessary to restore the surface. The opposing tooth may also be worn away by a ceramic bracket, just as porcelain on the occlusal or chewing surface of a tooth often grinds away the opposing tooth. For these reasons, ceramic brackets have not replaced metal brackets and should be used only when esthetics is of prime concern.

There is no reason for cosmetic or invisible braces to cost more. You will be told the brackets are more expensive, but the amount is minor compared to the total orthodontic fee. You will be told they require more time to apply, but the additional time, if any, is trivial.

Why Is Orthodontic Treatment So Expensive?

Aiming for perfection. One reason for the expense is that fully trained and qualified orthodontists are compulsively perfectionistic in the attempt to convert a malocclusion into an ideal occlusion. Ideal occlusion is based on the assumption that all teeth should align according to a theoretical norm, which may itself be abnormal since it is so rare. Precise control for repositioning the teeth is obtained by banding and sliding them along an arch wire into proper position. If movement is too fast, if too much force is applied, the nerves or roots or periodontal bone may suffer irreversible damage. Great care and patience must be exercised. The process is time-consuming and therefore expensive.

Unadjusted Labor Costs. Another reason is that fees are based on the cost of the doctor's time as though the doctor was performing all the treatment. In actuality, most orthodontists have assistants doing a lot of the work. Although the assistant's hourly cost is much less than the doctor's, the savings accrue to the doctor, not the consumer.

Unnecessary X-rays. Initial diagnostic and post-treatment X-rays increase the cost significantly. Cephalographic or full-sized head X-rays are said to be necessary for precise measurements and an accurate diagnosis. Orthodontists insist that without cephalographic (skull and jaw) X-ray measurements, they cannot perform a proper diagnosis and assure successful outcome of treatment. Like many assertions, this one has little scientific foundation. There has never been a solid study to determine if this is true. On the contrary, a study, irresponsibly ignored by orthodontists as well as public health and general dentists, concluded that three-fourths of orthodontic radiographs were of no value for either diagnosis or treatment planning.[30] These films not only add to the cost of treatment, they subject the patient to a nontrivial amount of brain radiation. Patients should not be subjected to these nonessential X-rays unless there are extenuating circumstances, such as a consideration of orthognathic surgery. In most cases orthodontists can design their treatment plan on the basis of the full-mouth X-ray films already taken by the general dentist and the plaster study models.

Expensive photographs and plaster models. Many orthodontic patients are charged extra for professional photographs and fancy plaster models of their teeth. They may be sent to a dental X-ray laboratory not only for cephalographs but also for lovely front, side, and occlusal photographs that make a nice "before" record of the malocclusion. If an orthodontist does not have a camera, you or a friend can take adequate before and after shots for both the doctor's and your own comparisons. These photographs may not be as good as those taken by a professional, but they are sufficient for the purpose.

Plaster study models provide an excellent record of the teeth at the beginning and end of treatment. Since they are not for public display, there is no reason to wax and polish them like works of art. The cost of necessary models and photographs should be part of the total fee, not an add-on.

Defensive dentistry. Orthodontists contend that the "standard of care" requires all these X-rays, photographs, and models. Many dentists understand them to be part of what is called defensive dentistry, a way of practicing that anticipates what will be needed to defend against a malpractice suit. But they were used long before malpractice became a concern of the profession, and the most effective defense against malpractice suits remains good treatment and good communication between doctor and patient. Another reason the excesses may have become commonplace is that they serve teaching purposes and help the practitioner pass specialty board examinations. These are not sufficient justifications for routinely subjecting patients to unnecessary radiation and unfair additional charges. Procedures to qualify for specialty board certification should have no bearing on the expenses that the patient will incur. A doctor who explains to a patient that before and after photos of the problem will be useful to the dentist in demonstrating his or her skills will likely find the patient willing, if not always eager, to cooperate. But the additional costs should be borne by the dentist, not the patient. When they are routinely passed along to the patient, they become, simply put, overcharges.

Limited Orthodontic Treatment

Most people—children and adults alike—are content if their front teeth are straightened and remain straight after treatment. For this reason, as long as the front teeth look good, complaints rarely arise if the posterior teeth are not perfectly repositioned. Considering that far more children and adults have disfiguring malocclusions than can be treated by the nearly 5,000 orthodontic specialists in this country and that most families cannot afford the cost of idealized full treatment, there is a place for partial or limited treatment.[31] After all, only partial correction is possible in many severe malocclusions. In others, after the treatment there is significant movement back to the original malocclusion.

Many general dentists as well as orthodontists are capable of providing what is to them compromise treatment at much lower cost than the $2,800 to $4,000 or more for full treatment. There is nothing wrong with working to correct the disfigurement of front teeth for someone who cannot afford total correction. The psychological value of limited improvement far outweighs the disadvantages of the untreated malocclusion.

Nonetheless, one must approach this limited approach cautiously. Training and experience in limited treatment is not widespread in the United States, although it is not uncommon in other countries where less precise removable and fixed appliances have been used successfully for decades. Not every dentist is qualified to provide even limited treatment. Before undertaking orthodontic treatment of any kind, you should ask to see plaster casts and photographs of other patients' teeth before and after treatment. (Former patients are entitled to confidentiality, so you should not be shown their faces.) You can judge the improvement at least in alignment of the front teeth. Find out if the general dentist works with an orthodontist for the review and supervision of cases. Find out if he or she belongs to a study group and what the qualifications of the leader of the group are. Find out how many full cases the dentist has treated and how many limited cases. And, of course, compare the fee with that charged by an orthodontist for full treatment. If it is not a half or a third less, it may not be worth the difference to opt for less than full treatment by an orthodontist.

Shopping Around

If you live outside major population centers, your choice will be limited to those few orthodontists practicing in your vicinity. While their fees usually are on the high side, costs can be budgeted over the years of treatment. A sizable down payment will be required, perhaps a third of the total fee. If you can manage that, the rest should be fairly easy, ranging from $25 to $50 a month.

Some orthodontists include the retainers and supervision during retention in the total fee. Others charge another $250, and some as much as $500, with additional charges for broken or lost retainers. All this should be discussed beforehand and written into a signed contract. If you live in a large city, there is no reason not to shop around since there can be a wide range in orthodontic fees. Many orthodontists who state that their customary fee is $4,000 are treating patients with dental insurance for $2500 if that is all the insurance pays. A check of the yellow pages might locate an orthodontic clinic that employs qualified specialists who charge as little as $1900 for full-banded treatment.

Don't be shy about checking their qualifications. Today, most orthodontists have received a master of science (M.S.) degree from graduate programs at dental schools, which indicates at least 2 years of specialized orthodontic training following their D.D.S. degrees. But, as noted above, there are also general practitioners capable of providing good orthodontic treatment. If you decide to go with a general practitioner make sure you check out his or her training and experience as described in the preceding section.

RECOMMENDATIONS

1. Don't create problems. Avoid cosmetic treatment unless there is a significant problem.
2. Good toothbrushing with regular toothpaste reduces or eliminates unsightly stains. Avoid prolonged use of more abrasive "tooth whitening" pastes and powders.
3. Do not replace functional amalgam fillings even if the enamel in a back tooth looks darker.
4. Do not ask for or accept composite fillings as a substitute for amalgam on chewing surfaces of bicuspids or molars or to restore worn incisal surfaces of lower anterior teeth, unless you are willing to pay the price for early replacement. They won't last long.
5. Avoid porcelain inlays on chewing surfaces of teeth that are not normally visible and can be restored with amalgam fillings or gold onlays.
6. Ask your dentist to consider bleaching before veneering or capping a discolored tooth.
7. Unless there is a *significant* cosmetic problem, don't waste your money bleaching your teeth.
8. Veneers are preferable to caps or crowns to correct minor irregularities of front teeth because there is less tooth grinding and less potential damage to the tooth and nerve.
9. Prior to treatment, discuss replacement fees and "goodwill" discounts if porcelain veneers or crowns fracture or fail prematurely.
10. Avoid orthodontic treatment of minor irregularities.
11. Do not accept cephalographic (head) X-rays for orthodontic diagnosis unless there is a severe malocclusion.
12. Do not pay extra for orthodontic photographs and study models from professional laboratories.
13. Avoid third molar extractions unless there is a third molar problem. Wisdom teeth do not cause initial or relapse "crowding" or overlapping of front teeth.
14. Get a second opinion about alternatives to bicuspid extractions if recommended for orthodontic treatment.
15. Orthodontic fees vary widely. Do not hesitate to get second opinions and multiple estimates.
16. If you cannot afford the cost of full orthodontic treatment, consider partial treatment from a qualified dentist to correct the major esthetic problem.

10

Replacement of Missing Teeth—

Bridges and Dentures

Almost everyone missing a front tooth wants it replaced, but is it necessary to replace missing posterior teeth? The answer depends on how many teeth are missing and whether or not the empty space presents a problem. If only one molar tooth is missing, for example, there is little if any benefit in its replacement.[1] It also depends on the patient's finances and, more often than not, whether there is dental insurance to defray at least 50 percent of the cost. Insurance may be the decisive factor, often accounting for treatment that otherwise would be considered nonessential, if not unaffordable.

The Economics of Bridges and Dentures

Replacement of missing teeth is very expensive and provides a major source of income to dentists. Because people are conditioned to pay for appliances and mechanical devices, it is customary to charge fees for prostheses that generate higher hourly income than for fillings. To be sure, crowns, bridges, and dentures are expensive because of the time involved and the added cost of laboratory construction, including the labor of the technician and the costs of materials. Nonetheless, when these costs are deducted from the total fee for the appliance, dentists earn more per hour for this kind of work than for most other services.

Because fees vary, reflecting the competitive dental marketplace, it is not a bad idea to obtain a few estimates whenever a lot of expensive bridgework is required. But price should never be the only determinant. As John Ruskin is quoted on the nineteenth-century marketplace:

> *There is hardly anything in this world that one man cannot make worse and sell for less. The person who considers price only is this man's lawful prey.*

One way to "make worse and sell for less" is to rush through treatment. Good dental technique requires careful attention to details, which takes more time and, not infrequently, repetition of a procedure or an impression until the correct result is achieved. The less time a dentist spends on a procedure for which a fee has been established, the higher the hourly income; therefore, the lowest-priced dentist may be less able to resist the temptation to cut corners. On the other hand, there is no guarantee that a high-priced dentist will be more conscientious. The goal, then, is to locate a dentist who is competent in technique and reasonable in his or her charges. This requires that the consumer have at least a basic understanding of the basis for treatment.

Preference for Fixed Bridges Is Natural

Fixed bridges are virtually indistinguishable from the natural teeth, in contrast to a partial denture that is bulkier and must be removed to clean around the metal-plastic base and clasps. Yet if the larger expenditure of multiple fixed bridges is beyond one's means, a properly designed partial denture can be as comfortable as fixed bridges.

If nothing is known of a dentist's skills, a removable bridge is the safest way to replace missing teeth. After all, if the fit is poor, it can always be thrown away. Not so with a fixed bridge that is cemented onto adjacent teeth that have been cut down for artificial crowns to which the missing teeth are attached. If the crowns are poorly done, the bridge will be lost in a few years along with the teeth.

How Permanent Are Bridges?

A good fixed bridge will last a decade or longer, many for over 20 years. When a bridge fails within a few years of placement, the reason is almost always poor dentistry, not patient neglect. Much less expensive **removable bridges** or **partial dentures**, as they are more commonly known, last as long as good fixed bridges if they are properly constructed and cared for. Patients who have resisted persuasive arguments to replace well-functioning partial dentures with fixed bridges have been known to wear the same appliance for 15 or 20 more years. An experienced dentist knows not to tinker with success and does not recommend replacements in the absence of obvious need.

Some fixed bridges, however, rival the Golden Gate in span, stretching from a back molar on one side to the last molar on the other side with too few supporting teeth in between. An "ear to ear" or "roundhouse" bridge costs thousands of dollars more than a removable bridge and seldom lasts longer. Too often these great bridges are monuments to the ambitions of the dentists but end up as disasters to their patients when they come loose and have to be removed

129

along with the teeth that have decayed extensively underneath. Nevertheless, if enough strong teeth remain, if good oral hygiene is maintained, and if the dentist is experienced and conscientious, and there is legitimate need, fixed bridges, large and small, are well worth the effort and the money.

Restorations seem to last longer when there is no dental insurance to pay for replacement. Willing patients and those with insurance may be receptive to suggestions that they replace crowns and bridges even when all that is required is a small gum line filling to repair a decayed margin.[2] Most insurance plans limit coverage for crowns, bridges, and dentures to once in five years. This seems like an arbitrary limitation, but it does help prevent the worst abuses.

There Needs to Be a Problem

Most often the decision to replace teeth should be made on a sense of *felt need* for improvement of appearance or function, though account should be taken of the future consequences of leaving things as they are. The consequences of losing a posterior molar are greatly exaggerated. While it is true that the adjacent and opposing teeth might shift towards the open space, the change is minimal. There is greater risk of iatrogenic damage to the adjacent teeth when they are cut down to support a fixed bridge than to the dentition if left alone. The dentist's responsibility is to evaluate the condition of the remaining teeth and the patient's ability to chew and otherwise function effectively. The dentist should also predict for the patient what will likely occur if the missing teeth are not replaced. Since dentists are trained to think in terms of restoring every mouth to an ideal state, patients cannot rely solely on professional recommendations. Before going ahead with bridgework, you should be convinced that there really is a problem that needs correction, not just an empty space that offends the dentist's sensibilities. (See the section below on *Restoring Chewing Surfaces.*)

Reasons for Replacing Missing Teeth

In addition to restoring function and appearance, replacement of missing teeth prevents other teeth from moving into the empty spaces, which in turn prevents periodontal breakdown and possible loss of other teeth. But teeth are not stacked in the mouth like a row of dominoes. Extraction of one or a few teeth does not necessarily lead to loss of other teeth. Except for appearance, functional reasons for replacing every lost tooth are exaggerated. Nevertheless, there are good reasons for replacements, such as the missing front tooth that discourages smiling or where insufficient back teeth remain for adequate mastication, causing the front teeth to be overworked and eventually to break down.

Early Loss of a Six-Year Molar: The Case for a Second Extraction

The permanent teeth that are most frequently lost in childhood are the first molars. If the child's second molars have not yet erupted, they can be an excellent replacement. For example, if a child's 6-year molar is extracted because of gross decay before the eruption of the second permanent or 12-year molar, the developing second molar will drift forward into the space of the first molar. But the opposing first molar will move up or down into the empty space, depending on which tooth was lost, upsetting the position of all the molars in that arch. To prevent supereruption of the opposing molar, it should be extracted at the same time, thereby allowing the upper and lower second molars a chance to replace the first molars. This also provides room for the third molars to erupt without difficulty. Even if the second molars do not replace the first molars perfectly, the condition will still be better than if only one first molar is extracted (Figure 10-1).[3]

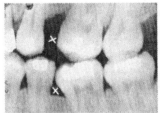

Figure 10-1 Upper and lower first permanent molars (x) were lost in childhood over 30 years ago. The second and third molars (wisdom teeth) have moved forward. The lower space is completely closed. The small upper space is not a problem.

Not All Teeth Supererupt

Teeth do not always extrude into open spaces. In a young person, there is a high probability of tooth movement into spaces vacated by extracted teeth. The older the patient, the less likely it is to occur, and then it is not always harmful. There is the example of a patient in his mid-fifties who had all his upper teeth and a lower partial denture replacing a few lost molars. The partial denture fit well but was a constant annoyance because he could not stop tongue-doodling with the appliance. Having been warned by his former dentist of the dire consequence of supereruption of the unopposed molars without the partial denture, he continued to wear it despite the constant annoyance. When he explained his inability to adjust, a more sympathetic dentist (the author) suggested that he try doing without the partial since he had enough teeth to chew with. Twenty-five years later he was still grateful for the suggestion. The other teeth had held up, and the unopposed upper molars, which were stabilized in bone, did not extrude downward. This kind of non-treatment is very successful because it does no harm and relieves the patient of discomfort, but it is not very popular among dentists because it provides them little economic satisfaction.

When to Replace a Missing Tooth

Assuming all the first and second molars are in normal occlusion and the lower first molar is extracted sometime during adolescence, the second molar frequently drifts and tilts forward into the space. The bicuspid in front of the space is less likely to drift backward because it is held in place by occluding with the upper teeth. At this early age, the upper first molar supererupts slightly down into the space below until further movement is prevented by contact with the shifting lower teeth in adjacent spaces. Quite often the teeth stabilize at this point, but it is not uncommon for small spaces to remain, which collect food particles and plaque, causing further tooth decay and periodontal breakdown. Thus, it is desirable to prevent shifting of other teeth by replacing the missing tooth soon after extraction. But there should be at least a two-month delay to allow the tooth socket to heal so that the artificial tooth (pontic) will fit snugly against the gum ridge. If the tooth is replaced immediately after extraction, the gum may shrink away from the pontic, creating a food trap that can be a constant annoyance.

What if the extraction was many years ago, and the teeth have already shifted so that the space is small and the situation has stabilized, as in Figure 10-1. What if the adjacent teeth are sound, with only small fillings or perhaps no filling at all? What if the bone support is strong and there is no periodontal breakdown around these teeth? What if you do not miss the tooth until your dentist reminds you of the small space and recommends a fixed bridge? Before consenting to a replacement bridge, consider the case for leaving well enough alone. If you face the circumstances described above, a bridge is not necessary and should not be done.

Restoring Chewing Surfaces

Many dentists insist that a full complement of teeth is necessary for proper mastication, a conclusion that is unrelated to reality. If too many posterior teeth are missing, replacement with fixed or removable bridges is generally advisable to balance the chewing table even though the need for replacement may not be felt. Otherwise there is a tendency to chew more on the front teeth, which can be very damaging since the incisors are designed for cutting food, not grinding. However, many people get along very well with a *shortened dental arch*, with as few as twenty teeth in occlusion.[4] Thus, having a bite from the second bicuspids on one side to the second bicuspids on the other side—two-thirds of the natural teeth in occlusion—is sufficient for adequate mastication and replacement of missing teeth is not essential.

For the Sake of Appearance

Almost everyone wants to replace a missing front tooth. Not so the old man who ran a cheap restaurant near my dental school in New York City. His missing upper central incisor provided a space that was just the right width to hold an ever-present cigarette. He could talk, smile, and chew gum without missing a puff. Since the cigarette was part of his face, replacing the tooth would serve no purpose.

We cannot be faulted for wanting to look our best, and that includes the appearance of our teeth, but we can be faulted for accepting or insisting on cosmetic treatment that has no cosmetic value. As an example, dentists often place a porcelain-covered (veneered) metal crown on an upper second molar instead of an unbreakable full metal crown. The only way anyone can see such a tooth is if you stand on your head with your mouth wide open and the other person kneels and peers in with a flashlight. It is just as foolish to have porcelain-covered metal crowns on lower second molars. The problem is that the porcelain veneer is so thin on these molar crowns that there is a high percentage of fracture. Porcelain veneers should also be avoided on the lower first molars since they are not visible in normal speaking and smiling. The best restoration for a molar, assuming a filling is not possible, is a gold onlay or a three-quarter or full gold crown, depending on how much of the tooth has to be restored. However, onlays and three-quarter crowns require more skill and may "show" some gold so they are becoming an art lost to the ubiquitous porcelain veneered metal crown.

Many people have small spaces between a few teeth, which may be the result of an extraction at a young age or simply related to the fact that the circumference of the jaw is too large for all the teeth to be held in contact. In the absence of functional or esthetic problems, grinding down healthy teeth at the risk of nerve injury to place a small bridge is potentially more harmful than ignoring the space. It is even more foolish if to see the space you have to hold a mirror six inches in front of your face and then grimace to lower the lower lip. This is quite different from the normal movements of the lips, which draw back over the lower front and side teeth when one smiles, rendering them even less visible than in normal speech. But there are some people whose teeth are visible back to the lower first molars. For them, replacement of missing teeth even where the space is small, or covering first molar crowns with porcelain veneers, makes esthetic sense.

Types of Bridges and Dentures

Fixed bridges. Fixed bridges are usually constructed of crowns on either side of missing teeth that are cemented to natural teeth, called abutments, and pontics or artificial teeth suspended between the crowns. Abutment teeth are reshaped to remove bulges so that the artificial crowns can fit over them to hold the bridge in place (Figure 10-2).

Fixed bridges usually replace one or two teeth. If three or more teeth are to be replaced, the abutments must have long and strong roots, or else they will be loosened by the additional stress. Long-span bridges sometimes require double abutments at one or both ends to share the load, particularly when the abutment teeth are short. But if the crowns and the roots are short, the patient is well advised to consider a removable rather than a long, overloaded fixed bridge.

When the space is small, five or six millimeters in width as in the case of a lateral incisor or small bicuspid, only one abutment or attachment tooth is necessary from which the pontic is cantilevered. The attachment teeth are usually covered by full crowns for maximum retention. By **retention** is meant the resistance of the bridge to loosening. If the crown is not made properly, the cement bond will not be strong enough to hold the bridge in place. The skill of the dentist and the design of the bridge—not the strength of the cement— determines success or failure. For this reason, bridges generally should be made with crowns on the abutments, rather than inlays or onlays, because the latter lack sufficient retentive strength. An exception would be a very small bridge, in which case strong onlays or three-quarter crowns on large teeth are satisfactory.

Most fixed bridges are made by fusing porcelain to a semiprecious or nonprecious metal base. Semiprecious metal avoids the risk of a hypersensitivity reaction to the nickel in some nonprecious metals and up until the late 1990s was relatively inexpensive. Containing palladium, the price of semiprecious metal now approximates gold, increasing the cost of crown fabrication by $60 to $90. To keep laboratory costs down as well as to maximize their own profits, many dentists use non-precious metal crowns. While the risk of sensitivity reactions is small, it should not be ignored and patients should be given the option of paying the extra cost for a semiprecious or precious metal crown. (See "Risk of Metal Hypersensitivity" in chapter 4.)

Since the porcelain veneer can chip or fracture, the occlusal or chewing surfaces of the bridge should be made entirely of metal. Also, porcelain on an occlusal surface, particularly if it is unpolished or unglazed, can act like a millstone, grinding away the enamel of opposing natural teeth.

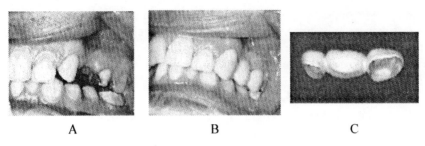

Figure 10-2 A. Teeth prepared to receive a fixed bridge replacing the upper left first bicuspid. B. Bridge cemented in place. C. Underside of a similar bridge replacing a lower molar.

An alternative to the conventional bridge. The **Maryland bridge**, named after the university dental school where it was developed in the 1970s, is an alternative to a small conventional fixed bridge.[5] It has the distinct advantage of requiring only minor modification of abutment teeth. Instead of grinding off all the enamel and some dentin, small metal wings are bonded to the inside enamel of the natural crown on either side of the pontic to hold it in place. Success is dependent on careful case selection, design, and bonding. The Maryland bridge is not suitable for replacement of more than one molar or a few anterior teeth. Too long a span results in torquing and breaking of the bond. But if only one or two small teeth are involved, and if the abutment teeth would not otherwise benefit from artificial crowns, the Maryland bridge is an ideal choice (Figure 10-3).

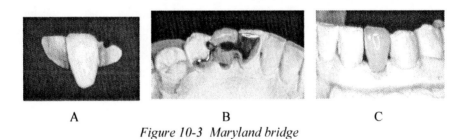

Figure 10-3 Maryland bridge

A. *Front view of the artificial tooth (pontic) and the lateral arms that are bonded to the supporting teeth on either side of the pontic.*
B. *Plaster model shows how the arms fit against the supporting teeth.*
C. *When the bridge is bonded to the teeth on the inside, only the pontic will be visible.*

Defective bridges. As with any restoration, the **bite** of a bridge must be correct. All the teeth should come together evenly and without interference or "tripping" over opposing teeth in lateral movements. There should be no high spots or sense of imbalance. Patients should never tell a dentist that they can get used to the bridge if the bite feels even slightly off center or high. A good dentist continues to adjust the bite until it feels just right.

If a fixed bridge comes loose in a few years, the cause is usually faulty design and poor abutment tooth preparation. Most often the crowns are not long enough and the attachment teeth are overtapered. Or in the case of the Maryland bridge, the attachment arms are too small or the bonding was defective. Sometimes a bridge can be recemented or re-bonded. If it comes loose more than once, it should be remade.

Gum line sensitivity following cementation is due to a crown that does not completely cover the surfaces of the tooth that were ground off or to an **open margin**. When a cavity develops in two or three years, the cause is most likely poor construction of the crown with a deficient margin at the gum line. This is especially true if the cavity is on the inaccessible **proximal** surface between teeth. A deficient bridge should be remade at no charge. A small gum line defect on the outside buccal or the inside lingual surface of a crowned tooth can be corrected satisfactorily with a filling.

Patients are often blamed for causing the cavity by eating too many sweets and not keeping the bridge clean. Since many people do not brush thoroughly, such accusations have a ring of truth to them. But it is the rare person who through neglect develops a gum line cavity around a fixed bridge so soon after placement. When such a cavity occurs, the dentist should not make the patient a scapegoat. If poor dental treatment is suspected, an independent examination (second opinion) should be obtained. Although dentists are reluctant to criticize colleagues, a good dentist will at least describe the problem and let the patient draw his or her own conclusion.

Removable Bridges—Partial Dentures

The removable partial denture is best suited to the replacement of a number of teeth that are missing all around the arch. Until recently, it was the only reliable choice where there were no posterior teeth to which a fixed bridge could be attached. (See the section in this chapter on implants for replacement of teeth in selected cases.) They also provide less chance of injury to the nerves of sound teeth because none have to be ground down for crowns.

A partial denture consists of **saddles** to hold artificial teeth, the underside literally saddling toothless ridges, a **base** or **bar** connected to the saddles in different parts of the mouth, and **retainers** or **clasps** to grip abutment teeth and hold the partial denture in place (Figure 10-4 A). **Rests** or small extensions of clasps sit on the occlusal or chewing surfaces of the abutments to prevent the partial from sinking into the tissue.

The base is customarily cast in a stainless steel alloy. This alloy has great strength, allowing the framework and clasps to be kept thin. Before the price of gold became too high, many partial dentures were constructed of gold. Prior to 1950, gold was a superior material because in those days the stainless steel was too brittle. The modern dental chrome alloy is not only stronger than gold but also flexible so that clasps can be adjusted and tightened from time to time. Gold no longer has any advantages in the construction of removable partial dentures unless one has an allergy to stainless steel.

Artificial teeth used on partial dentures are the same as for full dentures. Made of plastic or porcelain, the denture teeth are attached to the saddle base with pink denture plastic—**acrylic**—to resemble the gum tissue. The underside of the saddle, which fits on the ridge of the jaw, is also lined with acrylic. Since the ridge changes over time, this design permits periodic **relining** of the saddle to maintain a close fit.

Before constructing a bridge or partial denture, dentists are likely to grind off an extruded tooth to realign it with the other teeth, sometimes to the extent that root canal therapy and crown coverage become necessary. However, these teeth can be shortened slightly without inflicting nerve damage. The partial denture can also be designed with an irregular line of occlusion to accommodate extruded teeth. While it may be desirable to have an even occlusal plane, in practice the mouth really does not know the difference. If extreme extrusion has occurred in the back of the mouth, the partial can be designed with a thin metal chewing plate to restore function without having to crown or extract any of the natural teeth to make space for artificial teeth.

A   Partial upper denture   *B.   Full upper denture*

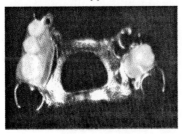 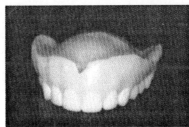

Figure 10-4 Removable Dentures

When to crown a clasped tooth.   Some dentists recommend crowning abutment teeth that will be clasped in order to reshape their contours and to help prevent future decay. Unless a tooth requires a crown for other reasons, such as extensive decay or fracture, the added expense is unnecessary. With few exceptions, clasps can be designed to fit attachment teeth even if tilted or out of normal position. Teeth can also be reshaped without crowning by selective reduction of excessive bulges to permit easy placement and removal of the partial denture as well as to brace the teeth securely. Decay of supporting teeth is minimized by proper design and good daily oral hygiene, including cleansing of the denture base and clasps, preferably after each meal.

Clasps usually can be designed so that they are not visible, even when smiling. But sometimes the clasps come so far forward or the patient's smile is so broad that they are truly unsightly. In such cases, crowns can be designed to completely hide a clasp. The very expensive precision attachments used years ago have been replaced by a **dowel and dimple** design that is less expensive and just as effective. The dowel is part of the partial denture and fits into a groove in the crown of the abutment tooth. A half-clasp with a **pimple** on the end encircles the inner surface of the crown where it is invisible. The pimple snaps into a small dimple, which is a corresponding concavity on the inside surface of the crown to hold the partial in place.[6] Since only visible teeth benefit from dowel and dimple design, conventional clasps can be used on all the other support teeth.

Single-tooth removable bridge. The unilateral removable bridge, also called a **Nesbit** after the name of the dentist who promoted it decades ago, is frowned upon by most dentists. Since only one tooth—occasionally two—is replaced, it is not uncommon for a patient to leave it out of the mouth from time to time. If it is left out a few days, the adjacent teeth sometimes shift ever so slightly so that the bridge no longer fits.

Since anything that happens rarely can happen, the danger of swallowing a small removable bridge if it dislodges while eating is something to be considered. Since the clasps are like little hooks, the concern is that surgery would be necessary if it got caught in the esophagus, stomach or intestines. Poorly fitted single crowns and onlays also come loose and not infrequently are swallowed, but they do not have clasps that could hook and prevent passage through the alimentary canal. Patients have also swallowed the needle-like files used for root canal treatment. Fortunately, these objects usually pass through the body without harm.[7]

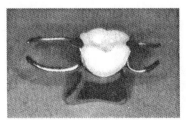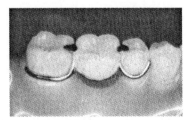

Figure 10-5 Unilateral removable partial denture replacing the lowe first molar.

Despite these concerns, a person who cannot afford a fixed bridge may be well served by a Nesbit until finances permit a fixed restoration. Sometimes it is a logical choice to solve a special problem, as in the case of a patient who had to lose part of an extensive bridge that had been made years before. Since he was recovering from a stroke, extensive treatment to remake the entire bridge was inadvisable. He was partially paralyzed and there was some doubt about his ability to remove and replace the little bridge. However, he was well motivated and mentally alert and the Nesbit functioned successfully until his death almost a decade later.

Even though fixed bridges are customarily recommended by dentists, many patients are satisfied with unilateral removable bridges Thus, it is not inappropriate to question the wisdom of grinding down perfectly healthy teeth to place a one-tooth posterior permanent bridge, which, if poorly done, will last only a few years and might cause loss of the attachment teeth. A Nesbit might serve as well, provided that the clasped teeth and the appliance are kept clean. On a personal note, the author would rather have the space of a missing posterior tooth than the risk of swallowing a Nesbit bridge.

Proper fit. Maintaining a close fit is particularly important when the partial denture has a **free end saddle.** This saddle is partly tissue-supported because there is no posterior tooth to hold a clasp. Occlusal forces have to be distributed evenly over the teeth and gums. If the saddle does not fit properly, chewing forces the free end to sink down into the ridge rather than be supported by it. If the clasps are too tight or are improperly designed, the partial rotates and loosens the abutment teeth, eventually causing their loss. Partial dentures should be checked once a year by the dentist, or whenever they become bothersome, and adjusted and relined as necessary to maintain a balanced fit.

As with fixed bridges, poorly constructed removable bridges do more harm than good. If the clasps are put in the wrong position, they act as levers to loosen the teeth. A properly designed clasp that is too tight has the same effect. Thus, a removable partial denture should not snap into position. It should seat gently and be held in place without any sense of pressure. Likewise, its removal should require no more than gentle pressure and no movement of the support teeth. The saddles should be extensive and tight enough to keep all but the smallest particles of food from getting underneath. And, of course, the underside or tissue surface of the denture should be kept clean of debris that could cause or aggravate sores.

If the bite is incorrect or the base or connecting bars press too hard against the mucosa, sore teeth and tissue sores develop. Occasional discomfort is no cause for alarm since the bite or the area of the denture irritating the gum can be relieved easily by the dentist grinding away an insignificant amount of material. If frequent sores occur, the partial denture needs relining or replacement. The partial denture can be worn during the healing period because its cause, the impinging denture, has been relieved. A sore should heal completely within two weeks after denture adjustment. If it does not, further adjustment is necessary. Any sore that resists healing raises the suspicion of cancer and should be examined closely by the dentist.

To avoid shifting of abutment teeth, a partial denture should not be left out of the mouth for more than a day while waiting for an adjustment or for a sore to heal. Once the teeth shift, no matter how slightly, the partial may never fit again.

Full Dentures

Many people expect to lose all their teeth eventually because their parents ended up with dentures. They think all their dental problems will be over with false teeth–also called a *plate*. Such is not the case. Among the big sales items in drugstores are denture adhesives and do-it-yourself reliners, proving that denture wearers are constantly troubled with loose fits and sore gums.

The number of edentulous (toothless) persons in the United States is decreasing. Among the reasons are the reduction of tooth decay and consequent tooth loss and the increasing availability of dental insurance to pay, at least in part, for expensive restorative treatment rather than extractions. With proper dental care, few people should lose all their teeth. Nevertheless, by age 65, one out of three people (33 percent, down from 46 percent 20 years ago) of the population is edentulous.[8] When all the permanent teeth are lost in the same arch (upper or lower), a full denture is necessary to restore function and appearance (Figure 10-4 B).

Some patients ask for dentures as a deliverance from their fear of dental treatment. Good dentists should be able to assuage their irrational anxieties. They will persuade their patients to keep at least a few strategic teeth that can be clasped for support of a removable partial denture. They will not extract sound teeth. Extracting healthy teeth at the request of a patient is essentially *mutilation by consensus.*[9]

Immediate dentures. If the remaining teeth cannot be saved, it is customary to have an immediate denture placed at the same time that the front teeth are extracted. The back molars and bicuspids will have been removed at least a month earlier to allow healing and better control over the construction of the new denture. Since the underlying bone and gums continue to shrink following extractions, an immediate denture gradually loosens and has to be relined. The permanent relining should be delayed for at least six months to allow complete ridge healing. During the interim, the denture can be tightened with a soft, gel-like lining material called **tissue conditioner**. Tissue conditioner can last several months and may also be used as a semipermanent reliner by a denture wearer who otherwise never gets a satisfactory fit.

Dentures have a way of breaking on Saturday night just before going out to dinner or when one is about to leave for work. Therefore, if you can afford it, the immediate denture should be replaced by a new one and the immediate denture kept as a spare. A completely new denture allows improvement of the bite, of the overall fit of the denture base, and of the appearance of the artificial teeth.

An immediate denture does not have to be replaced if the fit is satisfactory after the gums have healed and the base has been relined. A duplicate denture can be made of inexpensive base and tooth acrylic by the dental laboratory at a fraction of the cost of a new denture. It can be worn for a short time while the regular denture is being repaired. When not in use, the duplicate denture should be stored in soapy water or a dilute denture cleaner to prevent the plastic base from drying out and losing its fit.

Overdentures. When a tooth is extracted, the top part of the bone that surrounded the root is resorbed while the lower part of the tooth socket fills in with new bone. In other words, there is a leveling process that reduces the crest or height of the alveolar ridge. When many teeth are extracted because of advanced periodontal bone loss, the entire ridge flattens out, making denture retention and stability very difficult. This is more likely to occur in the lower jaw where the entire alveolar ridge is resorbed, leaving a thin, horseshoe or U shaped jawbone termed an **atrophied mandible**. The only way to achieve any degree of stability on an atrophied mandible is to build up the ridge artificially with a graft or by inserting an implant with posts to support the denture base. (See the discussion below of grafts and implants in this chapter.)

As long as roots are present, resorption of the alveolar bone is slowed if not completely prevented. Even where teeth are too weak to support a denture, it is sometimes possible to save a few roots, ideally of the cuspids. The top parts of the roots may be left above the gum for direct support of the denture—now called an overdenture—or they may be cut off to the level of the bone and covered over by the gum. Either way, the roots remain, giving support not only to the denture above but also to the alveolar ridge bone. Although this principle applies to both arches, it is particularly relevant to the lower arch, or mandible since that is the location of most denture problems.

More positive retention is obtained by inserting special attachments (connectors) into these roots. The connectors stick out above the gum and snap into the overdenture base. The attachments should be designed to allow minor movement of the base caused by chewing without torquing and loosening the roots. Another concern is decay of the exposed roots. All surfaces must be kept clean and free of plaque to prevent root decay.

The main disadvantage of an overdenture is the expense of root canal therapy and connectors, or of implants if there are no roots remaining. If connectors are not used, the opening to the root canal can be filled with amalgam, avoiding the cost of a gold cap that some dentists place over the stump, ostensibly to prevent decay. But the stump, capped or not, will decay if meticulous oral hygiene is not maintained. Application of fluoride gels and rinses will also inhibit decay.

Some patients report a better sense of "feel" with an overdenture, more like chewing on natural teeth, but there is no certainty that an overdenture will be significantly more satisfactory. Many people never adjust completely to any type of denture. Nonetheless, there is little to lose and perhaps much to gain, provided initial costs are kept to a minimum. Cutting off the crown at the level of the bone, filling the root canal, closing the canal with amalgam, and then suturing over the gum tissue sounds complex, but it is actually quite simple. It costs about as much as an extraction, a single root canal filling, and a small amalgam filling—about $500 in year 2002 dollars. Connectors increase the cost per root by another $150. If more than two roots are to be retained, the dentist should be asked to reduce the charges for the additional roots. After all, it does not take four times as long to do four teeth or twice as long to do two teeth when all are done at once.

If a partial denture is supported by too few natural teeth, the teeth may eventually loosen. Anticipating their loss, which is by no means certain, some dentists recommend an overdenture so that at least the roots will be preserved to support the underlying ridge bone. Good strong cuspids (canines or eye teeth) are sometimes cut in half to make an overdenture when they could have been retained to support a partial denture. If the remaining teeth are strong enough to avoid a full denture, neither extraction nor removal of the crown of the tooth for root retention should be done. If only two lower cuspids remain, neither one wiggles on finger pressure, and the x-ray film shows close to 50 percent of bone remaining about the roots, a conventional partial denture is the treatment of choice.

The natural look. Dentures are made of an acrylic base and porcelain or plastic artificial teeth. Artificial teeth come in a variety of shapes and colors to match real teeth. Denture teeth look unreal if set too straight. They can be set into the base with slight irregularities that impart a more natural look. Some patients, anticipating a new denture, ask for bright white teeth, regardless of the shade of their natural teeth and skin tones. Teeth that are too light look flashy instead of blending into the color of the face. Healthy teeth have a light yellow hue, becoming slightly more yellow with age.

The color of the denture base should also be natural. Denture acrylic is usually light to medium pink, but it can be tinted darker to match a patient's gums. An extra charge for tinting a denture base is unwarranted since it costs no more to produce in the laboratory. There is no sense paying extra for a clear plastic palate on the upper denture. The palate is not visible, and if it could be seen, the clear acrylic would look more unreal than the pink of the denture base. However, characterized front teeth that simulate stained enamel fracture lines or slight mottling or a gold inlay effectively disguise a denture look. The cost for characterized teeth is about $75 more than a regular set of denture teeth; the laboratory cost of an inlay in a denture tooth is also about $75.

Advice to senior denture wearers. If a denture is comfortable but requires replacement because the teeth are badly worn and chipped or the base has cracked and been repaired a number of times, it should be duplicated as closely as possible. If you are 60 years old, the teeth should not be set as though you were still 20. Don't expect the dentist to eliminate all the wrinkles around your mouth by making the teeth and the denture bases longer—what dentists call "opening the bite." The bite should be opened only if the previous dentures are so short that your mouth overcloses, making you look prematurely older. Even so, there are limits to how much the bite can be opened to lengthen your profile and smooth out your wrinkles. Improvement can often be obtained by thickening the peripheral borders of the dentures to plump out lips and cheeks that appear to have fallen in, but the wrinkles of age cannot be so easily erased.

Denture Problems

Movement in action. The upper denture with a full palatal base is more easily tolerated than the lower horseshoe shaped denture. It fits on the broader, more solid base of the hard palate, whereas the lower ridge is narrower and the gum tissue is thinner and more fragile. The lower denture seldom seals like the upper denture, so that it is easily displaced by action of the tongue, cheeks, and lips along the borders of the denture base.

Although the upper denture feels more secure and almost always fits tighter, both upper and lower dentures actually move and rock during chewing, swallowing, and talking. In a sense, there is no such thing as a tight denture. Some are simply better or worse than others. The success of dentures is as much due to the ability of the patient to adapt as to the skill of the dentist. Even a properly fitted denture may not be successful, and sometimes a poorly constructed one is completely satisfactory to the patient. But the risk of failure is always greater if the bite is incorrect or the denture base is undersize.

Denture adhesives. Denture adhesives provide a little more security but should not substitute for a proper fit. A well fitting upper denture rarely needs an adhesive. Since a comparable fit is seldom achieved with a lower denture, an adhesive can help for a few hours. There is no general advantage of one type of adhesive over another. Some people prefer powders, others pastes. Whatever works best is best.

Many people, especially the elderly, wear their dentures only for appearance, removing them to eat. Without teeth to chew, the pleasure of eating is severely diminished. If food is not cut into small pieces, attempting to swallow it whole is dangerous. Death from suffocation has happened all too often when a large piece of steak lodged in the throat, cutting off the airway. But the more common complaints deal with the misery of being unable to chew without pain or to laugh

143

and smile and speak without a denture coming loose, and of the distaste for the gobs of adhesive powders and pastes that literally gum up the works.

Diminished taste and gagging. New denture wearers occasionally complain about the lack of feeling when the palate is completely covered, but they soon get used to it. Some patients complain of loss of taste, since 25 percent of taste buds are located on the hard and soft palate. However, this complaint is rare because most taste buds are located on the tongue. Then there are the gaggers, people who simply cannot tolerate the denture extending onto the soft palate, the **postdam** area, which provides the suction or seal of the upper denture. A few people cannot even tolerate the plate covering the center of the hard palate. While it is preferable to cover the entire hard palate for maximum stability, with extension of the postdam two or three millimeters onto the soft palate, it is possible to make a horseshoe-shaped upper plate that leaves the palate bare.[10] A horseshoe palate usually will decrease retention, but it may be the only solution for an otherwise uncontrollable gagger.

The inaccuracy of articulation. Some dentists claim that to make the best dentures and bridges requires a special device, an expensive anatomical articulator set to the measurements of the patient's natural jaw movements. This adds hundreds or even thousands of dollars to the cost. Any additional accuracy obtained by special measurements transferred to complex articulators is lost in the imprecision of the fabricating process. In addition, the slight movement of every denture on the viscous oral tissue renders such accuracy meaningless. There is no reason to pay the extra cost of anatomical articulation. The same result is obtained by any skilled dentist using a simple laboratory articulator.

Functional artificial teeth. It makes no difference what kind of teeth or base materials are used. Only the front denture teeth need to look exactly like natural teeth. The bicuspids and molars also have to look natural on the visible sides but not on the occlusal or chewing surfaces. Chewing surfaces should not have high cusps that lock in the bite and limit the free movement of dentures from side to side. Patients have less trouble if chewing surfaces are flat, albeit with special grooves to assist cutting, shearing, and grinding food. Even these grooves are not too important since teeth just barely touch on chewing. It is more the pressure of the posterior teeth that tears and grinds food particles, not the cutting edges. Some artificial posterior teeth are designed as cutting bars to improve chewing efficiency. Magnets in reverse or repelling position can be set in opposite dentures so that the dentures seat more tightly as they come together. Nevertheless, none of these devices provide reliable solutions for some denture wearers, no matter how good the device seems in theory. To some problems there simply are no easy solutions.

Relines and Remakes

How long should dentures last? Some people have worn the same dentures for decades without needing relines. They are the exceptions. Most denture wearers benefit from refitting every few years. The inside of the old denture is ground out and relined with new acrylic plastic that bonds perfectly to the outside base. On average, a denture should last five years or longer. Regardless of its age, a denture that satisfies a patient should not be changed. New dentures, like new shoes, never fit the same. One can seldom go back to the old denture with the same comfort if it has been out of the mouth for weeks or months and the new denture has somehow changed the tissue adaptation. By the same token, do not blame your dentist for a new denture that does not fit the way you remember the old denture fitting years ago. You and your mouth are no longer the same.

Soft tissue relines. Because the hard denture base rubs on the soft tissue or skin of the mouth, denture wearers are likely to develop occasional sores The dentist provides relief by grinding away a small amount of the denture base to reduce the pressure over the sore spot. If sores occur frequently, the denture can be relined periodically with a plastic that is semisoft or rubbery in consistency. The material gradually hardens. It is also more porous than hard acrylic and may retain unpleasant odors. But a soft reline can provide relief for months at a time.

For some denture wearers there are no permanent solutions, not even when permanency is measured in months or a year. They are the likely purchasers of the do-it-yourself reline pads available at drugstores. These replaceable cushions help some individuals, but they generally fit poorly and may accelerate the shrinkage of the underlying bone. A better solution is to have a dentist place a soft **tissue conditioner** as an inexpensive temporary liner in the denture. The material is mixed to a creamy consistency and spread on the underside of the denture, where it sets like foam rubber.

The tissue conditioner provides immediate relief from painful sores and markedly improves retention of the denture. It may be comfortable for only a few weeks or months as the material gradually hardens, and then the denture loosens again and new sores develop. Instead of looking for a permanent reline, patients with this kind of recurrent problem should have the tissue conditioner replaced as needed by the dentist or a trained assistant. Think of it as going to the hairdresser every month or having a car serviced every two or three months. Patients can also be taught to apply the material themselves at home, with periodic checkups by the dentist to assure the oral tissues are healthy. Both patients and dentists have to get over the idea that there is anything permanent about a denture base.

Because soft liners are porous, microorganisms settle into the material, increasing the risk of yeast infections. This can be prevented by soaking the dentures daily for 15 minutes in a disinfectant solution.

Care of Dentures.

Denture materials are essentially the same as plastic and porcelain dinnerware. Soap and water clean them as well as commercial denture cleansers. Commercial denture cleansers or household chlorine bleach diluted one to 10 parts of water are convenient for overnight soaking and disinfection. Do not use harsh abrasives such as scouring powder that scratch the surface or full-strength bleaches that leach the color out of the plastic. The denture should be cleaned often, preferably after each meal. Small round brushes are handy for cleaning the inside of partial denture clasps, and larger denture brushes are available to reach inside the denture base.

Some dentists recommend leaving dentures out of the mouth at night to give the gums a chance to recuperate, but there is no clear evidence that doing so makes any difference. Most important, dentures should always be kept in soapy water or denture cleaning solutions when not worn. If the base dries out, the acrylic shrinks and distorts, affecting the fit adversely. The base also becomes more brittle.

Annual tissue examination. Even though dentures fit all right and there are no apparent problems, denture wearers should still have an annual dental examination. It takes a dentist only a few minutes to examine the oral tissues for changes and for sores that might become cancerous. Denture wearers should be particularly wary of a painless sore in the mouth. Of course, if it does not hurt, how is one to know it is there? This is one of the reasons that periodic dental examinations are recommended. It is also a reason why a denture wearer should regularly feel around his or her mouth, particularly under the tongue, to detect breaks in the tissue or painless "ulcers."

Ordinary sores caused by the pressure and movement of dentures heal in 10 to 14 days after adjustment of the denture by the dentist. If a sore persists despite repeated relief of the denture base, the problem is more serious. The constant irritation of a denture, particularly around the underside of the tongue, can cause cancer. Oral cancer represents about 3 percent of all cancers and 2.4 percent of cancer deaths.[11] Suspicious areas should be examined by an oral pathologist or an oral surgeon with a biopsy for microscopic examination of the tissue. Delay could be catastrophic.

DENTAL IMPLANTS

The ideal implant attaches to the jawbone like the root of a tooth. It supports the crown of an individual tooth or serves as an abutment for a fixed bridge. Multiple implants can be inserted into the jawbone to hold a full denture. While there has been significant improvement in the design of dental implants, they lack two essential features that can limit their longevity: an elastic attachment membrane similar to the periodontal ligament, and an epithelial attachment. (See chapter 2 for a description of these structures.) The elastic membrane cushions the shock of chewing, grinding, and clenching forces applied to the root, and the epithelial attachment seals the tooth where it extrudes through the gum to prevent bacterial invasion and infection. Careful design and placement minimizes adverse forces on the "root" of the implant. Frequent professional prophylaxis and meticulous home care are essential to keep the tissue tight around the attachment post, although the implant seal will never be as complete as a true epithelial attachment.

An implant inserted into the bone is firm at first, with new bone growing into the irregularities of its design. In time, the supporting bone begins to resorb, and the implant loosens to the point where it must be removed. The problem is not simply that the material is basically incompatible with bone. The same resorption and loosening takes place with an inherently compatible implant, one's own tooth that has been knocked out and replanted. The problem is the 150 or more pounds per square inch of biting force, which inevitably breaks down both the rigid, nonelastic attachment of an artificial implant and a reimplanted natural tooth. Nonetheless, newer materials and improved surgical techniques have increased the success rate of implants significantly, but failures are not infrequent, particularly when placed in the upper arch. One study demonstrated a failure rate as high as 20 percent in the maxilla, compared to only 5 percent in the mandible.[12] These figures may be low since many, if not most, failures go unreported.

Types of Implants

Osseous-integrated (bone) implants. The osseous-integrated implant is the current rage in dental implantology, representing a major advance over older methods. Success is critically dependent on careful patient selection and surgical technique. The implant consists of a small perforated titanium or ceramic cylinder that is placed into a hole drilled in the jawbone. The gum tissue is sutured back over the implant, where it remains undisturbed for three to six months as new bone grows into and around the cylinder. After the implant has become firmly fixed in the bone, a post is screwed into the cylinder. The post sticks up through the gum for attachment of a single tooth, a bridge or denture.

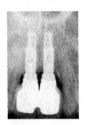

Figure 10 Osseous-integrated implants supporting splinted porcelain-fused-to-metal crowns replacing the missing maxillary central incisors.

Multiple implants are necessary for large fixed bridges and for dentures. Since there are two surgical procedures, first to place the implants, second to uncover them and insert the posts, the cost for the surgery and implants ranges from a few thousand to over $10,000. Then there is the added cost of the bridge or denture.

Subperiosteal implants. The periosteum is the tough fibrous membrane that covers bone. A subperiosteal implant is a thin metal framework that is placed under the periosteum next to the bone. While the periosteum is usually strong enough to hold the implant in place, the frame is sometimes stapled to the jawbone by long pins. The procedure requires two fairly extensive operations. In the first, the underlying jawbone is uncovered for an accurate impression. The implant is constructed in the laboratory and then inserted during the second operation.[13]

The subperiosteal implant is used almost exclusively for denture wearers with atrophied mandibles where the ridge has worn completely flat. Four posts stick out of the gum and fit into the base of the denture to stabilize and retain it. The main cause of failure is the inflammation and infection that sets in around the posts and gradually extends to loosen the entire implant. The implant also loosens under the heavy pressure of the denture, but it can provide substantial improvement if not complete satisfaction for a few years to persons otherwise described as "denture cripples."

Implants Are Not Forever

Advocates of implants promise an end to partial and full denture miseries. Newspapers, senior citizen magazines, radio and television present advertisements by dentists claiming to be experts in dental implantology. Unfortunately, the reader of such ads too seldom tries to confirm the training and certification of these experts. But even the best dentists working on the best patients will have implant failures; dental implants are foreign objects, and the body is prone to reject them.

Success and failure are relative terms. If life with a lower denture is miserable and the price is affordable, a subperiosteal or osseous-integrated implant is a success even if it provides only a few years of improved comfort.

Is it worth thousands of dollars for implants to hold one or two posterior teeth that a patient could probably do without? If only money were at risk, the answer would be relatively simple. The patient can either afford it or not. But there is also the risk of nerve or sinus injury, or extensive bone degeneration around the implants as they loosen, destroying even more of the base bone and leaving the patient with more of a problem than before. While the improvements in dental implants have been impressive, the potential for harm should not be underestimated. Implants should not be undertaken unless more conventional and less risky alternatives have been unsuccessful.

Such caveats are unlikely to deter the true dental cripple, the totally frustrated denture wearer who cannot imagine things being worse than they are. Nor should they because implant supported dentures can be quite successful, compared to the alternative of no support.[14] Before embarking on an implant, however, you should investigate the dentists' qualifications. Ask about their training. Find out how many implants they have done and over what period of time. Ask to see checkup X rays on their patients' implants. If they claim a success rate close to 100 percent, it is because they have performed too few or have only just begun to do them. It is 5- and 10-year success rates that indicate whether or not a dentist is sufficiently qualified to deserve your confidence.

GRAFTS FOR DENTURES

Prior to implants, the only way to increase the underlying support for dentures was to build up the ridge, using either bone or skin grafts. More recently, an artificial bone graft procedure called **ridge augmentation** has been introduced. These types of grafts continue to have limited effectiveness, as evidenced by ongoing efforts to develop better remedies.

The **bone graft** serves two functions. It improves denture retention and reinforces a lower jaw that has been weakened by complete resorption of the dental ridge, leaving only a narrow, thin mandible that can fracture from the slightest blow The graft is formed from a section of a rib or hipbone (iliac crest) that is shaped in the form of a U to replace the ridge. Hospital surgery is required to obtain the graft and then to insert it beneath the gum.

The **skin graft** is a roll of skin taken from the abdomen or thigh that is sutured in place over either the upper or the lower jawbone, forming a ridge to support a denture. Although not as hard or firm as a bone graft, skin grafts also improve denture retention.

Artificial bone grafts are composed of a special material, commonly hydroxylapatite to those who enjoy tongue twisters, that is placed beneath the periosteum, the tough fibrous membrane enveloping bone. The surgery is relatively simple compared to bone or skin grafts, both of which require hospitalization. Artificial bone grafts or ridge augmentation can be done in the private dental office. The procedure consists of making a minor incision through the gum tissue and separating the periosteum from the bone by tunneling an instrument along the length of the dental ridge area, thereby creating a space into which the artificial bone is injected. The material sets hard in a few weeks, during which time fibrous tissue grows into it, intertwining with the graft to stabilize it.

The relative ease of placement and the lower cost give artificial grafts a distinct advantage over bone and skin grafts. The value of any graft remains sharply limited, however, because it does not provide the positive retention of an implant. The most one can hope for is some support from the built-up ridge, some increased stability for an intrinsically movable denture.

Natural and artificial bone grafts can be combined with implants to significantly improve denture retention, as long as the grafts and implants are not rejected. To the edentulous person with severely atrophied jaws, any improvement is a godsend. If the graft implant permits wearing of an otherwise unwearable denture, if it strengthens the jawbone to reduce the risk of fracture, if it prevents a lower denture from impinging on nerves that can trigger shooting pains or create facial numbness, clearly it has value beyond the measure of dollars.

RECOMMENDATIONS

1. A single missing posterior tooth usually does not have to be replaced unless there is a sense of need.
2. If a first permanent (six-year) molar is extracted in a child before the second molar has erupted, the opposing first molar should also be extracted.
3. Wait at least two months before replacing an extracted tooth with a fixed bridge to allow complete healing.
4. If occlusion extends from the second bicuspid on one side to the second bicuspid on the other side, there is adequate chewing surface, and replacement of missing molars is not essential.
5. A Maryland bridge should be considered, especially for anterior teeth, to avoid grinding down support teeth that are caries-free or have only small fillings.
6. The chewing surfaces of bridges should be made of metal, not porcelain, to avoid chipping and fracturing of the occlusal veneer and to minimize wear on opposing teeth.
7. If a cavity develops on the inaccessible proximal surface of an abutment crown, the bridge usually needs to be replaced. But if the cavity is on an

accessible buccal or lingual surface, a filling to repair the defect is better than replacement of the entire bridge.

8. If a "permanent" bridge becomes defective around the margins of abutment crowns in a few years after placement and cannot be fixed with fillings, it was probably defective initially and should be replaced at no charge or at a greatly reduced fee.

9. Removable partial dentures are preferable to long-span fixed bridges where many teeth are missing in different parts of the same arch.

10. Sound teeth clasped by partial dentures do not have to be crowned unless there are special cosmetic problems.

11. Do not struggle to adjust to a bridge or partial denture that does not feel right. The dentist's responsibility is to make it right.

12. Extracting healthy teeth for replacement by full dentures should be avoided.

13. Two strong cuspids are sufficient to support a partial denture.

14. Regular dentures inevitably require repair, and denture wearers should have a spare or duplicate denture for temporary use.

15. Even if all the teeth are lost, retention of roots, usually in the cuspid area, slows down ridge resorption.

16. Attachments placed in mandibular roots or implants increase the retention of lower overdentures significantly.

17. Unless there is a retention problem with an upper denture, overdenture attachments and implants in the maxillary arch are not of much value.

18. Anterior denture teeth should be set with slight irregularity to simulate a natural look.

19. Do not replace a comfortable denture. The new one may never be the same.

20. Avoid extra charges for anatomical articulators and other special bridge and denture fabrication techniques.

21. A conditioner or soft tissue reliner applied professionally as often as every two months provides significant relief for chronic denture sores and also increases retention.

22. If a sore persists for more than two weeks after denture adjustment, have it examined to eliminate the possibility of cancer.

23. Denture wearers, like people with natural teeth, should have annual oral cancer screening examinations.

24. Implants should be considered when there are no reasonable alternatives such as a conventional fixed bridge, or to provide support for a lower denture for patients who cannot function successfully with a conventional denture.

11

Endodontics—
Root Canal Treatment

Fear of toothache is literally rooted in our heads. From ancient times to the present, people have suffered excruciating pain, large swellings and infections, and even death from abscessed teeth. The simplest remedy is removal of the offending tooth, which usually brings prompt relief and everlasting thanks to the skilled dentist, especially one who performed a painless extraction. However, if the tooth was of strategic importance and could have been saved with root canal therapy, thanks is not what should have been offered.

Many teeth can be saved by removal not of the tooth but of the pulp tissue contained within the tubular root canals and sealing them with an inert material to eliminate bacterial infection. Retaining the natural tooth avoids the need for a fixed or removable bridge to replace it, or the tooth may be needed as an abutment to support the replacement of other teeth. It is not necessary to save all teeth with degenerated nerves, but when a tooth is of strategic importance, endodontic treatment is a particularly valuable dental service.

Indications for Root Canal Therapy

Nerve degeneration. Degeneration of the dental nerve is the primary reason for root canal treatment. It is most frequently caused by untreated bacterial decay that destroys the enamel and dentin and infects the pulp tissue. (See chapter 3.) A sharp blow to the tooth can also precipitate nerve failure, sometimes years after the initial trauma. Nerves may degenerate long after teeth have been filled or capped, especially if the original decay was deep. Infection in a deep periodontal (pyorrhea) pocket may extend to the nerve, requiring a combination of endodontic and periodontic therapy to save the tooth. Or nerve degeneration might be due to poor dental treatment. For example, if a dentist drills deeper than is necessary to remove decay, cutting close to or into the pulp chamber, the nerve will degenerate. The pulp may be irreversibly damaged when overheated during drilling or when the tooth is ground down excessively for a crown restoration. This kind of injury is called **iatrogenic** (meaning caused by the doctor or medical procedure, from the Greek word *iatros*, "physician"), and while it does not occur often at the hands of a good dentist, it is far too common in some dental practices. Although pulpal degeneration can occasionally follow any dental procedure performed on a tooth with deep decay, if a number of teeth "abscess" following fillings or crowns, an independent review of the pretreatment films should be obtained. If these films show the pulpal degeneration to have been predictable, the dentist was not likely at fault and should not be held accountable. If poor treatment appears to have been the cause, the patient is not only advised to find another dentist but also to advise the first dentist that he or she will be held accountable. At the very least, the dentist responsible for the iatrogenic injury should pay for the remedial care. Most dentists will be eager to come to some accommodation with you rather than have you consult a lawyer about bringing a malpractice suit.

Intentional devitalization. Root canal therapy is sometimes necessary to eliminate hypersensitivity due to extreme attrition that has worn away one-third to one-half of the tooth's crown. For example, if a front tooth, usually in the lower jaw, is worn down so rapidly and severely that secondary dentin cannot form quickly enough to insulate the vital nerve, removal of the nerve relieves intolerable sensitivity to temperature and chewing. Normally, if a tooth is sensitive to both hot and cold temperature changes *and* the discomfort disappears immediately afterward, root canal therapy is not needed.

Vital nerves are also removed in roots that are to be retained for support of overdentures. (See chapter 10.) This should only be considered if the teeth in question, usually the cuspids, are not strong enough to support a partial denture. Overdenture attachments may be placed in roots that are long enough to resist loosening by the denture.

Diagnosing Nerve Degeneration

Dentists use the term **nonvital** to describe the condition of diseased pulp tissue, abhorring the popular jargon of **dead nerve** or **dead tooth**. While it is true that a nonvital pulp is a dead nerve, a tooth is not dead as long as it has a sound root attached to a live head! To make sure the root stays sound, the dead nerve tissue must be removed and replaced with an inert filling material.

Different diagnostic indicators are employed by dentists to assess tooth vitality. They include the following: history of acute or chronic pain; response to hot and cold temperatures, percussion, and minute electrical current; pain on chewing; the color of the tooth; and the appearance of the root and its surrounding bone in the X-ray film.[1-2] The dentist must differentiate between normal sensitivity to temperature changes or chewing, frequently caused by cavities or defective fillings or crowns; pain that indicates minor inflammation of a nerve that can be reversed without root canal therapy; and signs and symptoms indicating that, short of extraction, only root canal therapy will alleviate the pain or infection.

Sometimes a simple response to aspirin helps assess the significance of pain. After receiving fillings, most people experience mild sensitivity to temperature changes, which gradually diminishes and disappears after a few weeks. There may even be a mild toothache that is relieved by aspirin. This type of **hyperemia** or minor inflammation often reverses itself as the nerve heals. When aspirin does not relieve the pain, the dentist has more reason to believe that nerve damage may be irreversible.

History of Pain

Pain response is highly subjective but less so for a toothache than for many other injuries and infections. The reason is that the nerve is enclosed in a very restrictive pulp chamber and narrow root canals. An acutely inflamed pulp has little room for swelling. Pressure quickly builds up against the nerves within the pulp to produce a severe toothache, but pulps may also degenerate slowly, causing chronic, mild episodes of pain or no pain at all.

Sometimes a patient can point only to the side of the face that hurts without being able to identify the specific tooth. Pain also has a way of disappearing temporarily when a patient appears at the dentist's office. Dentists are usually able to identify the offending tooth even though the ache has gone, though in some cases it may be necessary to wait for the recurrence of discomfort.

Then there is the problem of misdirected pain. A classic example is the patient who complained of a toothache in the lower right jaw. It had been hurting off and on for six months. She pointed to the same second molar every time she came to the office, but the tooth never hurt when the dentist, in this case, the author, tested it. The X-rays and diagnostic tests were negative; all the lower teeth were alive and healthy. By chance, another dentist in the group practice checked her upper teeth. As soon as the last upper molar was probed, pus oozed out of a chronic abscess that was referring pain to her lower jaw. This patient had so firmly but unintentionally misdirected the author, that he overlooked what turned out to be the obvious. The remedy was a simple extraction of the upper molar, which was beyond redemption by endodontic treatment.

Response to Temperature Changes

Because thermal response is so often misinterpreted, patients must be wary of "instant" root canal therapy to treat tooth sensitivity. There has been an alarming increase in the number of teeth receiving root canal therapy with a diagnosis of "sensitivity to hot and cold." One of the worst examples is of a patient who underwent root canal therapy because his bicuspid was still sensitive to "cold" four or five days after a small amalgam filling had been placed in the occlusal groove. The fee, in year 2002 dollars would be over $900, which included not only root canal treatment but also a post and crown, all of which was unnecessary.

Sensitivity to cold and hot temperatures is normal after receiving a filling. The dentist should have waited at least two or three weeks for the thermal sensitivity to diminish. If it continued to be severe, then the correct treatment would have been removal of the small amalgam filling, placement of a sedative zinc oxide-eugenol or IRM temporary filling for a few weeks or months, and then refilling after all temperature sensitivity had disappeared. Sensitivity to both hot and cold temperatures is a normal nerve response. It increases during periods of heavy clenching and bruxing, diminishing on cessation. If one cannot stop clenching and bruxing, a plastic **occlusal guard** should be worn to protect the teeth and relieve the symptoms.

Large cavities and defective or broken fillings allow cold air and hot and cold liquids inside the tooth. Sensitivity is eliminated with new fillings. Teeth also become sensitive if the enamel is worn off too quickly. Gum line grooves due to abrasive toothbrushing or simply too much toothbrushing produce areas of sensitivity. Less toothbrushing and use of a desensitizing toothpaste or topical application of a fluoride varnish often relieve the symptoms.

A healthy nerve that is sensitive to cold air or liquids is not always sensitive to heat, but if a healthy tooth is sensitive to heat, it will almost certainly be sensitive to cold as well. When heat produces pain and cold immediately relieves that pain, the nerve is irreparably damaged, though not completely nonvital, which is the reason pain is experienced. Heat applied to the tooth increases the pressure of fluids within the tiny dentinal tubules or causes the gas of a gangrenous pulp to expand, stimulating remnant vital nerves and producing pain. When cold is applied, the fluids or gases contract, the pressure is relieved, and the pain disappears.

Patients with this condition report that hot coffee makes the tooth ache but a mouthful of cold water or whiskey chases the pain away. If the dentist applies heat against a normal tooth, the reaction is mild. As the heat penetrates an infected tooth, however, the pain builds up to a severe ache.

Response to Percussion

When a dental nerve becomes inflamed, the periodontal ligament attaching the root to its bony socket may also become inflamed and swollen, causing the tooth to extrude ever so slightly. Bringing the teeth together will then be painful. The patients' usual complaint is that they cannot chew on that side even though they do not know exactly which tooth hurts. The dentist performs a percussion test by tapping on each tooth in the area with a hard object, such as the handle of the dental mirror, to locate the one that is sensitive.

This response indicates something is wrong but not necessarily that root canal treatment is required to correct the problem. Teeth become sensitive to biting pressure and percussion from clenching and bruxing or from minor changes in position that put them into **traumatic occlusion**. Traumatic occlusion may cause or result from periodontal bone loss around a tooth. Adjusting the occlusion by grinding away small areas on the crown of the sensitive tooth or the opposing teeth is usually sufficient to eliminate a traumatic bite.[3] An occlusal guard should be constructed for a habitual clencher or grinder to minimize the traumatic wear and pressure.

A **cracked tooth** is sensitive to biting pressure but not necessarily to percussion. (See chapter 4, Cracked Tooth Syndrome.) If the crack extends into the pulp chamber, root canal therapy is necessary along with full crown coverage. But one should be wary of too quick a diagnosis of a cracked tooth. Quite often the problem is traumatic occlusion.

Response of a "hot" tooth to percussion is quite another matter. Here the sensitivity to tapping is not mild but results in a sharp, acute pain and ache that indicates serious infection of the nerve and inflammation of the periodontal ligament at the tip of the root. The condition is not reversible. Even if the pain disappears, the nerve continues to degenerate; an abscess or granuloma will develop if root canal treatment is not done.

Electrical Pulp Test

Vital dental nerves respond to minute electrical currents applied to the outer surface of the tooth. Pulp testers transmit low levels of electricity through a small conductive tip pressed against the enamel. The intensity of the electrical current is gradually increased until a minor sensation or tingling is felt. If the tooth fails to respond or tingles only at the higher current levels, the tooth is most likely nonvital. Some teeth with very large fillings or very small nerves fail to respond even though the remaining pulp tissue is still vital. Also, some nerves become nonvital but remain sterile so that root-end breakdown and infection do not occur. For these reasons a negative electrical pulp test does not necessarily mean that root canal treatment must be done. But if there is a complaint of pain in the area, the electrical pulp test frequently identifies the problem tooth when other tests fail.

Tooth Color

The color of a front tooth is sometimes a dead giveaway that the nerve has degenerated. Some types of bacteria infecting the pulp produce substances that stain the dentin. Since enamel is translucent, the discolored dentin underneath shines through, and the tooth turns dark yellow, gray, or black. A traumatic injury, even a slight blow, can lead to pulpal degeneration without pain. The first symptom may be the observation of discoloration years after the event.

Discoloration in front teeth, obviously more noticeable, should not be confused with discolored fillings on back teeth. The usual cause of discoloration in a bicuspid or molar is a dark, corroded amalgam filling. There is no reason to replace a discolored filling unless it is highly visible and visually objectionable. Large areas of dental decay also discolor front and back teeth; here removal of the decay and restoration with fillings, onlays, or crowns is needed.

Radiographic (X-Ray) Diagnosis

The dental X-ray film is usually the clincher in deciding on root canal therapy. What the dentist looks for is abnormalities at the tip and along the sides of the root. If the normally thin periodontal ligament is thickened, and particularly if a black "hole" appears around the root tip, degeneration of the nerve is confirmed. Thickening of the ligament is not always indicative of a dead nerve. A tooth that has been loosened by traumatic occlusion or periodontal bone loss will also show an enlarged periodontal ligament space. That is why other factors such as pain on percussion, electrical pulp tests, and tooth color must also be evaluated in arriving at a correct diagnosis.

One of the reasons dentists recommend full-mouth periapical X-rays every five years or so for patients with a lot of fillings and crowns and prior root canal treatment is to look for "abscessed" teeth. X-rays reveal abnormal lesions that develop without any symptoms. A dark (radiolucent) spot at the tip of the root is usually diagnostic of nerve degeneration, but not all such radiolucent areas are pathological. The skull contains many holes (foramina) through which pass large nerves and blood vessels. The X-rays show them as dark spots. Sinus cavities appear as much larger dark spaces. These natural anatomic structures are often superimposed over the tip or apices of roots, giving the untrained eye the illusion of abscesses. When X-ray pictures are taken at different angles, the normal dark spots appear to move to new positions, much as a shadow shifts along the wall as the source of light changes. A true apical lesion remains "attached" to the root in the different X-ray films.

When apical pathology appears in the X-ray as a dark circular area or radiolucency at the tip of the root, patients are usually told they have an abscessed tooth even though the lesion might be a granuloma or a cyst. For it to be a true **abscess**, there must be infection and pus formation. A **granuloma** is a more or less circumscribed area of fibrous tissue and inflammatory cells, called **granulation tissue**, that is relatively dormant. Both dental abscesses and granulomas usually heal when their cause, a degenerated nerve, is removed. A

cyst is a lesion filled with a fluid that is enclosed within a sac lined by epithelium. Surgery is necessary for its elimination.

Although important for revealing an abnormal condition, the X-ray film is not too helpful in differentiating among these three lesions, particularly when they are small, since they all appear as gray or black circles around the tips of the root.[4] Many lesions that are diagnosed as cysts because of their relatively large size turn out to be granulomas or abscesses. Granulomas tend to be fuzzy in outline, in contrast to cysts, which are usually round, well-defined dark areas surrounded by a white "ring" representing the outer wall or lining of the cyst. To know for sure, the tissue removed at surgery is sent to a pathology laboratory to be examined microscopically. If it shows an epithelial lining, the outside wall of a cyst sac has been positively identified. Other than for obtaining positive identification, microscopic examination serves little purpose. As long as the lesion heals by filling in with new bone, which may take six months or longer following root canal therapy or surgery, and then either is smaller or no longer visible in the check-up X-ray, it matters little what it was.

A common radiographic misdiagnosis is of abscesses on lower front incisors. Occasionally, a nonpathologic condition occurs along the root tip of one or more of these small teeth that is called a **cementoma**.[5] Cementomas begin as dark, round areas in the X-ray that eventually calcify to become more dense, at which time they appear lighter rather than darker, somewhat like small pearls at the tips of the roots. Cementomas frequently form simultaneously below all four roots. Diagnosis is easy, particularly if the teeth have never had fillings or traumatic injuries that might cause nerve degeneration. Nonetheless, some dentists confuse cementomas with abscesses and do root canal therapy, posts, and crowns on these innocent teeth. Electrical pulp testing is very useful in differential diagnosis of teeth with suspected superimposition of foramina, sinuses, and cementomas. These teeth always test vital. They respond normally to hot and cold, and they are not sensitive to percussion.

No single diagnostic tool provides 100 percent diagnostic accuracy. It is the combination of patient complaints, responses, and nonresponses to the various thermal, percussive, and electrical tests and radiographic evidence that must be sifted through to arrive at a correct diagnosis.

Types of Pulpal Therapy

Endodontic or root canal therapy refers to complete treatment; the entire pulp chamber and root canals are filled with an inert material. Sometimes more limited pulpal therapy such as pulp caps and pulpotomy can be done to preserve the tooth. Limited treatment is particularly appropriate for baby teeth, which have to last only a few years before exfoliating.

Pulp cap. Removal of deep decay sometimes results in penetration of the pulp chamber by a small, pinpoint **pulp exposure**. The pulp may also be exposed inadvertently by the dental drill during a cavity or crown preparation. Rather than proceeding immediately to complete removal of the nerve, the dentist has the option of performing a direct pulp cap to cover the small exposure with a calcium hydroxide paste or glass ionomer cement that seals off the pulp and protects the nerve. Although many exposed nerves gradually degenerate, not every tooth with a pinpoint pulp exposure should have root canal treatment. Unfortunately, economics sometimes plays a part in the diagnostic decision. If the patient has dental insurance, some dentists may elect to remove the entire nerve rather than settle for the fee of a pulp cap, only $40 to $50.

Exposure of the nerve can be avoided by an indirect pulp cap, wherein the soft decay is removed, leaving a small amount of leathery decay that is covered with the calcium hydroxide or glass ionomer material. Active decay usually ceases once the gross decay is removed and the tooth is sealed from saliva. Meanwhile, the pulp forms a protective layer of secondary dentin beneath the decay. Pulp degeneration is much less likely with an indirect pulp cap.

A two-step indirect pulp cap procedure called **remineralization** or **recalcification** can be used in a grossly decayed tooth that still has a live nerve.[6, 7] Most of the decay is removed during the first visit. A temporary filling is put in the cavity for two or three months, allowing the pulp to form new dentin. Then the remaining soft decay is removed and the tooth is filled or crowned. The charge for remineralization is about $100 to $150.

Some dentists charge for a "pulp cap" beneath every filling. What they are really doing is placing an insulating lining beneath the filling material. The insulator may be a cement base, a thin layer of calcium hydroxide, or a coating of varnish. In fact, cavity varnish should be applied beneath all fillings and crowns. Insulating cements and varnishes should be included in the fee for the restoration. Unless the decay is visible in the X-ray film to within one millimeter of the nerve or there is a direct pulp exposure, a charge for pulp capping is excessive and should not be paid by the patient or the insurance plan.

Pulpotomy. In the past, pulpotomies were usually limited to children's primary teeth.[8] But the technique is also applicable to decayed or injured permanent teeth of young children and adolescents. The objective is to retain deeply decayed primary teeth until they exfoliate naturally. In the permanent tooth, the goal is to maintain the vitality of the remainder of the pulp, which then allows the root to fully form. Instead of removing the entire nerve, only the pulp within the large pulp chamber is removed. A pulp cap material, calcium hydroxide or MTA (mineral trioxide aggregate)—a recently developed material that may be superior to calcium hydroxide and glass ionomer cements—is placed over the nerve stumps leading into the root canals, and the tooth is filled or covered with an inexpensive preformed stainless-steel or plastic crown.[9] Because a pulpotomy can be done in about 15 minutes, once anesthesia has been established, the charge is much less than for complete root canal treatment, ranging from $85 to $150.

Pulpotomies are not recommended for fully developed permanent teeth except as a temporary procedure Even if the nerve tissue remaining in the roots of a baby tooth gradually degenerates, the roots are being resorbed as the tooth exfoliates But if the nerve in the root canal of a permanent adult tooth degenerates following pulpotomy, as is more likely, an infection around the root eventually develops, requiring full root canal treatment or extraction.

Compromise treatment. Years ago, dentists attempted to mummify the nerve in root canals by inserting a pellet of cotton soaked in a preservative such as formocresol. The technique proved extremely unreliable and caused extensive damage if the caustic solution spread to the bone outside the tooth. Despite the criticisms of poor treatment, many teeth survived with incomplete root canal filling. In recognition of this fact, a compromise method known as the Sargenti technique, after the name of the Swiss dentist who developed it, achieved some popularity as well as notoriety in the 1970s and 1980s.[10] Nowadays one rarely hears about it, but because it is so easy to do, it is probably still being done.

The Sargenti technique utilizes a specially formulated paste that is inserted into the pulp chamber and main root canals. Conventional enlargement, cleansing, and filling of the canals with a dense material such as gutta-percha are abandoned. While there were many documented successes, many failures also occurred. In extreme cases, material was forced through the tooth into the main nerve canal of the lower jaw, causing permanent damage and numbness (paresthesia) of the face.[11]

Since success of properly performed conventional treatment has been well documented, the only legitimate reason to utilize a shortcut method is to save money and teeth for patients who cannot afford the cost of full treatment. There is nothing wrong with attempting a pulpotomy in a permanent tooth—unless a caustic and destructive chemical like the Sargenti paste is used—when for economic reasons the only other alternative would be an extraction. In such cases the patient should be fully informed of the compromise and the greater risk of failure.

Pulpectomy—root canal treatment. The goal of root canal treatment is the complete removal of the tooth's pulp tissue—pulpectomy—and filling of the pulp chamber and root canals with an inert material to seal or **obturate** the multiple minute holes or foramina at the apex. This is accomplished with small reamers and files shaped like tapered spirals that are moved up and down and around in the narrow canals until all the pulp tissue has been removed and the canals are enlarged enough to be filled.

Most dentists use hand held stainless steel files and reamers to enlarge and clean out the canals. However, nickel titanium files have been developed that are much more flexible and resistant to breakage than stainless steel files. They can be used in a slow speed rotary instrument similar to a dental drill, which is much easier and less finger fatiguing than hand files. The nickel titanium files are more costly and the special electric or air driven rotary endodontic drill is quite expensive, but the combination reduces the time it takes to prepare the tooth for the root canal filling. Therefore, these improvements should not necessarily result in a higher fee. It should also be emphasized that excellent results can be achieved using either type of files and, in fact, dentists often combine both rotary and hand filing techniques.[12]

In order to protect the tooth from contamination by the bacteria in saliva, as well as to protect the patient from accidentally swallowing one of these pin-like reamers or files, the dentist should apply a rubber dam. The rubber dam is a 5 inch square of latex or similar rubbery material in which the dentist punches a small hole or a series of holes, forming a mask over the mouth through which the tooth or teeth protrude, thus isolating the tooth being treated from saliva.

The rubber dam can also be applied when filling and drilling teeth to prevent accidental swallowing of broken drills and excess filling material. Too many patients have swallowed these sharp root canal files because some dentists are too lazy or incompetent to place the rubber dam. Although most of these instruments will pass through the alimentary canal and be excreted without damage to the patient, swallowed files that lodge in the esophagus (throat) or the stomach or even the intestines, require surgery for removal. If a dentist does not protect the patient with the rubber dam, then he or she should tie a long piece of string or dental floss to the files and reamers so that an advertantly swallowed instrument can be retrieved immediately. To provide less protection for a patient is malpractice.

A more common risk of root canal treatment is the breakage of a file or reamer within the root canal. If the instrument, which looks like a spiraled safety pin, binds when being rotated in the canal, it can break. If it breaks about midway, it may be possible to remove the fragment. If only the small tip fractures, it is often impossible to remove. The dentist may recommend leaving the tip in place, since it may serve as part of the root canal filling. In the event that pain persists or a periapical lesion occurs, an apicoectomy (surgical removal of the root tip) and retrofilling (sealing the canal at the apex) can be done. But not all teeth can be saved this way. If the file breaks in a molar and reinfection occurs, an apicoectomy might be inadvisable because of the risk of permanent nerve injury and paresthesia or sinus damage, in which case the tooth will have to be extracted. (See *Surgical Endodontics* below.)

Files do not break often but it happens often enough that you should be aware of the risk. The cause may be a manufacturing defect or metal fatigue that results from over-usage. Since the metal files and reamers can be sterilized, they are reused. It is safe to use a file three or four times, after which they should be discarded. But even new files can break. Therefore, it is difficult to determine if the fault is due to a manufacturing defect or the dentist's over-usage or improper usage of the instrument.

Ideally, the root canal filling should be about one-half to one millimeter short of the apex or tip of the root. It can also extend a little beyond the tip, again no more than one millimeter. If the filling is too short or too long, healing of the apical lesion may not take place or a new lesion may develop. Patients experience more postoperative pain if the filing or the final filling extends beyond the tip of the root into the surrounding bone. That is why slight underfiling and underfilling is preferred.

To achieve the proper length of the root canal filling, one that is neither too long nor too short, the apex or tip of the root must be located. The traditional and still most common method is to place a small reamer or file up into the canal and then to X-ray the tooth. The file shows up in the film, just like a metal filling, and allows the dentist to assess its proximity to the apex and thus measure its length. As many as 5 or 10 measurement X-ray films may be taken throughout the process, particularly on multi-rooted teeth. A measuring device to reduce the need for the X-rays is an electronic apex locator that uses minute electrical currents to determine the length of the root. As apex locators become more accurate, the number of measurement X-rays will be reduced, but both methods of measuring canals may be necessary to assure an ideal outcome.

Some teeth have canals that are blocked or the roots are so tortuous that ideal treatment is not achieved even by specialists. The canals are filled as well as possible, usually without complication afterward. However, if a large, straight canal is not sealed near the root tip, poor treatment is a reasonable conclusion.

The entire endodontic procedure may be accomplished at one sitting if the pulp tissue is not gangrenous or completely degenerated.[13] One-visit treatment is usually, but does not have to be, limited to the single-rooted anterior teeth because the canals are relatively easy to enlarge and clean out. Multirooted teeth, especially the molars, often require two or three visits, sometimes more, to obtain the best results. The problem for the consumer is that dentists, including endodontic specialists, charge the same fee whether the treatment is completed in one or three visits. The incentive, then, is to do it in one visit for the higher hourly earning. On the other hand, if the dentist charges per visit, the incentive is to extend treatment over two or three visits. This is the dilemma the consumer faces in a fee-for-service system.

The reason root canal treatment takes—or should take—so much time is that all remnants of the infected pulp tissue must be removed and the canal thoroughly cleansed and dried before it is filled. Bacterial cultures of root canals used to be done frequently but were found to be meaningless. Root canals do not have to be absolutely sterile when filled. They need to be dry to obtain a seal. The real key to successful treatment is adequate enlargement and filling of the central and lateral root canals to assure that all organic debris is removed and replaced by an inert substance.

The filling material has to be placed carefully to seal the apex of the tooth as well as condensed laterally against the walls of the canals to seal the small auxiliary, canals. Lateral condensation is extremely important because the root canal is not a single hollow tube. Rather, it is a relatively large, irregularly tapered cylinder with many tributary canals resembling the root of a plant with its myriad lateral filaments. Incomplete sealing of the lateral canals is one of the major reasons for root canal failure. On the other hand, excessive condensing forces can also fracture the roots. The measure is gentle but firm pressure.

Types of Root Canal Fillings

The best root canal filling material is made of **gutta-percha**, which comes from a tree of the same name. It resembles malleable rubber that has been preformed into large, medium, and small tapered cones, also called *points*. The smaller cones are the size of narrow pins. Multiple cones are inserted into the tooth in stages. A warmed instrument is inserted alongside the points to compact them against the sides of the canal to fill its lateral tributaries. Special filler cements are also used to enhance the sealing properties of the gutta-percha. Slight overfilling of the gutta-percha into the bone surrounding the root is well tolerated.

Silver points, once popular, are no longer recommended to obturate root canals because they depend on a special cement to seal the tooth. Lateral condensation is not possible with silver points, so the canals are not filled with pressure, as is the case with gutta-percha. Because the cement does not fill all the irregularities of the canal, the endodontic failure rate for silver points is much higher. Silver in contact with body fluids eventually tarnishes and corrodes. It is more likely than gutta-percha to cause pain and fail in the event of overfilling. Nonetheless, silver points may still be used by some general dentists to fill the very narrow and tortuous canals of molars Some dentists may also still use silver points in the relatively straight and easy canals of incisor teeth, where they are clearly contraindicated.[14] Though easier to place than gutta-percha points, they are a risky second choice and are not used by endodontists or conscientious general practitioners. They are no longer considered an adequate endodontic filling material.[15]

In addition to magnifying lenses attached to eyeglasses that many dentists use, some endodontists now have special intraoral microscopes that enable them to view the interior of a tooth in greater detail, revealing fractures or cracks that might not be seen by the naked eye. There is no evidence that the microscope improves the rate of endodontic success. More likely it will be used to justify higher fees.

Other techniques have been developed that use special gutta percha heating systems, instruments and cones to achieve successful obturation, but none thus far have proved superior to the conventional gutta-percha points and technique described above. Regardless of the material used, the same principles of thorough cleansing and filling of all the canals to or near the apex of the root apply. When all is said and done, it is the skill and diligence of the dentist, not this or that technique, that is of critical importance.

The Post-treatment Root Canal X-ray

When treatment is completed, you should be shown the final X-ray film. The gutta-percha filling appears as white lines in the center of the root canal. It should look solid and fill the entire outline of the canal. If the filling appears "loose" so that the dark outline of the canal is still visible, then it is a poor filling.

Since underfilling or overfilling happens even with good technique, patients should be informed of the difficulties and the possibility of failure. Payment should be withheld if the final X-ray shows gross overfilling and discharge of material into the bone around the roots. This condition should be reviewed and corrected, if possible, by an experienced general practitioner or specialist.

The final X-ray is taken immediately on completion of treatment, not only to assure adequate filling of the canals but also as a baseline record to be compared with checkup films in three or six months. Sometimes healing takes longer and may not be evident in an X-ray film until a year or more has passed. At the very least, the follow-up X-rays should not show an enlargement of the dark area—the periapical lesion beyond the tip of the root, indicating that the condition has gotten worse.

How Painful Is Root Canal Therapy?

If root canal therapy is needed, it should be done even if there is some pain. However, the stories of extreme suffering, not only with respect to root canal therapy but for all dental treatment, should be quickly put to rest, thanks to anesthetics that grant effective relief from most dental pain.

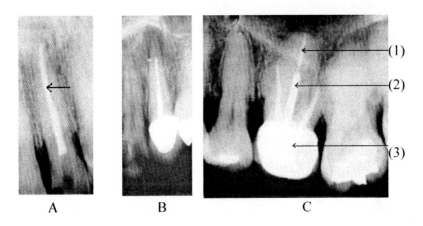

A   B   C

Figure 11-1 A. X-ray showing a well-condensed gutta percha filling (arrow) in an upper lateral incisor that has a single root canal. Note good fit to the root tip. B. Note short gutta percha filling with a large circular pathological lesion at the tip of the root that could be a granuloma, an abcess or a cyst. C. Molar root canal filling: (1) one of three canals of 3-rooted upper first molar filled with gutta percha; (2) metal post in large palatal root; (3) porcelain-metal crown restoring the tooth showing excellent fit at the margins.

After the local anesthetic injection has taken hold, quickly relieving the toothache, initial treatment is usually painless. Unless a large swelling and infection are present to interfere with the local anesthetic, "novocaine" is sufficient to control the pain. The dentist then drills a small hole into the pulp chamber to permit removal of the nerve tissue and allow pus, if present, to drain out of the tooth. Pain from a large abscess is also relieved quickly by lancing to allow the pus to drain out of the gumboil. Unless there is a significant infection such as a large abscess, antibiotics should not be prescribed. Some dentists prescribe antibiotics routinely for all root canal therapy even in the absence of infection, which is bad medicine.

Because the nerve will have been removed at the first visit, anesthesia is seldom necessary on subsequent visits. If the nerve is already degenerated, initial treatment can also be done without an anesthetic. Some patients are so tense, however, that dentists inject a local anesthetic just to relieve their anxiety. The final appointment, at which time the canals are filled, is also usually painless

Acute pain is sometimes experienced following the first treatment. A quiescent infection may flare up if the area is disturbed by penetration of the files and reamers or the cleansing solution beyond the tip of the root. Filler or sealer pastes that are used along with gutta percha points can also be irritating if extruded beyond the apex into the bone. Some teeth begin to hurt after filling even though treatment has been done correctly. Apicoectomy—removal of the root tip—may then be required to provide ultimate relief. But these episodes are exceptions to the general rule that endodontic therapy quickly relieves the pain of toothache and causes very little pain itself. For the most part, root canal therapy is no more or less uncomfortable than having a complex filling.

Post-treatment Pain

Pain should be completely gone by the time root canal therapy is finished. The tooth may be sensitive to pressure for a few weeks, however, particularly if the root has been overfilled. As long as the discomfort is minor and gradually diminishes until it disappears, there is nothing to worry about. Minor pain following treatment is usually alleviated by analgesics such as aspirin, ibuprofen, or acetaminophen. More severe pain is relieved by codeine and other narcotics. If chewing discomfort or an ache persists for more than a few weeks, and especially if it becomes more severe, retreatment, root surgery (apicoectomy), or extraction will be required.

Surgical Endodontics—Root Surgery

Root surgery is not necessary in conjunction with routine endodontic therapy. It is seldom necessary even in the presence of large granulomas and abscesses. After removal of all the toxic tissues inside the tooth and creation of a good apical seal, the body's defense cells eliminate the infection in the bone without having to subject the patient to the additional trauma and expense of surgery. Healing within the bone usually takes place in a few months. If the follow-up X-ray film taken six months or a year later shows no increase in the size of the lesion, it may be observed for a longer period since in some cases complete healing takes two or three years. Some lesions never disappear because they are filled with connective tissue rather than new bone, which is just as satisfactory. And, of course, if the lesion becomes smaller and disappears, as is usually the case with good treatment, nothing further need be done.

If after conventional root canal therapy the lesion appears enlarged in the follow-up X-ray or pain persists after the canals have been filled, surgical intervention may be necessary. Root surgery should not be taken lightly. There is an inherent risk of damage when surgery is performed, particularly on the roots of molars and bicuspids. The mandibular nerve lies in a canal just beneath the roots of the lower molars and bicuspids where it can easily be injured by the chisels, drills, and curettes used to remove the root tip. This type of surgery risks permanent numbness (paresthesia) of the lip or chin and should be avoided unless required to remove a cyst or tumor. The tips of the upper posterior teeth often protrude into the maxillary sinuses. Surgery in this area could result in a chronic sinus infection. While these injuries do not occur often, their consequences are very real to those individuals who experience them.

Before jumping into surgery, consider conventional retreatment. Post-treatment pain more frequently follows root canal therapy that is done in one visit. A poor gutta-percha filling can be redone. Apical surgery should be a last, not a first, resort. The alternative to this kind of surgery may be the loss of a tooth, never an attractive alternative, but the risks of apical surgery, especially on molars and bicuspids, should be weighed carefully.

The average person does not possess the expertise to diagnose cysts and other pathological lesions, but one can recognize a large radiolucency—a large black "hole"—around the apex of a tooth in the X-ray. Unless the dentist is fairly certain the lesion is a cyst, apical surgery is not justified at the time of initial treatment. If the checkup X-ray shows a new lesion or an increase in the size of a preexisting lesion after competent root canal filling, and a post has been placed in the canal that prevents retreatment, surgical intervention—an apicoectomy or an extraction—are your choices.

Apical curettage. Apical curettage is usually done in conjunction with an apicoectomy. A flap of tissue is raised over the area and the outer layer of bone is removed, revealing the tip of the tooth and the lesion. Curettage is then performed with a small, spoon-shaped instrument that scoops out the infected tissue and the sac lining if it is a cyst. The flap is repositioned and sutured into place. Healing is usually uneventful, although there may be some swelling immediately afterward.

If the pathology is identified as a cyst, the procedure is called a **cystectomy** although its removal is no different from an apical curettage. The size of the lesion rather than its name should determine the extent and the expense of the surgery.

Some dentists, including oral surgeons, have microscopic examinations done on all tissue that is removed. Routine biopsy makes no sense for the common variety of abscess, granuloma, or small cyst that is easily removed in its entirety at the time of surgery. It is an example of rote behavior that contributes to excessive health care costs. But if the lesion is large and has an unusual, irregular appearance in the X-ray film, microscopic examination should be done to determine the type of pathology and if further treatment is required. Cancer is quite rare in these areas and would appear as a large, diffuse, grayish radiolucency that does not have a direct connection to the root of a specific tooth. Apical curettage is also done to get at the apex of the root in order to remove excess root canal filling material and cement that has squeezed through the apex into the surrounding bone and appears to be causing a periapical lesion. Gutta-percha can be resealed at the apex by burnishing it with a hot instrument. An extruding silver point can be cut off and the apex retrofilled.

Apicoectomy and retrofilling. If chronic pain persists after good root canal treatment or the root has not been filled adequately and cannot be refilled, or there is evidence of damage to the root by the infection, the tip of the root may have to be removed. An apicoectomy is relatively simple on the upper front teeth because of the ease of access. The roots of other teeth, particularly molars, are more difficult to reach, and attempting to do so risks damage to adjacent sinuses in the upper arch and to the mandibular nerve in the lower arch, as previously noted.

The initial surgery is the same as for an apical curettage. A flap is raised to expose the bone over the root, which is then removed to expose the tip of the root. Since there is an apical lesion, the area is curetted. The root tip is then removed with a dental drill. To assure that the apex of the tooth is completely sealed, a small hole is drilled into the remaining end of the root to permit placement of a **retrograde filling**. Silver amalgam is the material most commonly used, but other non-metallic materials are likely to be developed in the future. Regardless, amalgam is extremely well tolerated as an apical filling.

A retrograde filling is no different from an amalgam filling on the opposite end of the tooth, the occlusal surface, which usually costs $50 to $75. Yet the charge for a retrograde filling is about $150 in addition to the apicoectomy fee of $300 to $450. There is no real justification for such a large disparity in the fee for an amalgam filling. The charge becomes even more onerous when applied to a multirooted tooth.

Root amputation and hemisection. The upper first and second permanent molars usually have three well-defined roots to support their large crowns. The two buccal roots, so named for their proximity to the cheek side of the tooth, are small in comparison to the lingual or palatal root, which provides the major support for the molar. If the buccal roots have lost their bone support because of periodontal disease, one or both roots can be removed, leaving the large palatal root to retain the tooth. The remaining stump of the buccal root can receive a reverse pulp cap, avoiding the expense of root canal therapy. If the pulp degenerates before the tooth has to be extracted, endodontic treatment of the other roots can be done at this later date. With or without root canal therapy, 40 percent of teeth with root amputations do not last more than five years.[16]

Lower molars have two large roots, occasionally three. If one of the roots has suffered extensive periodontal bone loss or decay but the other is sound, amputation of the diseased root allows retention of the tooth. The remaining root must have root canal treatment, however, since the trauma to the pulp of a lower molar is much greater than with a buccal root amputation of an upper molar. Root amputation may be only temporarily successful. The remaining root eventually loosens and has to be extracted if it is not strong enough to withstand the occlusal forces on the crown. Also, the area beneath the crown will decay if it is not kept meticulously clean.

Quite often the lower molar develops a deep periodontal pocket between the two roots that cannot be kept clean. The pocket is eliminated by cutting the tooth in half—**bicuspidization**—thus making two teeth out of one. Each root then requires root canal therapy and a separate crown. If only one of the roots is sound, the other is extracted, a procedure called **hemisection**. It is also necessary to cap this half-crown, thus doubling the cost of the root canal filling and hemisection. If both roots are retained and capped, the cost is that much greater.

Many of these teeth do not last more than a year or two, and at least 40 percent are extracted in less than five years; therefore, the tooth must have high strategic value to justify the cost. The combined fees for hemisection, root canal therapy, a post, and a crown are almost as much as replacement of the entire tooth with a fixed or removable bridge Since the remaining portion of the tooth is invariably weaker than a full tooth, retention makes sense only if the tooth is the last one at the end of the dental arch. It is particularly advantageous when the hemisected root is strong enough to serve as an abutment for a small-span fixed bridge.

These exotic solutions—root amputation, bicuspidization, hemisection—should be considered only in carefully selected cases where there are no reasonable alternatives and the patient is willing to pay the price, knowing that it is probably only a temporary solution to the problem. If the tooth is not of strategic importance, however, it would be better removed and replaced, if replacement is needed, by a fixed bridge supported by teeth with sound roots.

Restoration of Endodontically Treated Teeth

Many dentists contend that an endodontically treated tooth becomes brittle, and therefore a crown is necessary to prevent its inevitable fracture. There is no evidence that endodontically treated teeth are more brittle than nontreated teeth.[17] If gross decay was present before treatment there is greater risk of fracture because the tooth has lost structure and been weakened by the decay. Some teeth are more prone to fracture, such as the upper bicuspids, but any tooth with a large cavity or filling can fracture. Even teeth without fillings fracture. But most teeth do not fracture, including those with root canal fillings. It simply makes no sense to crown a tooth on the expectation of an event that might not happen. To crown every endodontically treated tooth at least doubles the cost. A crown should be done only when there is an existing fracture or when the tooth is so hollowed out by decay or previous fillings that refilling is not practical.

Endodontically treated teeth turn dark if the pulp tissue is not thoroughly removed. It matters little in the back teeth, but a front tooth turning brown or black is unsightly If the stain is not too severe, the tooth can be bleached to normal color at much less expense than applying a porcelain cap. The technique is simple. The filling on the underside of the tooth is removed, remnants of the pulp are drilled away, and a pellet of cotton saturated with bleach is sealed inside the tooth for a few days or weeks. This treatment may have to be repeated a few times before the tooth regains good color. Then the cotton is removed and the tooth is refilled. The tooth can also be bleached externally using bleach activated by a high intensity ultraviolet light. (See also chapter 9, *Bleaching*.)

When the outcome of root canal treatment is questionable because of a large abscess or extensive bone loss around the roots, crown restoration should be delayed until healing is evident in the checkup X-rays. A temporary filling or preformed plastic or stainless steel crown can be placed to last the year or so required to be sure the root canal therapy has been successful. A dentist who insists on immediate placement of a permanent crown ought to offer you a credit for the cost of the crown toward replacement costs if the tooth has to be extracted later on.

Dowel posts and buildups. A dowel post and buildup is not necessary for an endodontically treated tooth unless the crown has been largely destroyed by decay or fracture.[18] If there is insufficient tooth structure remaining after root canal treatment, a post is cemented into the root one-third to one-half its length. The part of the post rising above the root is built up and shaped like a tooth that has been prepared to receive a crown. Increased retention is thus obtained to prevent the cap from coming loose.

Dowels are prefabricated in many sizes, but some dentists prefer to have a laboratory-constructed post that includes a core or stump to hold the crown. If a prefabricated post is used, a **core buildup** is attached to the part of the post that sticks out of the tooth to create a stump. Buildups are usually composed of composite, although amalgam may also be used in posterior teeth. If there is no post, small pins can be cemented into the tooth to strengthen the buildup. Composites can also be bonded to dentin, eliminating the need for pins. There should be only one charge for a post and buildup, ranging from $150 to $250. If only a buildup is done, the charge should be about half this amount.

Prefabricated dowel posts cost less than cast posts because they are cheaper to manufacture. When properly fitted, prefabricated posts are more effective in securing crowns.[19] A preformed post can be placed immediately after a root canal filling to hold a temporary crown. Many dentists place posts in every endodontically treated tooth without regard for need. Unfortunately, for a dowel post to be of sufficient thickness and length, the root canal must be enlarged. But if the circumference of the root is small, it will end up weakened rather than strengthened by the post, increasing the risk of root fracture from a sharp blow or heavy biting force. Dowel posts are of more value in badly decayed or broken anterior teeth but are needed less often in bicuspids or molars unless the crowns have been destroyed to the level of the gum.

Years ago it was customary for dentists to place **cement bases** to protect nerves or to fill up the cavity prior to construction of a crown. Many dentists now charge separately for cement bases, renaming them buildups. An additional charge is not appropriate unless half the crown is destroyed by decay or fracture. The consumer's only defense is to ask the dentist to justify all procedures and the fees they generate. Patients should also ask to see an X-ray of the completed root canal therapy with the dowel post in place. Too often the dowels are little more than pins the thickness of paperclips that fit so poorly into the canals as to be worthless. If it looks like a paperclip that extends only a few millimeters into the root, it serves no purpose, and the charge should be waived.

The Strategic Tooth

A good dentist evaluates the importance of the tooth and helps you decide if the additional expense of root canal treatment is worth it. And expensive it will be when the combined cost of root canal treatment, a post and a crown are added. The fee for root canal therapy ranges from $350 to $450 for a front tooth, and $450 to over $900 for a molar, with crowns costing $390 to $600 and more. Add another $150 for a post and the decision to save a single tooth can cost well over $1000.

No explanation is needed to define a front tooth as strategic or the last molar as nonstrategic when all the other teeth are present. On the other hand, if many back teeth are missing and the last molar is faced with either root canal therapy or extraction, its strategic importance as an abutment support tooth for a fixed bridge or removable partial denture cannot be overemphasized. Between these two extremes are teeth of varying importance, depending on their position, function, and visibility, and the number of other missing teeth.

If all the other teeth are healthy and only one tooth requires root canal treatment, the cost may not be prohibitive to the average pocketbook. Quite often it is a toothache—technically called **pulpitis** or **pulpalgia**—that brings the patient to the dental office for the first time in years, in which case many teeth need fillings and crowns. Saving one tooth at great expense must then be evaluated in relation to the cost of saving a number of other teeth. Dentists do not always weigh the strategic value of a tooth. They have difficulty recognizing that a patient is often better off with the removal of badly decayed, broken, and infected teeth. Heroic and highly remunerative efforts are made to save teeth that are eventually and predictably lost to further decay. Sometimes the removal of the most frequently decayed tooth—the first permanent molar in a child between eight and eleven years of age—allows another one to take its place. Extraction of a child's badly decayed 6-year molar allows the second and third molars to move forward to replace the missing tooth. Removal of a badly decayed second permanent or 12-year molar at an early age often allows the third molar or wisdom tooth to take its place.[20] (See chapter 10 for a more complete discussion of molar extraction in children.)

Many adults have teeth that have decayed into the roots, creating the probability of future extraction no matter how well root canal treatment and crown restoration are done. The cost of replacing such a doubtful tooth with a fixed bridge might be only one-third more than root canal treatment, a post, and crown, with a much better chance for long-term success. But if the tooth is of strategic importance, if it is a back molar with missing teeth in front of it, if the decay is not too far advanced into the roots, if the cost is not beyond one's means, the tooth should be saved.

Why Endodontic (Root Canal) Treatment Is So Expansive

Any skilled general dental practitioner can do good root canal treatment, particularly of the single-rooted anterior teeth. Many also treat bicuspids and molars as well as specialists. And that is the point! Endodontics is not really a legitimate specialty, no more so than pedodontics and periodontics. All these so-called specialties are part of the province of general dentistry. There is no highly specialized body of knowledge and treatment that distinguishes them from dentistry in general. It is simply a matter of learning and practice.

To be sure, these specialists can do the job faster and better than most general practitioners because that is all they do. And to make sure that they garner the market, they limit the amount of training the students get in dental school. That is why so many general dentists decline to do molar and bicuspid root canal treatment. They lack the training, experience and confidence. Thus, specialists being in short supply can raise their prices as high as the market will bear. The middle and upper class, which has insurance and/or sufficient surplus income, can afford the price. The lower middle class, the working poor and, of course, the very poor, will lose these teeth, including those of strategic importance that could avoid true dental disability.

RECOMMENDATIONS

1. Only teeth that are functional and of strategic importance warrant the time and expense of root canal treatment. Discuss the pros and cons with your dentist before starting treatment.
2. When gross decay extends into the roots, long-term prognosis is poor, and the combined cost of root canal treatment, posts, and crowns may be better applied to replacement of the tooth, which may be necessary in the end whether or not the root canal treatment is undertaken.
3. Do not allow final filling of the root canals until pain and infection have been eliminated.

4. Don't take antibiotics for routine root canal treatment in the absence of an acute abscess or infection.
5. Avoid silver points for root canal fillings.
6. Avoid the one-visit paste-filler (Sargenti) technique, except as a temporary procedure until you can afford conventional treatment.
7. Obtain an independent second opinion if a number of teeth that had been filled or crowned by your dentist undergo nerve degeneration.
8. If a recent filling is hypersensitive to temperature or causes mild toothache, ask your dentist to replace it with a temporary sedative filling until symptoms subside rather than immediately resorting to endodontic treatment.
9. Before accepting root canal treatment because of percussion sensitivity, request occlusal adjustment to lighten the bite and see if the discomfort subsides.
10. Avoid root canal therapy for "cracked tooth syndrome." If a tooth is actually cracked, placement of a crown is usually sufficient, unless the crack extends to the pulp.
11. Avoid pulpotomy on fully formed permanent teeth except as a temporary treatment. Do not accept an extra charge for a pulpotomy, often called "open & medication," in conjunction with root canal treatment. It should be included in the fee for the RCT.
12. Ask to see the final X-ray film to be assured that a dense filling seals the apical one-third of the root.
13. Avoid the risk of nerve or sinus injury by apicoectomy for a small periapical lesion if the roots of the tooth extend into the maxillary sinus or near the mandibular canal, particularly if traditional retreatment can be done.
14. Avoid a general anesthetic for endodontic therapy and root surgery. Local anesthetic injections are sufficient.
15. Ask to see the post-treatment X-ray film of a cemented dowel to be assured it is substantial and fits into at least a third of the root.

12

Oral Surgery—Extractions

Removal of teeth, also called exodontics, is a big business, so big that it supports the second largest group of dental specialists, about 6,000 oral surgeons. In comparison there are 8,600 orthodontists, 4,500 periodontists, 3,400 endodontists, 3,800 pedodontists, and 2,900 prosthodontists. However, the majority of the 119,000 general practitioners in the United States also do extractions and root canals and make dentures and treat children. [2]

Routine extractions do not require the services of a specialist. Most teeth, including those impacted, can be removed by an experienced general dentist with a local anesthetic. It has been noted elsewhere that there has been a general deterioration in the education of general dentists. With the increasing emphasis on specialization, the schools provide minimal training of general practitioners in exodontics, as well as the other so-called specialties, so they are likely to refer all but the simplest extractions to oral surgeons. This significantly increases the cost to the patient and/or the dental health insurance plan.

Oral surgery is one of the true specialties in dentistry, requiring advanced knowledge in many aspects of medicine and skills that are not part of the general dental curriculum. However, it is not exodontics that distinguishes oral surgeons but rather their extensive training in maxillofacial surgery, which includes treatment of fractures of the jaws, cysts and carcinomas, reduction or enlargement of the jaws for correction of gross orthodontic malocclusions, and reconstructive or plastic surgery for the repair of cleft palates and oral-facial structures damaged or destroyed by traumatic injuries and cancer. They are also trained to administer intravenous (I-V) sedation and general anesthesia.

Nevertheless, the major part of an oral surgeon's income derives not from maxillofacial surgery but from the extraction of normally developing third molars with I-V sedation or general anesthesia, a procedure that can be done by any competent general practitioner with a local anesthetic. There is no other major medical or dental specialty except perhaps plastic surgery that makes so much money out of so little pathology.

Types of Extractions

It is absolutely essential that consumers become informed about the basic types of extractions and the procedure codes used to identify them to avoid being overcharged by oral surgeons. The table below summarizes the procedures and the classification of extractions adopted by the American Dental Association and the American Association of Oral and Maxillofacial Surgeons.[2] It is used by insurance companies and other responsible agencies to determine benefit payments and to identify fraudulent billing, although it is not an exaggeration to state that most oral surgeons get away with over-billing more often than not. Following is a more detailed description of each type of extraction:

Routine, simple, uncomplicated extraction (7110). A fully erupted tooth that is removed whole.

Surgical or complicated extraction (7210). An erupted tooth that cannot be removed whole because the clinical crown has been destroyed by decay or fracture. Extraction requires elevation of a flap of gum tissue and removal of a small amount of bone to gain access to the remaining root(s). Also, a tooth that crumbles or fractures during extraction and requires additional surgery for removal. These teeth can be quite difficult to remove, justifying a higher fee, but the dentist or oral surgeon is overcharging if every tooth is billed as a "surgical" extraction.

Soft tissue impaction (7220). Usually a third molar or wisdom tooth that is not fully erupted. Removal requires an incision of the overlying gum tissue to allow grasping with a forceps or positioning of a lever-shaped instrument called an exolever or elevator to force the tooth out of the socket. Most of these teeth are not true impactions since they erupt normally if left alone.

Bony or partial bony impaction (72 30). Most commonly an adolescent's unerupted third molar before its roots have developed or where there is not enough room in the dental arch for the tooth to fully erupt. Removal requires incision of the overlying gum tissue, elevation of a flap of gum tissue to allow removal of overlying bone, and removal of the tooth in one piece. Cuspids (canines or eyeteeth), bicuspids, and supernumerary or extra teeth are also frequently impacted. Some are removed whole, others require sectioning.

Bony impaction (7240). A tooth that is completely covered or embedded in bone without possibility of eruption because it is lying sideways or at an angle against an adjacent tooth. Removal requires incision through the gum, elevation of a flap of gum tissue, removal of the overlying bone, and sectioning or cutting of the tooth into smaller pieces to facilitate removal.

CLASSIFICATION OF EXTRACTIONS AND IMPACTIONS

Procedure Code	Description
7110—Extraction, routine	Uncomplicated removal of a whole tooth.
7210—Extraction, surgical	Removal of an erupted tooth requiring some removal of bone or separation of roots.
7220—Impaction, soft tissue	Extraction of an unerupted tooth that requires incision of overlying gum tissue.
7230—Impaction, partial bony	Extraction of an unerupted tooth that requires incision of overlying gum tissue, elevation of a flap, removal of overlying bone, and removal of the tooth without sectioning.
7240—Impaction, full bony	Extraction of an unerupted tooth that requires incision of overlying gum tissue, elevation of a flap, removal of overlying bone,and sectioning of the tooth for removal.

Institutionalized Overcharging

Some general practitioners and many if not most oral surgeons have institutionalized overcharging by routinely classifying extractions as more complex than they actually are. Many oral surgeons also administer a general anesthetic or I-V sedation as a matter of routine, often at a cost greater than the extraction, even though a local anesthetic injection, often referred to as a *shot of novocaine,* is adequate and safer. Uninformed patients have no way of knowing if they are being overcharged, and most insurance companies and public agencies are indifferent to the abuse.

One study by a dental insurance administrator revealed that 62 percent of claim statements (bills) submitted for insurance payments by oral surgeons in California contained overcharges.[3] In nearly 50 percent of extractions, the oral surgeons claimed that the surgery to remove the teeth was more complex and should be paid at a higher fee than was justified by the actual procedure. Analysis of bills submitted to Blue Shield of Pennsylvania, one of the largest insurance companies in the country, revealed the same overclassification and overcharging for extractions.[4] Although these studies were done a number of years ago, dental consultants reviewing billings, including the author, have observed the same pattern up to the present.

The table below shows the increase in cost with the increase in complexity of extraction. It illustrates the potential for overcharging by overclassifying the procedure and what it costs the consumer out-of-pocket or through higher premiums for dental insurance.

COST OF EXTRACTIONS[*]			
Code	Description	Cost ($)	Increase (%)
7110	Extraction, routine		90
7210	Extraction, surgical	150	67
7220	Impaction, soft tissue	175	94
7230	Impaction, bony (whole tooth)	250	178
7240	Impaction, bony (sectioned tooth)	350	289 (100%)

*See the table in chapter 15 for the range of *Selected Dental Fees in the United States*, which vary widely between and within geographic areas.

If a routine extraction is charged as a surgical extraction, the fee increases by at least two-thirds (67%). One of the easiest and fastest extractions, taking no more than a few minutes, is the soft tissue procedure (7220). Yet many oral surgeons charge them as "full bony" impactions (7240), thereby doubling the fee that should be charged.

The panoramic x-ray film in Chapter 6 (see Figure 6-5) shows the four normally developing third molars. If these four unerupted wisdom teeth are removed, and the two upper ones are charged as full bony impactions (7240), even though they are simple soft tissue extractions, you or your insurance will be overcharged by as much as $350. Most of these teeth will erupt normally, at which time the extraction, if needed, would—or should—be charged as a routine, uncomplicated procedure at a cost of approximately $90 each. Extracting them prematurely with the additional expense of general anesthesia at $175 or more means that the overcharge is even greater than described. By any standard other than the profession's and the insurance companies' acquiescence, this type of institutionalized overcharging would be classified as fraud.

Institutionalized Overtreatment

Unnecessary extractions. The decline in the decay rate associated with water fluoridation, fluoride toothpastes, and improved oral hygiene has greatly reduced the need for extractions. Yet dentists still prescribe extraction of wisdom teeth in the mistaken belief they are practicing good prevention. Some children and,

177

more frequently, adolescents and adults are routinely referred for their extraction, despite the fact that the normal eruption period for these teeth is between 16 and 25 years of age. Any tooth in an adolescent or young adult that is in an upright or nearly upright position in the jawbone and that is still in its formative stage of development is not an impacted tooth. Some orthodontists routinely prescribe extraction of unerupted wisdom teeth prior to treatment. Many third molars that are truly impacted could also be uprighted and brought into functional position by the orthodontists.[5]

Many dental X-rays are improperly angulated so that the images of teeth are distorted and superimposed on each other. Normally erupting teeth appear impacted or likely to impact. Properly angulated X-ray films also give the appearance of teeth erupting at an angle that is often misinterpreted as impaction. Checkup X-rays taken a few years later will show that these teeth are straightening up and continuing to erupt normally, if they have not already come into the mouth. The first and second permanent molars look exactly the same as third molars in their formative stages of development and eruption, yet dentists do not call them impacted years before they are due to erupt.

If the dark outline of the developmental or follicular sac that the crown of the tooth grows in is more than two millimeters wide, patients are told it is a cyst. This diagnosis is presumptive. The width varies, and even though the follicle appears on the wider side of normal, classification as a cyst during the eruptive years is usually premature.

Wisdom teeth's role as a cause of cysts, abscesses, root resorption of adjacent teeth, and even of cancer is greatly exaggerated. Studies have shown that only 6 percent of wisdom teeth can be classified as diseased by any definition; only 3 percent as abscessed; less than 3 percent are cystic even by the loose definition described above; and root resorption of adjacent teeth is found in barely one-half of 1 percent (.68 percent) of unerupted and truly impacted third molars.[6]

Unnecessary radiographs. Patients are usually referred to oral surgeons by their general dentists on the basis of diagnostic X-rays. These X-rays should be given to the patient to bring to the oral surgeon so that it will not be necessary to repeat the radiation exposure and the charge at the surgeon's office. Only if the original diagnostic films are insufficient or of poor quality should additional films be taken. Panographs are unnecessary if the referring dentist's periapical radiograph of the individual teeth shows the whole root and surrounding bone. A good periapical film provides more detail and is sufficient to determine the position of the tooth for purposes of extraction. Oral surgeons sometimes take postsurgical panographs following a difficult extraction; this makes little sense since a single periapical X-ray provides a better picture.

Before accepting the additional X-rays, patients should make sure they are necessary and do not duplicate X-rays already taken by the general dentist.

Before paying for a panograph, make sure the film is not a gray or white blur and that the images of the teeth and jaws are visible and well defined. The oral surgeon probably will have no further use for the panograph after the extractions since the patient is not likely to return in the near future. Therefore, the panograph or a duplicate should be sent to the general dentist for diagnostic review. The film should be kept in the patient's folder for future reference.

Unnecessary general anesthesia. Most extractions are done painlessly by general practitioners with injection of a local anesthetic, which is included in the fee. Yet over 90 percent of insurance bills submitted by oral surgeons contain a fee of $175 or more for a general anesthetic or intravenous (I-V) sedation. Preying on people's fears, the surgeons seldom give patients a realistic choice. Though reducing patients' conscious anxieties during the extractions, general anesthesia places patients in greater jeopardy for the following reasons:

1. An unconscious patient is more easily subjected to excessive force that can stretch and damage the temporomandibular joint and fracture the jaw.
2. The extractions can be described afterward as more difficult to justify higher fees.
3. General anesthesia for the removal of wisdom teeth (third molars) increases the risk of mandibular nerve damage.[7]
4. General anesthesia, as well as I—V sedation, is more easily overdosed and can result in permanent brain damage or death.[8]

Postoperative Complications—the Risks of Extractions

Pain and swelling. An extraction is an insult to the dentition and an injury to the mouth: an insult because it usually results from personal neglect or poor dental care, and an injury because of deteriorating dental health and the trauma of treatment. Even though extraction relieves the major pain of toothache, lesser pain will be experienced for a day or two afterward, gradually disappearing. Swelling around the area of the extraction is not uncommon. If it does not gradually diminish over the following two or three days, infection should be suspected. Likewise, pain after the anesthetic wears off should diminish and disappear after a few days. Many over-the-counter analgesics are available to relieve minor postoperative pain and reduce fever. (See chapter 13.) If pain persists, if it is not relieved by the ordinary analgesics such as aspirin or ibuprofen, if it gets worse and develops into a dull ache, a postsurgical infection—most frequently a "dry socket"—is setting in.

Some dentists and many oral surgeons routinely prescribe antibiotics for extractions even in the absence of systemic infection. Antibiotics have no value for a healthy person following an extraction. However, if one has a prosthetic (artificial) heart valve or hip joint or a history of rheumatic fever or heart valve damage, prophylactic antibiotic therapy is recommended to prevent infection around the valves and joints. The recommended antibiotics for patients not allergic to penicillin are amoxicillin or cephalexin (two grams orally one hour prior to treatment). For patients allergic to penicillin, clindamycin is recommended (600 mg orally one hour prior to treatment). Other antibiotics can be used on consultation with the patient's physician. It is generally recommended that persons with these conditions be protected by prophylactic antibiotics for any treatment that causes bleeding and introduction of bacteria into the bloodstream, including scaling of teeth during a prophylaxis.[9]

Following a difficult extraction, an ice pack placed on the face over the area minimizes swelling. The pack should be held on and off at 15- minute intervals over a 2-hour period. Cold has little effect after 2 hours. Patients should not eat or rinse following an extraction; otherwise, the blood clot that has formed in the tooth socket might be disturbed. After a few hours, light rinsing to keep the mouth clean is all right. The best mouth rinse is warm water, with half a teaspoon of salt per glass. Commercial rinses have no special therapeutic effect. It is important to remember that gradual diminution of pain and swelling indicates proper healing. If swelling and fever worsen and pain develops into a dull ache, additional professional care is necessary.

Bleeding. It takes 8 to 15 minutes for a firm blood clot to form in the tooth socket following an extraction. Some minor oozing of blood may continue, but it usually stops after 20 minutes of biting pressure on a gauze pack. Blood mixes with saliva and appears more voluminous than it really is. However, if bleeding persists and is not stopped by repeated gauze pressure, biting for 20 to 30 minutes on a tea bag moistened in hot water usually works. Tea contains tannic acid, which coagulates blood or acts as an astringent to constrict the blood vessels. The tea bag application can be repeated a few times until bleeding stops. If it does not, further professional treatment and suturing of the extraction wound will probably be required.

Failure to treat continuous postextraction bleeding can be catastrophic. Take the case of a 17-year-old girl who had 4 normally developing third molars extracted on recommendation of her general dentist. The extractions were easy, but heavy bleeding occurred that night in one of the lower tooth sockets. It stopped by the time she was examined by the oral surgeon the following day but then hemorrhaged again the second night and continued to bleed off and on for the next 10 days. Whenever she or her mother telephoned the oral surgeon, they were told that postextraction bleeding was normal, that the amount was exaggerated because it mixed with saliva, and just to keep biting on cotton. On the tenth night there was again severe hemorrhaging. and the young lady was brought to a hospital emergency room. While in the waiting room she suffered cardiac arrest, the sole cause of which was excessive blood loss. Fortunately, she was in the right place at the right time and was immediately resuscitated. This near-tragic event could have been avoided with prompt and proper treatment of the hemorrhaging tooth socket or, more particularly, if the unnecessary surgery had never been performed.

Most episodes of prolonged postextraction bleeding occur in persons with otherwise normal blood clotting and cannot be explained. Just to make sure nothing is wrong, a patient experiencing excessive bleeding should have a complete blood examination even though the extraction eventually heals.

Trismus. Trismus or difficulty in opening the mouth frequently is caused by extraction of lower third molars. It may also follow prolonged dental procedures that overstretch and traumatize jaw muscles and joints. Trismus usually disappears in a few days. Exercising the jaw every two or three hours by opening as wide as possible for a few minutes, short of pain, prevents further tightening and limitation of jaw movement. If trismus persists or becomes worse, an infection may be setting in, and the patient should return to the dentist or oral surgeon for further treatment.

Dry sockets and sinus infection. Complications can follow any extraction. Apart from the usual pain and minor swelling of a normal extraction, the most common problem is dry socket. Technically, a dry socket is an alveolar osteitis or inflammation of the bone that lines the tooth socket, in which a blood clot does not form but rather disintegrates. Thus, the socket is not really dry but rather appears empty when the clot breaks apart. A dry socket happens most often after removal of a mandibular third molar, but other extraction sites are also at risk. It develops three or four days after the surgery and is extremely painful. Although the pain is usually localized around the area of the extraction, it frequently may extend to the ear. Body temperature generally remains normal, unlike osteomyelitis (see below), which causes fever because of the deeper infection of the bone marrow.

It may be three or four days before patients suspect that something is wrong. At first there is a dull ache that is not relieved by analgesics such as aspirin or ibuprofen. The pain gradually increases until it is quite severe. A foul taste emanates from the wound, and there may be difficulty in opening the mouth. Treatment usually is not difficult and can be accomplished without an anesthetic. But if the pain or the anxiety is very great, local anesthesia may be necessary to allow the dentist to clean out the wound. The disintegrated blood clot is removed by irrigation with warm saline solution or water. Following debridement, or cleansing, a drain is placed, consisting of a piece of gauze dipped in a sedative solution. Irrigation and replacement of the drain may be necessary every three or four days, sometimes more often, after which healing is uneventful.[10]

Routine administration of antibiotics for extractions and minor postoperative complications is contraindicated. Antibiotics are not necessary for a dry socket unless the condition does not respond to local treatment and a more serious bone infection such as osteomyelitis is suspected. An antibiotic should be administered if there is the slightest suspicion of a sinus exposure during the extraction of an upper tooth. Sinus infection is almost certain to occur if the sinus membrane is torn or punctured during an extraction. The upper posterior teeth, particularly the molars, have roots that are often in close proximity to or extend into the maxillary sinuses. If the sinus is exposed to oral bacteria following an extraction, an infection can develop within hours. It is imperative that antibiotic therapy begin at once to prevent permanent damage.

The first clear symptom of an infection is a sense of fullness in the affected sinus, extending in a line from the ear to the nose. Pressing the skin over this area may be painful. As the infection progresses, a foul-smelling discharge erupts through the nose. Pain and fever may be mild during the initial infection. If the infection is not recognized and treated immediately, the sinus membrane may eventually be destroyed. The infection can also extend toward the base of the brain and ultimately cause death. If the patient survives, severe sinus headaches and neuralgias may recur for the rest of his or her life.

Such was the situation of a young man in his late twenties who had a deeply impacted upper wisdom tooth removed by an oral surgeon. He had been referred for the extraction of the opposite tooth, a partially erupted upper right wisdom tooth that was bothering him. Since the third molars on the upper and lower left side were impacted, the surgeon decided to remove them as well, even though they were causing no problems. The upper left molar was lying against the sinus wall, reason enough to leave it alone because of the high risk of sinus involvement.

The day following the surgery, the patient complained of pain on the left side, including swelling between his ear and nose. The oral surgeon prescribed a strong narcotic painkiller. The pain persisted. More pain- killer was prescribed. The patient reported a bad taste in his mouth, fever, and chills. A few days later he was examined by the oral surgeon who decided he had a dry socket in the lower left molar extraction site. For the next three weeks the doctor treated the socket. He ignored the patient's persistent complaints of pain and swelling below the left eye and along the cheekbone, of a foul-smelling nasal discharge, and of high fever and general malaise. He continued to treat the lower socket and refused the patient's request for an antibiotic since dry sockets do not respond to antibiotics.

The patient went to his general dentist who referred him not to another surgeon for a consultation but back to the same oral surgeon. Nearly a month after the extractions, the patient was on his way home from the oral surgeon's office after having been told the dry socket was healed and no further treatment was required. On the freeway he began to feel extremely dizzy and disoriented and insisted his wife drive him to the hospital. The emergency room physician ordered a head X-ray, which revealed that the left sinus was completely filled with pus. Emergency surgery saved his life.

This was only the beginning of a series of surgeries to heal the sinus. The facial nerves and sinus membrane were permanently damaged. Years afterward he continues to experience frequent severe and debilitating sinus headaches and paroxysms of shooting pains in his head and jaws. He will likely be afflicted for the rest of his life.

The oral surgeon was well trained and on the teaching faculty of a local dental school. He was on the staff of a number of hospitals. He had published articles in journals and chapters in books on oral surgery. He was well respected in the community, but he was so sure of his diagnosis that he failed to listen carefully to the patient's complaints.

The patient, however, was also at fault. He should have realized at some point that the doctor was not listening to him and that the treatment was ineffective. Too often patients are reluctant to seek help elsewhere, fearing to offend their doctor. Whenever an infection is unresponsive to treatment, one should not hesitate to obtain a second opinion. In fact, good doctors will encourage their patients to do so.

Paresthesia. One of the most unpleasant postsurgical consequences is paresthesia, or numbness of the lip, chin, cheek, or tongue on the side of the extraction. Paresthesia is possible with any extraction, but it is most common in the lower jaw following removal of a wisdom tooth. It is like having a lower anesthetic injection that never wears off or wears off only partially, so that the lip and chin or tongue remain numb or continue to tingle. In addition to constantly drooling and accidentally biting a numb lip or tongue, the patient experiences a diminution in the lip's sensory function, which is so important in speech and in kissing.

Paresthesia is caused by injury to the nerve, usually the mandibular or lower jaw nerve, but the lingual nerve of the tongue may also be affected. The risk is small following a simple, nontraumatic extraction. It is greatest when the extraction is difficult and the roots of the tooth are close to the canal in the lower jaw, which houses the mandibular nerve. Most paresthesias are temporary, disappearing in a few weeks or months. But permanent paresthesia occurs in 1 percent of all impacted third molar surgery and may be as high as 7 percent when the impacted tooth is embedded vertically in the jawbone or lying at a 45-degree angle.[11, 12]

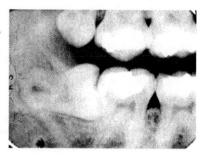

Figure 12-2 Impacted lower third molar with roots in close proximity to the mandibular nerve. Extraction risks permanent paresthesia and should be avoided unless there is a real problem.

Before consenting to the removal of asymptomatic third molars, every patient should be informed of the risks not only of injury to adjacent teeth, damage to the temporomandibular joints, fracture of the jaws, and postsurgical infection, but also of the higher risk of paresthesia. Patients with permanent paresthesia often suffer great emotional distress. Had they known the risk they would have refused removal of third molars that were causing no discomfort. Every patient and every dentist should ask if the risk of paresthesia is worth the removal of teeth that are causing no harm.

Osteomyelitis. Osteomyelitis is one of the more serious postextraction complications and requires prompt recognition and treatment with heavy doses of antibiotics.[13] It results from infection spreading beyond the tooth socket into the marrow spaces of bone. Osteomyelitis is distinguished from a dry socket by the presence of deep pain within the jaw, elevation of body temperature, generalized weakness, and malaise. Radiographs are not diagnostic in the early stages. As the infection spreads further in the bone marrow, the X-ray film reveals a diffuse, irregular radiolucency (dark areas). Eventually, a sequestrum, or separating section of bone, will be visible. As soon as osteomyelitis is suspected, a bacteriological culture should be taken to identify the specific organisms so that proper antibiotics can be administered. If the relief of symptoms is not prompt and especially if the swelling extends beneath the lower jaw into the throat, hospitalization for intravenous administration of antibiotics and incision and drainage in the area of the spreading infection is imperative. Failure to institute these measures promptly risks extensive swelling in the throat, which can close the trachea and cause death by suffocation. The infection can also spread rapidly to the heart and lungs, likewise with fatal consequences.

A Final Caveat

Surgery contains inherent risks no matter how well performed. When the need is based on specific diagnosis of infection, trauma, cysts, or chronic pain associated with an impacted tooth, the benefits clearly outweigh the risks and the need for surgery is obvious. But there is no reason to subject oneself to the risks of iatrogenic injury and infection by acquiescing to functionally unnecessary—FUN—surgery. As the saying goes: *If it ain't broke, don't fix it!*

RECOMMENDATIONS

1. Do not have an extraction unless there is a specific problem.
2. Avoid third molar extractions unless related to a specific pathological condition.
3. Avoid unnecessary radiation and charges by bringing X-ray films taken by the general dentist to the oral surgeon.
4. Avoid overcharges by carefully reviewing the criteria for classification of extractions.
5. Avoid general anesthesia for routine extractions, impactions, and surgery that can be done with a local anesthetic.
6. Do not accept a panographic X-ray for removal of teeth, including wisdom teeth, if periapical films are available unless there is suspicion of a special problem.
7. If pain, swelling, and fever increase after oral surgery, additional treatment is necessary.
8. Obtain a second opinion if prolonged bleeding and infection do not respond to postsurgery treatment.
9. Avoid antibiotics for routine extractions, including non-infected wisdom teeth.
10. Patients with valvular heart damage and artificial heart valves or joints should take prophylactic antibiotics beforehand for dental surgery or any treatment that causes bleeding, including dental prophylaxis.

13

Drugs and Anesthetics
Dentists Are Doctors, But...

Improvements in equipment and materials have made dental care easier, less painful, and more effective, but what dentists do has not changed significantly in the past 50 years, with the important exception of more recognition and treatment of periodontal disease. Dental treatment still consists largely of prophylaxis, fillings, crowns, extractions, root canal therapy, and replacement of missing teeth with bridges and dentures. All these services require intensive hands-on work by dentists, dental assistants, and dental hygienists, supported by laboratory technicians who fabricate crowns, bridges, and dentures.

Although one thinks of filling a tooth as a mechanical procedure, it is actually surgery because a live structure is being cut to remove the disease or decay. Otherwise, there would be no drilling pain without an anesthetic. Periodontal treatment requires mechanical cleansing of root surfaces to remove plaque, tartar deposits, and diseased cementum and is also a minor surgical procedure. More advanced periodontal treatment involves cutting and reshaping the gum tissue and alveolar bone that encircles roots in the jaws. And no one can mistake the surgical character of an extraction.

These are the reasons the dental degree, D.D.S., means doctor of dental surgery. Some dental schools confer a D.M.D. degree, doctor of dental medicine, but the training is exactly the same as the D.D.S. The D.M.D. degree was introduced to identify dentistry more closely as a specialty of medicine, but it should be clear from the introduction to this chapter that dental practice is much different from medical practice, consisting almost entirely of surgical and prosthetic treatment. Medicine, as distinct from medical surgery, relies heavily on drugs to alleviate symptoms, control infections, and effect cures. Nevertheless, just as physicians overprescribe drugs, so do dentists, particularly those who want to "play doctor."[1]

Antibiotics

Prophylactic therapy. Dental treatment frequently forces bacteria present in the oral cavity into the bloodstream, a condition known as **transient bacteremia**. The bacteria are destroyed by the blood's defense cells before they do damage; therefore, prophylactic antibiotic therapy is of no value for a healthy person without special needs.[2] Even for conditions that traditionally call for a prophylactic antibiotic, there is controversy over its necessity and effectiveness. While it is believed that some conditions risk serious infection following dental treatment, the occurrence of such infections is quite small even when antibiotics are not administered. It may be that the risk of injury or death from antibiotic-resistant bacteria or anaphylaxis, a system-wide allergic reaction to these drugs, is almost as great as from bacteremia. To compound matters further, minor spontaneous bacteremias occur all the time from such innocent activities as toothbrushing, dental flossing, and normal chewing.

Given the uncertainty, it is nonetheless advisable to follow the current guidelines for prophylactic therapy for conditions that risk serious infection. Patients who have heart valves damaged by rheumatic fever and mitral valve prolapse with murmur are particularly at risk. The reason is that bacteria can lodge and proliferate on damaged heart valves causing a life-threatening heart infection, **infective endocarditis (IE)**.

Treatment that causes minor bleeding produces transient bacteremia, which is harmless to a normal, healthy person. To a susceptible person, there is risk of serious infection from gingival curettage and root planing, gum surgery, apicoectomy, crown preparation, and even the subgingival scaling that is part of a routine prophylaxis. Although a local anesthetic injection can introduce bacteria into the bloodstream, it is not sufficient to require prophylactic antibiotics. Routine fillings do not present a threat.

Currently the preferred prophylactic antibiotic is amoxicillin. If fever develops after treatment, the patient should immediately obtain additional antibiotic therapy from the dentist or physician.

The following tables contain conditions for which prophylactic antibiotics are currently indicated and the recommended dosages.

Antibiotic Prophylaxis For Various Medical Conditions[*]	
Previous infective endocarditis	Isolated secundum atrial septal defect
Cardiac valve prosthesis	Coronary bypass surgery
Rheumatic heart disease (RDH)	Previous rheumatic fever without RDH
Hypertrophic cardiomyopa thy	Congenital pulmonary stenosis
Cardiac transplant with valve dysfunction	Cardiac transplant without valve dysfunction
Mitral valve prolapse with valve dysfunction [a]	Mitral valve prolapse without valve dysfunction
AV Shunt for hydrocephalus	Coronary artery disease
Kawasaki disease with valve dysfunction	Kawasaki disease without valve dysfunction
Mitral valve surgery	Cardiac pacemakers and implanted defibrillators
Indwelling catheter (right heart)	Physiological, functional, innocent heart murmurs
Idiopathic hypertrophic aortic stenosis	Orthopedic pins and screws
Congenital heart disease 　Aortic stenosis 　Bicuspid aortic valve 　Coarctation of the aorta 　Complex cyanotic heart disease [d] 　Patent ductus arteriosus 　Systemic pulmonary artery shunt 　Ventricular septal defect	Orthopedic joint prostheses [b]
	Six months or longer after surgery without residua for [c]: 　Atrial septal defect 　Coronary artery stents 　Noncoronary artery grafts [e] 　Patent ductus arteriosus 　Ventricular septal defect
Surgically repaired intracardiac lesions with residual hemodynamic abnormalities	HIV/AIDS
Systemic lupus erythematosus with valve dysfunction [f]	Asplenia
Myeloproliferative disorders with valve dysfunction [g]	
Osteogenesis imperfecta with valve dysfunction [h]	

a. Antibiotic prophylaxis for regurgitation, myxomatous degeneration, thickened and/or redundant valves particularly in males over age 45.
b. Antibiotic prophylaxis should be considered for such patients with inflammatory arthropathies (rheumatoid arthritis, systemic lupus erythematosus); disease, drug or radiation induced immunosuppression; insulin-dependent (Type 1) diabetes; first two years following joint replacement; previous prosthetic joint infections; malnourishment; hemophilia.
c. Lesions with minimal or no hemodynamic abnormality.
d. Includes single ventricle states, transposition of the great arteries, tetralogy of Fallot.
e. Prophylaxis may be considered for large vascular grafts (aorta).
f. Including possibly other collagen disorders.
g. Including polycythemia vera, essential thrombocytopenia, anogenic myeloid metaplasia.
h. Including Marfan's syndrome, Ehlers-Danlos syndrome, Hurler's syndrome, pseudoxanthorna elasticum.

[*]From: T.J. Pallasch, "Antibiotic Prophylaxis: The Clinical Significance of Its Recent Evolution," *Journal of the California Dental Association* 25 (1997): 619-32.

Dental Procedures and Endocarditis Prophylaxis[1]		
Antibiotic Prophylaxis Recommended		
Dental Extractions		
Periodontal procedures including surgery, scaling and root planning, probing and recall maintenance		
Dental implant placement and reimplantation of avulsed teeth		
Endodontic (root canal) instrumentation or surgery only beyond the apex		
Initial placement of orthodontic bands but not brackets		
Intraligamentary local anesthetic injections		
Prophylactic cleaning of teeth or implants where bleeding is anticipated		
Antibiotic Prophylaxis Not Recommended		
Restorative dentistry (fillings, crowns with or without retraction cord, unless significant bleeding is anticipated)		
Local anesthetic injection (nonintraligamentary)		
Intracanal (nonsurgical) endodontic treatment; post replacement and buildup		
Postoperative suture removal		
Taking of X-rays or oral impressions for study models or removable appliances		
Orthodontic appliance adjustment		
Shedding of primary teeth		
Prophylaxis with light scaling-significant gingival bleeding not anticipated		
Prophylactic Antibiotic Regimens for Dental Procedures		
Situation	**Agent**	**Regimen[2]**
Standard General Prophylaxis	Amoxicillin	Adults: 2.0g; Children: 50 mg/kg[3] - orally one hour before procedure
Unable to take oral medications	Ampicillin	Adults: 2.0 g intramuscularly (IM) or intravenously (IV); Children: 50 mg/kg IM or IV within 30 minutes (min) before procedure
Allergic to penicillin	Clindamycin or	Adults: 600 mg; Children: 20 mg/kg - orally one hour before procedure
	Cephalexin, or Cefadroxil or	Adults 2.0 g; Children: 50 mg/kg - orally one hour before procedure
	Azithromycin or Clarithromycin	Adults: 500 mg; Children 15 mg/kg - orally one hour before procedure
Allergic to penicillin and unable to take oral medications	Clindamycin or	Adults: 600 mg; Children: 20 mg/kg - IV within 30 min before procedure
	Cefazolin	Adults: 1.0 g; Children:25 mg/kg IM or IV within 30 min before procedure

[1] Adapted from T. J. Pallasch, "Antibiotic Prophylaxis: The Clinical Significance of Its Recent Evolution," *Journal of the California Dental Association* 25 (1997): 619-32.

[2] Total children's dose should not exceed adult dose. No second doses are recommended for any of these prophylactic regimens.

[3] 1 kg = 2.2 pounds.

Because so many conditions may warrant prophylactic antibiotic therapy, it is extremely important that patients report chronic diseases or conditions to their dentist and give complete and accurate medical histories. Patients should also inform the dentist of medications they are currently taking.

Indications for Antibiotics. Although antibiotics are designed to fight bacterial infections, not all infections require antibiotic therapy. An abscessed tooth is usually cured by the removal of the infected pulp (root canal therapy), sometimes with drainage of the abscess, or extraction, in which case antibiotics are not required. In the presence of fever or a large swelling, antibiotic therapy is usually a proper precaution.

Thus, antibiotics should not be prescribed for routine root canal therapy or for routine extractions, including removal of impacted teeth. It is not uncommon for a dry socket to develop following the removal of a lower third molar or other difficult extraction. Dry sockets require local treatment—cleansing of the extraction wound and placement of sedative dressings (drains). Systemic antibiotics are not necessary unless the condition fails to respond to local treatment. Many oral surgeons routinely administer antibiotics for complex extractions, but this adds unnecessarily to the cost and risks inducing drug sensitivity or anaphylactic shock. On the other hand, if the extraction creates an opening into the maxillary sinus, immediate antibiotic therapy is imperative to prevent a sinus infection.

Bacteria can spread into the bone from an existing abscess or from the trauma of an extraction. When bacteria gain a foothold in bone marrow, an osteomyelitis, or bone infection, is present. This condition must be treated promptly by antibiotics, most commonly penicillin V or amoxicillin. Hospital-ization may be necessary to permit continuous intravenous (I-V) administration of antibiotics; surgery may be necessary to remove the infected bone.

An abscess can also spread or be spread during surgery through the soft tissues of the jaw, and down into the throat causing a life-threatening infection called **Ludwig's angina**. Though less common today than before the era of antibiotics, these infections are not rare, and fatalities can result from delayed recognition and inadequate treatment. Any infection that fails to respond in a few days and appears to be spreading requires prompt reevaluation, sensitivity tests of the infectious bacteria to identify effective antibiotics, and prompt administration of the chosen drug.

Effect of antibiotics on teeth. With the important exception of tetracycline, antibiotics do not have a permanent effect on the developing teeth. Tetracycline causes permanent gray, yellow, or brown discoloration of teeth in the fetus when taken by women in the last half of pregnancy, by infants, and by children up to eight years of age. Although the teeth remain structurally strong, they can be extremely unsightly. Dentists and most physicians are now aware of this contraindication for tetracycline and prescribe alternative antibiotics. But mistakes can be made if the parent is not alert to the danger. Women should also be aware that antibiotic therapy may inactivate birth control pills, even though there is not clear proof that it does.[3]

Antibiotics are not for common-variety viral infections. Herpes simplex virus produces cold sores on the lips and ulcers on the gums. Severe eruptions cause fever and malaise although more often the symptoms are acute pain to touch and to spicy foods. Herpes simplex virus is resident in most mouths. Sores are likely to recur periodically at times of stress, during or following a cold, and with excessive exposure to sunlight. There are no cures for cold sores and therefore no reason to take antibiotics. Local treatment is generally ineffective. Cold sores gradually heal of their own accord in 10 to 14 days. (See chapter 5 for a more complete discussion of herpes infections and other oral diseases.)

Antibiotics and yeast infections. A healthy mouth is host to numerous bacteria, viruses, and yeasts, all of which live together in ecological harmony. Prolonged administration of antibiotics upsets this balance. Since antibiotics kill bacteria that feed on other organisms such as the yeasts of monilia and candidiasis, the yeasts multiply to produce a heavy coating on the tongue called **white hairy tongue**. These yeast growths may also occur on the palate, the inside of the cheeks, and at the corners of the mouth. Treatment is by topical application of another antibiotic, usually nystatin, four times daily until symptoms disappear. Clotrimazole is another effective fungicide for topical application. In more resistant cases, systemic ketoconazole may also be prescribed in addition to the application of topical fungicides.

Among the early oral manifestations of acquired immunodeficiency syndrome (AIDS) is **hairy leukoplakia** of the tongue. Superficially it looks like a yeast infection (moniliasis), but the yeast infection is relatively smooth in comparison to the hair or filamentous overgrowth along the top and sides of the tongue characteristic of hairy leukoplakia. Since the condition is symptomless, it is often first observed by a dentist or dental hygienist. Anyone who has recently been on antibiotics may be assured that the appearance of a white-coated tongue is more likely to be a yeast infection than the hairy leukoplakia of AIDS.[4]

Resistant strains. Antibiotics are a boon to mankind, but indiscriminate use is a bane. One of the major problems is desensitization of bacteria. Administration of an antibiotic for every minor infection allows bacteria to develop resistant strains. Then when the drug is truly needed, the resistant bacteria are no longer affected. Many strains of bacteria have become resistant to penicillin and other antibiotics. Patients should not ask for and densists should not prescribe antibiotics frivolously. No one should accept a prophylactic prescription in the absence of a specific diagnostic need.

Drugs to Control Pain and Anxiety

Fear of dental pain is so common that it affects people even before they have their first experience with a dentist. Drilling on teeth is intrinsically unpleasant, much like the screeching of chalk on a slate board. Even if treatment is relatively painless, it is still generally unpleasant.

Most people are able to overcome their fears and accept periodic dental care although it may take repeated positive experiences before the anxiety is significantly reduced. Extremely frightened children and adults with anxieties at the level of a phobia should be introduced to treatment slowly. In extreme cases, the child's first appointments may be only visits to meet the doctor and "nurses" and to observe the tranquillity of the dental office. But sooner or later one must experience the real thing. Then it takes a gentle but firm control of the situation by the dentist to overcome the patient's anxieties and to prove that fear of the dentist was unwarranted. Once encouraged past this point, the patient enjoys a sense of great accomplishment, of having overcome a major hurdle in the path to self-control and maturity. The effect is the same in both adults and children.

Overcoming fear of the dentist does not mean there will never be some anxiety over dental treatment. It means that the anxiety will be minimal and not directed at the person—the dentist—who is there to help.

A good local anesthetic injection is all that is necessary to provide virtually painless treatment. Most dental injections amount to no more than the tiny pinprick of the needle and do not hurt. However, if anesthetic solution is injected too rapidly, with too much force, the pain is unnecessarily severe. A good dental injection takes 30 to 60 seconds to complete and will be fully effective in 3 to 5 minutes. Patients frequently complain of the lingering numbness afterward, but it is a small discomfort compared to the pain that otherwise would be experienced.

Pain associated with dental conditions ranges from mild sensitivities to hot and cold temperatures to the severe pain of toothaches and acute infections of the gums. Analgesics such as aspirin are usually sufficient to alleviate mild aches and discomfort. Narcotics are prescribed for more severe pain.

As with antibiotics, drugs to relieve pain and reduce anxiety should be used sparingly. The choice of drug should always be based on the principle of *adequacy*, the least amount of the least powerful substance sufficient for the purpose.

Generic versus proprietary drugs. Generic drugs have a distinct advantage over proprietary brand-name drugs: They are cheaper. They are also just as effective.[5] Although manufacturers suggest that their brands are of a superior quality, the active chemical ingredients are the same. There is no reason to pay for higher priced brand-name drugs unless one believes the hype of advertisements.

Analgesics

Analgesics are medicines that usually relieve pain without entirely depressing the central nervous system. The most popular analgesics are aspirin (acetylsalicylic acid) and acetaminophen. These are often combined with other analgesics such as phenacetin and caffeine to potentiate the effect. Aspirin is the first choice for the relief of dental pain. It is inexpensive, nonaddictive, and well tolerated by most people, and for some it is just as effective as codeine. Aspirin should always be swallowed to relieve pain, never held directly on the gum where it causes ulceration and sloughing of the mucosa. An aspirin burn looks worse than it is and the mucosa heals uneventfully once the irritant is removed.

Aspirin should not be used by patients with a history of peptic ulcers. To avoid the risk of Reye's syndrome, a rare but serious illness that may result in mental retardation or death, children recovering from chicken pox or flu should not be given aspirin. Many aspirin alternatives are available, such as **acetaminophen** (Datril, Percogesic, Phenaphen, Tylenol), **propoxyphene** (Darvon), and **ibuprofen** (Advil, Motrin, Nuprin). These have analgesic and antipyretic (fever-reducing) qualities similar to aspirin's. They may be tolerated better by those who experience gastrointestinal side effects with aspirin. As with aspirin, prolonged use of ibuprofen can cause stomach ulcers and prolonged bleeding.

Narcotics. **Codeine** is a commonly prescribed narcotic in dentistry, usually in combination with aspirin, acetaminophen or other analgesics. Patients should first try aspirin alone since it may be quite adequate. **Percodan**, a synthetic narcotic, is more potent. Percodan contains aspirin and therefore should be avoided by those who have aspirin sensitivity. **Demerol** is another morphine-type narcotic sometimes prescribed for the relief of pain; however, it works much more effectively when given by injection than when taken orally. It is more likely to be used in dentistry as a pretreatment sedative.

Since narcotics are addictive, they should be taken no longer than required for relief of pain. Codeine is the least addictive, which makes it the first choice for those who can tolerate it. Other narcotics such as opium, heroin, and morphine are either too potent or too addictive for routine dental use.

Narcotics relieve pain by depressing the central nervous system. An overdose produces unconsciousness, stupor, coma, and death. Even an average small dose is likely to reduce alertness and induce drowsiness. To avoid injury to themselves and others, narcotized patients should not drive automobiles and should avoid work that requires alertness.

Oral tranquilizers and sedatives. The best tranquilizer is an empathetic doctor and a good local anesthetic injection. Once the patient's mouth is numb, most anxiety about impending treatment vanishes. But so many patients are so fearful of dentistry that even the thought of a simple injection brings on an anxiety attack. It is easier for a dentist to prescribe drugs to relieve anxiety and render the patients more passive during treatment than to take the time to build up their confidence and assuage their fears. Anxious patients, including children, can often talk out their fears with a receptive dentist without resorting to drugs. For those who cannot, mild tranquilizers and sedatives make sense.

The most commonly used drugs to reduce anxiety and induce drowsiness or sleep are tranquilizers (Valium, Librium, Xanax) or barbiturates (Seconal, Nembutal, and phenobarbital). Chloral hydrate, also known as "knockout drops," is a quick-acting sedative that is still used for otherwise uncontrollable infants and young children, although hydroxyzine (Atarax or Vistaril) is now considered safer and therefore it is more commonly used.

Patients should inform their dentist if they have taken a tranquilizer or sedative prior to treatment. Without such information the dentist might give them the same or another drug, resulting in overdosage or a poor drug interaction. Doctors who overprescribe drugs are, like their patients, seeking an easy way out of dealing with anxiety. Repeated and prolonged use of narcotics, tranquilizers, and sedatives can be addictive. People who rely on drugs for every dental visit and every anxiety producing situation are risking gradual descent into the hell of addiction.

Local Anesthetics

Pain control in dentistry improved tremendously with the development of effective local anesthetics. Like many innovations, pain control was initially introduced as an elective procedure. In the late 1920s and early 1930s, dentists charged 25 or 50 cents a shot. However, those were hard times, and if patients did not have the money, not only did they suffer but so did the dentist inflicting the pain. Dentists soon realized that numbing the patient's tooth relieved them of the struggle, the tension, the anxiety, the increased blood pressure, the sweating forehead and palms as the patient suffered and squirmed out from under them. It was also a good practice builder. The community soon learned who the painless dentists were. It was not long before patients were given novocaine at no charge, to everyone's benefit and relief.

Types of Local Anesthetics

Novocain is the proprietary name for one of the first local anesthetics; the word novocaine has become the universal name for all local anesthetics. The substances used today vary from one brand to another, the more common ones being xylocaine (lidocaine) and carbocaine. They may contain a small amount of epinephrine (synthetic adrenaline). Epinephrine is a vasoconstrictor, narrowing the blood vessels to reduce the blood flow to the area, so the anesthetic solution remains concentrated in the tissue longer. Some physicians recommend that patients with heart disease receive epinephrine-free local anesthetics, believing that the synthetic adrenaline can be harmful. An anesthetic with epinephrine produces deeper, longer lasting anesthesia, reducing the patient's anxiety. Since anxiety induces the body to secrete it own adrenaline into the bloodstream, nothing is gained by avoiding epinephrine in the anesthetic. On the contrary, if the anesthesia wears off too soon and pain is experienced, more natural adrenaline will be pumped into the bloodstream than the minute amount contained in the anesthetic solution. Patients with heart disease can well tolerate a local anesthetic that has epinephrine in the small amount of 1:100,000 (one part epinephrine to 100,000 parts anesthetic chemical). Higher content epinephrine (1:50,000) should not be used.

Allergy to novocain is rare. Some patients report a sensitivity or allergy to a local anesthetic characterized by itching or swelling. These reactions are not common and can be avoided when encountered by switching to another solution with a different chemical formula. True allergy to a local anesthetic is extremely rare. If in doubt, an allergist can test the various anesthetics to identify one that is tolerated by the patient.

In years past it was not unusual for an anxious or fearful patient to experience syncope (fainting) after the injection. This was due to rapid, if momentary, blood loss from the brain when the patient was seated in an upright position. Syncope from a dental injection has been virtually eliminated with patients lying in a semiprone position in the modern reclining dental chair.

Types of Dental Anesthetic Injections

Infiltration. Infiltration anesthesia is obtained by inserting the needle under the mucosa covering the bone on the outside of an upper tooth and slowly injecting the solution. The solution infiltrates through the thin, porous plate of bone to the nerves supplying the tooth. Both the tooth and the tissue around it become numb in a few minutes. If the tooth is to be extracted or if periodontal treatment is being done in the upper jaw, the inside palatal tissue is also anesthetized by injecting a few drops of solution opposite the tooth. A palatal injection may be slightly painful because this tissue is so thick.

Interligamental. Many people object to facial numbness from a local anesthetic that may last for hours after treatment is completed. An alternative is to inject the solution directly into the periodontal ligament that attaches the tooth to the bony socket. The patient feels no numbness with interligamental anesthesia and no pain from drilling, provided it works. Not all teeth can be anesthetized this way, in which case infiltration or block anesthesia is used.

Nerve block. This type of injection aims at the nerve supplying a number of teeth. It is used most frequently in the mandible, where the large mandibular nerve supplies half the lower jaw on each side. Mandibular nerve block injections require greater anatomical knowledge and skill in order to place the needle deeper into the tissue behind the last molar on the inside of the jawbone where the solution can reach the nerve trunk. A good lower injection numbs all the lower teeth, gum tissue, and skin on one side within three to five minutes.

If anesthesia is not fully effective in five minutes, the injection usually has to be repeated or some pain will be felt on drilling. Some dentists regularly fail to obtain anesthesia with the first injection, attributing the failure to some aberration in the shape of the patient's jaws or the position of the nerves. More likely it is the dentist's fault, not the patient's. If a dentist uses a needle that is too long, the solution may be deposited beyond the nerve, particularly in the lower jaw. A long needle also increases the risk of injecting too deeply behind the upper second molar and causing a hematoma (see below). To minimize these occurrences, dentists and hygienists should use needles no longer than 1¼ inches. Patients should not be embarrassed about asking that only medium-sized or short needles be used.

The reason for longer needles has historical roots. Prior to the 1950s, metals used for needles were more brittle. Before the days of disposable everything, the needles were sterilized in boiling water, sometimes sharpened by hand on a carborundum stone, and reused many times. Constant flexing during reuse occasionally caused the needle to break. A longer needle assured that the broken piece would extend outside the tissue where it could be grasped and removed. Otherwise, extensive surgery would be required to locate and remove the needle fragment before it caused serious internal injury. Today's circumstances are quite different. Not only are the needles flexible so that they can be twisted like pretzels without breaking, they are discarded after each patient. There is no longer any reason for a dentist to use a long needle.

Occasionally the needle passes through a **plexus**, or network, of blood vessels during an injection around the upper second and third molars. This injection is called a posterior superior alveolar or tuberosity nerve block. A large swelling immediately pops out on the side of the face, the result of a **hematoma**, or pool of blood, collecting in the tissues. It is similar to the black-and-blue swelling of a punch in the face. Apart from some transient discomfort, hematomas are harmless and disappear in a few weeks. A hematoma from a dental injection is most often due to faulty insertion of a long needle into a highly vascular area that skilled dentists know how to avoid.

The Importance of Aspiration

Dentists and hygienists are well trained to protect against accidental injection into a blood vessel. Aspiration is the opposite of injection. By pulling back on the syringe plunger, negative pressure is created that draws fluid back through the needle into the carpule (glass tube) of anesthetic. If blood appears, the needle is repositioned, with further aspiration to make sure there is no more blood. Then the injection is completed.

A small amount of solution inadvertently injected into a blood vessel may produce a momentary increase in heart rate because of the epinephrine in the anesthetic. If experienced, the patient should immediately signal the dentist to interrupt the injection. After a few moments, the heart rate will return to normal, and the dentist can resume the injection. These are occasional but unavoidable consequences of an injection and should not reflect adversely on the competence of the dentist or hygienist.

Nitrous Oxide Inhalation Anesthesia and Analgesia

The anesthetic effect of inhaling nitrous oxide gas (N_2O), known as "laughing gas," was first demonstrated by a dentist in the nineteenth century. Inhalation anesthesia revolutionized surgery, which previously killed as many patients from shock as from bacterial infection caused by nonsterile instruments and contaminated wounds. As late as the 1940s, dentists with little more training than a few hours instruction by the manufacturers of "gas machines" were still administering general anesthesia with N_2O. Unfortunately, not all patients woke up, and general practitioners gradually gave up nitrous oxide altogether.

As the profession recognized the dangers of general anesthesia, particularly when administered by inadequately trained dentists, general anesthesia in dentistry became the province of oral surgeons, nurse anesthetists, and physician-anesthesiologists. But many general dentists retained their interest in analgesia, which reduces the response to or sense of pain without rendering the patient totally unconscious. Once an extremely anxious patient is calmed by analgesia, the local anesthetic injection can be given painlessly.

By the 1950s, improved quality of the manufactured gas and protective mechanisms on the anesthesia machines increased the safety of administering N_2O analgesia by general dentists in their private offices. Previously the gas contained impurities that caused nausea and other side effects, and the machines too easily permitted overdosage. The modern analgesia machines automatically prevent administration of more than 50 percent nitrous oxide to 50 percent oxygen. Most patients reach the desired level of analgesia with 20 to 30 percent N_2O, always in combination with oxygen. When the dental procedure is completed, the patient breathes pure oxygen for five minutes to clear the body of residual N_2O.

Nitrous oxide analgesia is relaxing, calming, and soothing. Analgesia and general anesthesia can produce euphoria and hallucinations. The effect can be erotic, and patients have had sexual fantasies involving the dentist, as well as having dentists take sexual advantage of them in their weakened condition. To avoid unwarranted accusations and reassure the patient, a prudent dentist will have an assistant present throughout the entire analgesic or general anesthetic episode.

Sexual abuse is hardly the only danger of inhalation analgesia or general anesthesia.[6] Modern analgesia machines do not work with less than 50 percent oxygen in combination with nitrous oxide. That is fine as long as the right gas tank is connected to the right tube. Mix-ups are rare, but once in a while the nitrous oxide and the oxygen tanks are reversed. Although special tank fittings are designed to prevent reversal, there is no absolutely foolproof system. Patients have died when at the end of the treatment the pure oxygen they were given turned out to be pure "laughing gas."

Multiple drug overdose is more common. Children have been badly injured or killed outright by the synergistic effect of combinations of tranquilizers, sedatives, excessive local anesthetic injections, and nitrous oxide analgesia. One young dentist, in his first year of practice, gave a five year old patient an oral sedative, 10 shots of "novocaine," and nitrous oxide analgesia so that all the fillings could be done at one visit. The dentist did not know that 10 carpules or 18 cubic centimeters of local anesthetic solution is toxic for a small child and, in combination with sedatives, risks respiratory failure, cardiac arrest, and death. He did not use simple monitoring devices for blood pressure and heartbeats. The child died during treatment. Only after all the fillings were completed and the N_2O mask was removed did the dentist realize what had happened.

Properly administered, N_2O analgesia is a safe, effective means of reducing anxiety and pain during dental treatment, but it should not be used routinely. N_2O analgesia should be reserved for those with severe anxiety or special pain control problems.

Pediatric dentists and general dentists qualified for the administration of oral sedation in conjunction with N_2O analgesia can treat otherwise unmanageable children as young as 2-3 years of age in their own offices, without having to resort to hospitalizatin and general anesthesia. Unfortunately, there is a trend among the pediatric dentists to hospitalize these young children at great cost to the parents and increased profits to themselves because it takes less time to treat an unconscious patient. They charge out thousands of dollars of treatment for a few hours work that could be done in their own office with oral sedation and N_2O analgesia.

Intravenous Sedation, Twilight Sleep and General Anesthesia

The big sign over the dental office advertising Twilight Sleep or Pentathol plays on the fear but also the foolishness of anxious patients. To be sure, many people have had bad dental office experiences. Grownups remember how they were hurt by dentists when they were children or even as adults. Many have been frightened by hearing of patients who have died or suffered irreparable brain damaged from an overdose of intravenous Valium and pentathol or nitrous oxide alone or any of these drugs in combination with other drugs.

It is not only the twilight sleep dentists who pose a threat. Most oral surgeons in the United States administer I-V sedation or general anesthesia unnecessarily. Their use should be restricted to situations where local anesthetics are not effective.

The terms *intravenous* (I-V) *sedation* and *general anesthesia* are often used interchangeably. I-V sedation is the injection into a vein of Valium or other substances to produce twilight sleep, a light, heady, relaxed feeling approaching euphoria. The unconsciousness of general anesthesia can be induced either by gas inhalation or intravenous injection of anesthetic drugs. Ironically, even if I-V sedation or general anesthesia is administered, patients are given a local anesthetic injection to eliminate pain. The general anesthesia is for the **psyche**, whereas the local injection is for the **soma** or body. But there are better ways to handle the psyche. Oral tranquilizers and sedatives soothe the nerves of overly anxious patients without subjecting them to the inherent risks of intravenous and inhalation anesthesia. But the best tranquilizer is a good injection that produces effective local anesthesia.

Stay Awake!

Dentists extract hundreds of thousands of teeth using only local anesthetics, and that is the best way to go about it. Everyone approaches dental surgery with trepidation, but after the extraction it is not uncommon for a conscious patient to exclaim, "My God, I hardly felt a thing!" or "Is it out already? I can't believe it." Dental surgery, including complex extractions, seldom warrants I-V sedation or general anesthesia.

As long as the patient is awake, a doctor is less likely to force the mouth so wide open that the temporomandibular joints are injured or exert so much pressure with instruments that the jaw is fractured. While these injuries have occurred with local anesthetics, the risk is much less when the patient is present in mind as well as body.

Indications for I-V Sedation and General Anesthesia

There are a few indications for the use of I-V sedation and general anesthesia in dentistry. Local anesthetics are not always effective in the presence of an acute infection and swelling. Patients with advanced cerebral palsy and Down's syndrome may be unable to control their movements. Some patients are so frightened that intravenous sedation or general anesthesia is the only way the dentist can quiet them in the dental chair.

I-V sedation permits extremely anxious patients to tolerate extensive dental treatment over a long period of time. Yet, many dentists work on such patients for four or even six hours at a stretch, depending on good local anesthesia and a caring staff to make the experience tolerable. But there are some patients for whom I-V sedation is as much a benefit to the dental staff as to themselves. It may be the only way that extensive treatment can be accomplished.

Some children present great difficulty for dentists, particularly two- and three-year-olds suffering from **baby bottle tooth decay** (nursing caries) of their baby teeth. Virtually all of these infants can be handled in the dental office by a competent general dentist or a children's dentist—pedodontist or pediatric dentist—specially trained in the treatment of difficult children. The child is sedated, wrapped in a restraining "papoose board," and treated under nitrous oxide analgesia and local anesthetics.

Some pedodontists prefer to have a general anesthetic administered by an anesthesiologist in a hospital in order to treat difficult children. No doubt this is safer than office administration of a general anesthetic, but general anesthesia is inherently risky no matter who administers it. If a child is too young, treatment can be postponed for six months or a year, when he or she might be able to be handled in the dental office.

For a healthy patient undergoing routine treatment, including oral surgery, local anesthesia should be used for pain control. I-V sedation and general anesthesia are important additional tools, but they should be used only when the advantages clearly outweigh the risks.

RECOMMENDATIONS

1. Avoid prophylactic antibiotics unless recommended for specific preexisting medical conditions.
2. Tetracycline should not be taken by pregnant women or children under age eight.
3. Aspirin is the drug of choice for relief of minor dental pain but children recovering from chicken pox or flu should not be given aspirin.

4. Request prescriptions for generic rather than brand-name drugs to minimize expense.
5. Avoid unnecessary and excessive use of tranquilizers, sedatives, and narcotics.
6. Avoid nitrous oxide analgesia, and intravenous sedation for routine dental treatment including extractions and other types of oral surgery.
7. Don't let the oral surgeon sell you I-V sedation or general anesthesia for routine extractions, including removal of wisdom teeth.

14

How to Choose a Good Dentist
Caveat Emptor—Let the Buyer Beware!

A frequently asked question is how to choose a good dentist. It isn't like buying an automobile where you can visit a show room or take a test drive or read comparative ratings in Consumer Reports. There is no way to test out a doctor without risk, to see if he or she practices a *standard of care* based on evidence of need and effectiveness of treatment. One cannot depend on professional ethics, which too often is the victim of economic self-interest rather than the servant of the Oath of Hippocrates.[1] This chapter describes the different aspects of the problem and how one might choose between the different types of dental practices. It is not intended to undermine your confidence in the profession, but rather to demonstrate that confidence in your doctor should not be a *given.* It must be earned.

If you have dental insurance through employment, your choice may be limited to a list of participating dentists, but there is still that list to choose from. If one belongs to a union, the local may recommend one or more dentists who charge lower fees, but with indifference towards quality. Some people call the dental society or a dental school for recommendations. These organizations might offer names of dentists who need patients, but that is the only basis for their recommendation. Many people ask their friends or co-workers whom they go to. That is probably as good a start as any in choosing a dentist since at least the dentist has satisfied someone. Otherwise you thumb through the yellow pages.

Then what? Then you must protect yourself as best as possible from the greed and charlatanism of unethical doctors whom you may unwittingly have chosen. You must protect yourself from dentists who, though well meaning, are themselves victims of the short-comings of dental training and of the myths of dental practice. You must become an active participant in the decision-making process. To do so you must obtain some basic information about dental diseases and how to treat them. That has been the purpose of this book and if you follow its basic guidelines, you have a chance of protecting yourself and your family from the substandard and excessive practices of *modern* dentistry.

202

The Sine Qua Non—Confidence

Patients must have confidence in their dentist and feel comfortable with the office's receptionist, assistants, and dental hygienist, if there is one, to establish and maintain the long-term relationships that are fundamental to good oral health care. They have to believe that treatment will be of high quality and essentially pain-free. As long as the patient has confidence in the gentleness and humane concern of the dentist and the auxiliary staff, fears of dental treatment are easily overcome.

Next to fear of being hurt, anxiety over the high cost of dentistry is another obstacle that must be overcome. People who can afford it are more likely to seek early preventive treatment, even though too many delay because of fear. Others may put it off on the assumption that it will be too costly. Poor people often have no choice; they lack the money to pay for preventive treatment. Determining cost beforehand is not as difficult as it used to be. Some dentists advertise charges for examinations, X-rays, and cleanings. Dentists are less reluctant than they used to be to quote average fees over the telephone so that prospective patients can make comparisons. Price comparison is important, but price alone should not be the sole determinant in such a highly personalized service as health care. Low fees for exams, X-rays and cleanings are often a come-on, which is more than made up in overcharges for unnecessary treatment.

In a sense, it is not choosing a good dentist *per se* so much as choosing a good dental practice. Hygienists and assistants also perform direct contact services, and the attitude of front office personnel—receptionists, managers, collection clerks—often colors the entire relationship. No matter how good the dentist, if you do not feel confident and comfortable with the whole staff, you have not yet found the right office for your long-term dental care.

Managed Care

What was originally called *prepaid health care* and then *health maintenance organization (HMO)* and now *managed care*—and who knows what next year—is under siege. The original premises were that when you are sick, you are least able to pay for the high cost of health care and doctors' diagnosis and treatment should be independent of their income. Prepaying health care would alleviate these concerns in the same manner as home and car insurance. But responsibility for the design, organization and administration of prepaid health care was not intended to be removed from patients and doctors and turned over to commercial insurance companies.

The traditional prepaid health plans began in the 1930s as not-for-profit organizations, with both consumer and physician participation in determining and administering policies of health care.[2] During and particularly following World War II major prepaid health plans were developed and expanded in many areas of the country. There is Group Health Association (GHA) in Washington, D.C. (actually started in the 1930s) for federal employees, and Group Health Cooperative (GHC) of Puget Sound in Seattle, Washington. And, of course, there is the Kaiser Health Plan, begun during WW II by contracting with physicians to care for Kaiser employees in its own clinics (staff models), which were expanded afterwards to include other workers and their families and now covers 10 percent of the population of California. Dentistry was, and usually is, excluded from such programs with some exceptions such as GHA and Kaiser in Portland, Oregon.

Prepaid health care was strongly condemned by the medical and dental professions as "socialized medicine," pure, unadultered un-Americanism. Originally opposed even to indemnity medical and hospital insurance, that is, opposed to anything that might conceivably interfere with or intervene in the sacred *doctor-patient relationship*, the medical profession finally embraced fee-for-service indemnity insurance as a means of protecting private practice and slowing the growth of staff-model health plans. Dentistry followed at a slower pace, with 52 percent of the population having any kind of dental insurance today (See table below), compared to 85 percent with some kind of medical insurance, leaving over 42 million people with no medical and 135 million with no dental insurance at all, mostly the poor and "ethnic" populations.[3,4]

Unfortunately for everyone, health care costs continued to rise as a result of the population's increased utilization, its belief in all the hype of new treatments and cures for *everything* and especially its insatiable appetite for drugs. Enter commercial insurance and *managed care* ostensibly to control costs. Instead of effectively organizing health care services under one roof in staff model facilities

Estimated Number of Dental Plan Members, 1997*		
Type of Plan	*No. of Members*	*Percent*
Dental HMO	26,457,650	18
Dental PPO	24,460,062	17
Dental referral	5,453,264	3
Dental indemnity	90,640,826	62
Total:	147,011,802	100
*National Association of Dental Plans (NADP), 1998 Dental HMO/PPO Profile. Dallas, Tx.		

such as Kaiser did with great success, including a high level of patient satisfaction, managed care was based on a loose association of solo doctors in scattered offices called a "network," an Independent Practice Association (IPA) or a Preferred Provider Organization (PPO). Many doctors receive monthly capitation sums, sometimes with bonuses to minimize treatment. Others are paid a reduced fee-for-service. This was the price they were willing, or forced, to pay for the preservation of their separate private practices. But instead of maintaining their independence, they succumbed to management by the commercial insurance and managed care companies whose primary goals were paying enormous salaries to top executives and large dividends to investors. The only way to do this was to skim the cream, to minimize payments to doctors and services to patients.

Not all commercial or for-profit companies are bad. But enough of them, including the largest, badly exploited the doctors and patients, tarring and feathering the good programs with the same bad reputation. With costs continuing to rise despite the promises of managed care, competition among the various insurance or managed care companies resulted not in improved programs with improved coverage but bottom-line rates that would attract employers who paid bill. Even the good plans are forced to compete by lowering benefits or increasing out-of-pocket charges to patients. The predictable result has been increasing dissatisfaction of doctors and patients with the managed care of commercial insurance companies. But make no mistake about it. The overall populations covered by such plans as Kaiser and GHC are highly satisfied with their programs. It is these staff model health care plans that should be emulated about the country and expanded to include dentistry.

Managed Care in Dentistry

If you are fortunate enough to have dental insurance, your plan may offer indemnity fee-for-service insurance, a managed care panel or network of associated dental offices, or the staff model facilities of an HMO. These plans restrict the choice of dental offices, with promises of reduced costs and claims of quality care. The managed care office usually receives a monthly capitation payment for you and your family, which may cover examinations, X-rays, prophylaxes and fillings at no additional charge, but more often requires you to make small to large copayments to compensate for the low capitation rate. Some managed care offices are paid reduced fee-for-service if too few patients have been assigned to provide the dentists sufficient capitation and copayment income to cover the cost of providing treatment.

The dental network plans claim to screen participating dentists to weed out the bad apples. Unfortunately, quality standards are weak and weakly applied. Each plan tries to have as many doctors as possible on their panel to make them geographically accessible. Thus, the standard for selection becomes virtually *any willing provider*. What these plans are really promising is that if you choose from their panel you will save money. This is often more than an empty promise. It is fraud because the plans not only do not prevent overcharges, they often promote them to the panel dentists. The dentists are told that low capitation payments may be made up by *add-ons* and *up-grades*, such as selling you porcelain crowns or *bonded* composite fillings to replace your old, perfectly good amalgam fillings. They will tell you that the covered porcelain-metal crown, which you do need, is of poor quality, but for an extra $500 you can get the best, even though there is no practial difference between the two. Or, a routine cleaning that should be provided at no charge will be turned into "gingival curettage" and "subgingival irrigation" for an additional $200 to $300. Even selecting a dentist based on recommendations of friends or unions or administrators of health plans does not guarantee either a satisfactory relationship with a dental office, quality treatment or honest charges.

Most of the dentists on the network panels are solo practitioners who are not philosophically in agreement with the principles of managed care. They join because they have too few paying patients, because they fear this is the tidal wave of the future and if they don't join, others will and they will be left out in the cold. Other panelists may be employees of large practices owned by individual dentists or an HMO. They too may be resentful at being forced to work for a salary or not having their own practice. More and more dentists recently graduated from dental school seek employment in these large practices or work for private practitioners because they are heavily in debt from their education and cannot afford to start their practice.

And yet, there are many good dentists, true *doctors*, who function effectively in these types of practices, who are dedicated to helping people, whose ethics have not been destroyed by resentment or greed. There are still a lot of good people in this world, but it is not always easy to find them.

The large dental groups are more likely to be located in less affluent areas, catering to poor working people with dental insurance, offering to accept the insurance coverage as full or nearly full payment. Though many people would prefer to avoid the clinic atmosphere characteristic of many large group practices for the more traditional solo practitioner, their choice is limited by their income. Either way, we must learn to be intelligent participants in our own health care if we are to avoid being exploited by the monetary health care system.

The Secondary Negative Alternative

So, the world of dental care has changed and the dental consumer is hard put to sift through the various options and promises. Yet, we must make a choice. Perhaps the most important point to bear in mind is that one's first choice is not binding forever. Consumers have the right to alternatives in the event their first choice proves unsatisfactory. This **secondary negative alternative**—the right to reject a doctor and to choose another more to one's liking—is the essence of free choice.[5]

A person cannot make an intelligent choice without sufficient knowledge based on experience with a particular dental practice. Many plans assign patients to a specific dentist based on geographic proximity. There is nothing inherently wrong with ZIP Code assignment, provided that the patient is not bound to that doctor. It must remain the right of every patient to choose another dentist when a first assignment proves unsatisfactory. Only in this way will the dignity of the patient and the integrity of the plan be preserved.

TYPES OF DENTAL PRACTICES

As previously noted, few group practices existed prior to World War II, most of which were public health clinics employing part-time dentists for low-income people and indigents. The model for the young dentist was the solo practitioner working with one or two combination assistant-receptionists. There are now many group dental practices even though solo practice is more common. Before making a selection, you should know the advantages and disadvantages of each type of practice.

Solo Practice

The traditional solo practice consists of a single dentist who employs at least one assistant. The small office usually contains two dental chairs (operatories), a small waiting room, and a smaller business office. The more successful solo practitioners employ two, sometimes three, assistants, one of whom is the receptionist, and a part-time dental hygienist.

Advantages. A close doctor-patient relationship (DPR) is characteristic of a solo practice. The DPR extends not only to the dentist but also to the assistant and receptionist, who get to know patients more personally than in a large office. Because the dentist owns the practice, he or she has a direct interest in satisfying the clientele. The patient is assured continuity of care with the same person, thus enhancing the DPR.

Disadvantages. Few dentists are proficient in all aspects of dental treatment. Since their income is directly dependent on their own labor, solo dentists tend to attempt to do everything rather than refer patients to specialists. Fatigue and burnout occur in every occupation, including dentistry. Yet the need to produce income persists. Because there is no one else around to assure that quality standards are maintained, to stimulate professional involvement and to introduce new techniques, solo practitioners are the sole judge of whether or not the quality of their services is declining. Dentists also must have time to meet personal and family needs and for vacations. As a consequence, solo practitioners may not be there when their patients need them most.

But the greatest disadvantage may be that the fee-for-service practice, when *solo* as described above or *group* described below, needs a steady influx of new patients to make money. Today's high cost of maintaining a dental office forces the dentist to generate as much income as possible from each new patient. There is not much to charge a patient returning on periodic recall for a prophylaxis, unless a broken tooth requiring a crown is noted. But every new patient has high potential for creative diagnosis—replacing old fillings, exchanging amalgam fillings for composites, crowning that tooth with the big old amalgam, adding on the subgingival scalings and gingival irrigation. Dental practice management courses tell their students that the primary diagnosis for a new patient should be $600-700, and up. That is why you should always look closely in the eyes of the dentist as he or she is eying (examining) you. If you see $ signs in the pupils, consider a second choice.

Group Practice

There are many different types of group practices. Some are loose associations of dentists who share waiting rooms and receptionists with others in the group but otherwise function as solo practitioners, maintaining their own roster of patients. Others consist of a single owner-dentist who employs everyone else: dentists, hygienists, and office staff. Sometimes the dentists are salaried, but more commonly their income is a percentage, approximately 25 percent, of the money they produce for the firm, which is an incentive for *add-ons* and *upgrades* to increase their earnings—no different than if they owned the practice. Some group dentists are professional partnerships so that the dentists have a direct, personal interest in the success of the practice.[6]

Most groups are small, with only 2 or 3 dentists, 3 to 4 assistants, a receptionist, and possibly a part-time hygienist. An occasional large group practice employing 10 or more dentists, many assistants, receptionists, insurance clerks, hygienists, and laboratory technicians can be found in some large metropolitan areas. Specialists also combine in groups of 2 or 3. Many of the larger general dental practices employ specialists at least part-time.

Advantages. Group practices are often open longer hours and on Saturdays. Some offer early morning and evening appointments, the same as some solo practitioners. Patients have a choice of dentists and hygienists within the group. A parent, for example, might prefer one dentist in the group, the children another. Dentists can refer patients to a specialist within the group or to an associate who is particularly proficient in certain types of treatment. For example, some dentists are better at extractions, root canal and periodontal therapy, or the handling of children. Consultations between dentists are ongoing, and close professional association stimulates learning and improvement in techniques. Groups can better afford new and expensive equipment, replacement of old equipment, and advanced office systems since the cost is spread over a larger number of dentists, hygienists, and technicians.

Disadvantages. It is said in the profession that the only thing worse than a bad solo practice is a bad group practice. Both are plentiful. Many group practices are pure commercial enterprises without any redeeming features. Old equipment is barely maintained. Sterilization is minimal or deficient. Where groups are owned by commercial corporations rather than partnerships of the dentists, young dentists, heavily in debt from the high cost of their education, are employed to churn out the work. They may be required to produce as many services and to charge as many fees as possible to generate maximum income. These employee-dentists have little identification with the practice, much less with the patient, and are waiting for the day that they can afford to start their own solo practice. Review of the quality of treatment is a sham. Turnover in professionals is high, in some cases so high that the patients have no assurance that the dentist or hygienist they came to like will still be there when they return for a checkup.

This is the worst scenario, but some of these negative aspects are found in many dental practices that cater to working-class people with insurance. Nonetheless, the low-cost, high-volume group provides a genuine service to people who cannot afford other choices.[7] Much of the work is of acceptable quality even though far too much is so uneven that *professional* is the wrong word to describe it.

Advertising Practices

Advertising by doctors was long considered unethical. Doctors are supposed to be motivated by a desire *to do good*, not by a commercial incentive to make money. Until the late 1970s the American Dental Association and its affiliated state dental societies denied membership to advertising dentists, the implication being that advertising led to lower standards of care and unfair competition with ethical practitioners. However, the U.S. Supreme Court, in a case involving bar association attempts to keep lawyers from advertising, found that such attempts violated free speech by limiting the amount of information that could be made available to the public. Soon after, dentists who advertised were permitted to join the professional associations.[8] Now it is commonplace for dentists to advertise. Even the dental associations advertise on behalf of their members.

Advantages. A good advertisement provides essential information on office hours, scope of services, specialty care, and acceptance of insurance. While aggressive price advertising is still rare, some advertisers offer introductory packages—examination, X-rays, cleaning—at a special rate.

Disadvantages. An advertisement tells nothing of the quality of the practice. The larger and more flamboyant the advertisement, the more likely the emphasis is on mass production. Although the fees charged per service are lower than solo practitioners generally charge, the total number of services performed may be greater than needed, resulting in higher overall costs. Practices advertising twilight sleep, cosmetic dentistry, and one-visit comprehensive treatment are seldom interested in long-term maintenance care that does not generate high income. High sales volume is necessary to justify and pay for the advertising. While overtreatment is characteristic of many dental practices, the amount of overtreatment is likely to be greater in offices that advertise, and the quality of treatment must deteriorate with all the emphasis on volume production.

Prepayment (Capitation) Practices

A capitation plan is one in which the dental practice is paid so much a head (thus the word *capitation)* to provide basic dental care, no matter how much of this basic treatment is needed by the patient. Theoretically, this should create an incentive for more emphasis on preventive care and treatment.

The option of a capitation dental practice is usually restricted to employee fringe benefit dental insurance plans. The dental office receives as little as $3 to as much as $30 each month per employee or family that has signed up, with most plans near the low end of the scale. The capitation payment covers most basic services at no out-of-pocket expense or with small copayments. Larger copayments are required for crowns, bridges, dentures, and other complex services. Some large dental offices or associations of offices offer voluntary prepayment plans to individual subscribers who are responsible for their own capitation costs. By making small monthly payments, the capitation member is offered a choice of dental offices that provide examinations, X-rays, and prophylaxis at no charge and other services at much reduced rates. Though not exactly capitation, some plans charge an annual membership fee and discount rates for services, much like membership discount department stores.

Advantages. Since the dental office receives a monthly payment, the incentive to overtreat is reduced. Treatment not covered fully by the capitation plan is provided at lower fees. Conservative, preventive treatment can be emphasized. The incentive for high-cost treatment is not as great.

Disadvantages. By signing up with a capitation plan, patients have limited their choice of dentists. Since the dental practice is receiving monthly capitation payment whether or not patients receive treatment, there is no incentive to encourage the patient to have needed treatment. Most of these private practices are composed of a majority of fee-for-service patients who are given priority for appointments over the "captive" capitation patient. The reality is that patients who have chosen capitated network dentists who also serve fee-for-service private patients immediately become second-class citizens. Fee-for-service patients get an appointment within hours or the next day, at their choice of time. A capitation plan patient may have to wait a month or longer. The capitation payment provided the dental practice is often very small, and dentists make up the difference by adding treatments or suggesting more expensive treatments such as crowns instead of fillings that have patient copayments, a process already described and known in the trade as *upgrades* and *add-ons*. Thus, sadly, the promise of managed care to reduce overtreatment may be compromised by the dentists' need to make more money.

What to Look For in a Dental Practice

Methods of financing dental care appear less important than once thought because so much of dentistry is elective. Because of the large number of treatments offered on a copayment basis, many prepaid capitation dental plans are little more than modified fee-for-service plans. Methods of payment aside, the choice of a solo or a group practice should be based on general principles of good dental care and the satisfaction of patient needs. Even a solo dental practice is not really solo since assistants and hygienists are now permitted to perform many treatment functions previously performed only by dentists.

Consider the following factors before choosing a dental practice.

Office accessibility. The location and hours of service should be convenient. If adults are working, appointments may have to be in the early morning, in the evening, or on Saturdays. Older children can travel by themselves to the office if it is nearby or on a bus line. This is particularly important if a child is having orthodontic treatment that requires visits every 3 or 4 weeks for as long as 2 or 3 years. The office should have a 24-hour answering service with a dentist on call in case of emergency. If a solo dentist has been selected, he or she should provide a 24-hour telephone service and a referral arrangement with a colleague when he or she is unavailable.

How general is the general practice? A good dentist provides comprehensive basic care but is not necessarily skilled in all areas of dental practice. That is why a group practice that combines general practitioners with at least part-time specialists has the capability of providing an overall superior service. Although consultation and referral among solo dentists is not likely to be as frequent and as effective as in a group practice, it may be approximated where a number of dentists, including specialists, maintain offices in the same building. In this sense, scope of services is also an aspect of accessibility. Prospective patients should find out *what* and *when* referrals are made and *to whom* and *where*.

Is the dental staff qualified? Since all dental and dental hygiene schools in the United States and Canada are accredited, degrees from these schools assure at least adequate basic training. British, Australian, and New Zealand schools also turn out uniformly qualified dentists, but there are many other foreign dental schools that train dentists as well. Some areas of the country have a large number of foreign trained dentists who serve the enlarging immigrant populations. Dentists from unaccredited foreign schools may take short training courses in American dental schools, which help them obtain state dental licenses. The better training programs for foreign dentists require two full years of domestic study, after which the dentist is granted an accredited degree (D.D.S., D.M.D., or M.S.) in general dentistry or a specialty.

Unfortunately, dental school education has not improved over the past half-century. Instead of expanding the education and training of dentists, the profession has become increasingly specialized, even though some of the specialties are nothing more than greater proficiency in an area of restricted practice. The graduating dentist is poorly trained in treating children, extracting teeth, doing root canal treatment, making dentures and handling advanced periodontal disease. There are few post-graduate training programs such as internships and residencies for general practitioners. They must therefore *learn by doing*, by practicing in an unsupervised setting on their patients, or by limiting their own practice to the simplest procedures and referring more complex treatment to high-charging specialists.

Fortunately, dentists do not have to specialize to do complex extractions, root canals, and periodontal treatment, and handle young children and patients with physical handicaps. They can study the textbooks, expand their skills, and gain experience and become more complete general practitioners, having to refer only the most difficult cases. On the other hand, it seems that few dentists are willing to enlarge their scope of practice, having been inhibited by the specialists who have captured dental education and thus restricted the training of the general practitioner. They are also afraid of being sued for malpractice in our increasingly litigious society.

Thus, graduation from an accredited school or being licensed by the state does not guarantee that dentists are well trained or maintain high standards. How long a dentist has been practicing is also important. To have had enough experience, to have done enough extractions, root canal fillings, crowns, and dentures to become reasonably competent takes most dentists at least five years of clinical practice.

Qualifications of dental hygienists. Dental hygienists, being restricted to a narrower field of practice, are better trained in scaling and root planing than recently graduated dentists. Undergraduate training of dentists in such basic periodontal skills as root planing is generally inadequate even in accredited schools. Many dental hygiene schools have improved significantly in the last two decades with the liberalization of state laws that allow more intensive root planing and administration of local anesthetics by dental hygienists. There are now twenty-seven states that have come of age:[9]

Alaska	Kansas	Oklahoma
Arizona	Louisiana	Oregon
Arkansas	Maine	South Carolina
California	Minnesota	South Dakota
Colorado	Missouri	Utah
Hawaii	Montana	Vermont
Idaho	NebrAlaska	Washington
Illinois	Nevada	Wisconsin
Iowa	New Mexico	Wyoming

Some dental practices employ foreign-trained dentists as hygienists. Even though a dentist has managed to pass the state dental hygiene licensing examination, his or her skills as a hygienist are likely to be limited. Nevertheless, there are exceptions. Some dentists trained in unaccredited schools are not only satisfactory hygienists, they go on to become accomplished licensed dentists.

Dental assistant training. The training of dental assistants is also quite important. Many assistants are trained by their employer-dentists. Others have taken a short commercial course in dental assisting. A regular dental assistant is permitted to perform a few functions in the mouth. Dentists should not permit their assistants to take X-rays or final impressions, polish teeth, or place fillings unless they have received special training and are registered with the state dental board or licensing agency for these expanded functions. Assistants must pass a special examination in radiation safety to be allowed to take X-rays. Additional training and examination is required to become a Registered or Certified Dental Assistant (RDA/CDA); in those states that have removed prior restrictions, the RDA is permitted to polish but not scale teeth and to perform other noncomplex tasks in the mouth. Then there is the Registered Dental Assistant in Extended Functions (RDAEF), who is allowed to perform slightly more sophisticated procedures such as final impressions and application of pit and fissure sealants.[10] The reality is that these restrictions are often ignored, especially in solo practices because the licensing boards do not have the funds or manpower to enforce them.

Whether expanded functions are learned by assistants in special training courses or in the dental office is not the central issue. Competence is. Dental X-ray technique, for example, has been simplified with the use of mechanical alignment holders and can be taught easily in the dental office. The assistant may have received instruction in radiation safety, but it is the dentist who determines the frequency and number of X-rays. The assistant can know all about protecting a patient from peripheral radiation by using lead aprons and neck (thyroid) collars to cover the patient's body, but if the dentist prescribes routine bitewing X-rays every six months and full-mouth X-rays every two or three years, patients are still being overexposed.

Coronal polishing can be taught to anyone with reasonable dexterity in one day since it consists of no more than the removal of stains and soft plaque on tooth enamel with a rotating rubber cup containing a mild abrasive. Patients can do more harm to themselves with improper use of a toothbrush and dental floss. As for impressions of teeth, it is less important who does them than how well they are done. A good dentist will make sure the tasks are done properly by everyone in the office. In order to increase the odds of competency, however, it is recommended that assistants performing complex functions have completed a formal course of training and have received state registration.

Next to God—cleanliness and sterility. There is more to cleanliness in a dental office than clean floors and dust-free counters. The ambiance of the office can make one feel calm or anxious, elevated in mood or depressed. Entering a waiting room that is dark and dingy, with old, tattered magazines strewn about and shabby furniture, is hardly reassuring to a patient. Even worse is old dental equipment in equally dingy operatories. It is hard to understand why some dentists work 7 or 8 hours a day with old equipment and buy new cars every few years for a 15-minute drive to work.

Beyond the esthetics of the office, protection against transmittable diseases is the essential goal. Complete sterility cannot be obtained in a dental office environment, but the chance of inadvertent infection is minimized when some basic procedures are observed. Patients should be sure these procedures, outlined below, are followed:

- Disposable needles should be used for anesthetic injections.
- Carpules of unused anesthetic solution must be discarded, never used for another patient.
- All instruments contaminated with blood, such as scalers and root planing instruments, extraction forceps, and other surgical instruments, and most regular dental instruments should be completely sterilized in a steam, oil, or gas autoclave or a special high-temperature sterilizing oven, or they should be placed in a gluteraldehyde or other approved solution for a minimum of six hours, preferably overnight, to achieve sterilization. Sterilized instruments should be stored in packages that protect their sterility until ready for use.
- Other instruments such as mouth mirrors and explorers, if not contaminated by blood, can be sterilized in cold gluteraldehyde solution or similarly approved chemical for at least six hours, not in alcohol or a "germicide" solution.
- The handles on the dental light, the control buttons on the chair, all the switches touched by the dentist and assistant, and working surfaces

should be disinfected by swabbing with a gluteraldehyde or equivalent solution between each patient, and covered with barrier materials such plastic sleeves or aluminum foil.

- The dentist and dental assistant should wear protective gloves and face masks and eyeglasses when working on a patient.

Mercury contamination is another serious concern in dental offices, more so to office personnel than to patients who are exposed to it only episodically. Observance of small, shiny globules of mercury or silver-gray particles of leftover amalgam on cabinet tops where the amalgam is prepared or on instrument trays is a sign of sloppiness and a lack of regard for the potential toxicity of substances. It may also suggest a similar laxity in office sterilization procedures. Free mercury contamination should not be confused with bound mercury in amalgam fillings, which has been thoroughly investigated and proved safe.

Maintaining dental health—the recall system. Every dental office should have a recall system to remind patients when to return for a prophylaxis and checkup. How often you are recalled depends on your own dental health status. If you are dentally healthy and tartar forms very slowly and you rarely have new cavities, an annual prophylaxis and examination is sufficient. Minor gum problems or heavy tartar formation indicate the need for a prophylaxis at least every six months. Patients with significant periodontal disease require a good scaling every three or four months.

There is no need for routine examination by the dentist more than once a year. A conscientious hygienist examines teeth during the prophylaxis and scaling. If he or she discovers a cavity or feels that a patient requires more than a routine scaling, the dentist can be called in for a consultation.

A good recall system consists of more than a one-time reminder telephone call or postcard 6 or 12 months after initial treatment. In fact, for most people, adults and children, a 12-month recall is more than sufficient.[11] A patient who fails to respond at the 12-month recall should be reminded again at 18 months, and then again at 24 months. The 18-month recall is the most important because dental conditions such as cavities that have developed within the past year and a half can be treated before too much harm is done, but if delay is longer, advancing decay can infect the tooth nerve. Instead of a simple filling, the patient may then need root canal treatment and a crown.

Even though periodontal disease progresses slowly, too long a period between prophylaxes may lead to breakdown of the gums. Then more extensive and expensive root planing is necessary to remove the plaque and tartar deposits that have formed deep beneath the gum.

Most young children get along very well with an annual prophylaxis and examination. If a child has never had a cavity, forms little or no tartar, and has no stains on the teeth, an annual or 18-month checkup without a prophylaxis is sufficient. This frequency also holds for adults with minimal tartar and caries and no evidence of periodontal disease.

A good dental practice has an extended recall system that tailors the reminders to the patient's particular needs. Since dentists and hygienists tend to over-assess those needs, patients should not be afraid to question the frequency of recalls.

Minimizing X-rays. Patients have to protect themselves from excessive dental X-rays because the need for them is much less than usually recommended.[12] A full-mouth radiographic examination is indicated for a new adult patient who has not had a complete examination in a number of years. Otherwise, the dentist will fail to diagnose cavities, an "abscess," or periodontal disease that is not visible to the naked eye. Full-mouth X-rays should not be repeated in less than five years. If there are no special problems, if little treatment has been performed in the past that might have injured nerves, even five years is too often.

Dentists should not repeat checkup X-rays every 6 months, though many still do. Even annual bitewing X-rays are too frequent for someone past adolescence who rarely develops a cavity. Bitewing X-rays taken at the 18-month recall visit are sufficient for most adults for the simple reason that it usually takes that long for a cavity to grow so large that a filling is necessary.

Children need not be exposed to a full-mouth X-ray examination before 18 years of age unless some abnormalities are suspected.[13] Two posterior bitewing X-rays, one on either side, are sufficient at about age 4 when all the baby teeth have erupted but only if the spaces between the baby molars have closed. If the spaces are open, the dentist can see all tooth surfaces without X-rays. Children's baby teeth are "softer" than adults', and cavities can therefore develop more quickly. If the dentist suspects cavities are forming rapidly, a careful 6-month examination will reveal cavities large enough to require filling at that time. Like adults, most children need no more than an annual examination with or without a prophylaxis.

At age 18 a full-mouth X-ray series or a panographic film can be taken to review the adolescent's full dentition, including the developing third molars. However, you should avoid being pressed into hasty decisions about the wisdom teeth because at age 18 it is often too early to tell if they are likely to be impacted.

The recommended frequency for dental X-rays is based on the following guidelines:

Initial Adult

- full-mouth X-rays including 14 to 16 periapical films or a panographic film and 4 bitewing and three periapical anterior films.

Initial Child

- under 18 years of age: posterior bitewing films and periapical anterior films, if spaces between teeth are closed.
- over 18 years of age: full-mouth X-rays, as described above.

Recall

- at 12, 18, or 24 month intervals, depending on the patient's general oral condition, posterior bitewing X-rays with or without anterior periapical X-rays.
- full-mouth periapical X-rays and panographs not more than once in five to eight years in the absence of specific indications for more frequent X-rays.

As important as it is to minimize the frequency of X-rays, the quality of the X-ray should not be overlooked. The X-ray film should demonstrate a full range of contrast between black, gray, and white, the latter imaging metallic restorations. (See chapter 6 for illustrations of good dental X-ray films.) The film should not appear very dark or very light or all gray. The entire tooth should be visible in the periapical films. The crowns of the teeth should not overlap each other in bitewing films. Panograph films should also have good contrast and not be blurred. The small periapical and bitewing films should be mounted in cardboard or plastic holders for easy viewing and storage.

What to Avoid

The character of dental practice has changed from a small professional office to an aggressive business. Even ethical dentists are not immune to the pressures of making money and thus oversell their goods. Patients should always ask detailed questions to be sure work is justified by need.

Avoid twilight sleep. A much safer procedure for a highly nervous or hypersensitive patient is a mild sedative or tranquilizer a half hour before the appointment and nitrous oxide inhalation during treatment. This produces a pleasant analgesia. Few individuals need I-V sedation. It is a rare patient who does not become sufficiently tranquilized simply by a good local anesthetic injection that effectively numbs the dental nerves.

217

Avoid cosmetic dentistry, bleaching bonding. Dentists who advertise these procedures are appealing to the consumer's vanity and pocketbook. They recommend plastic and ceramic veneers, composite bonding, and porcelain crowns to smooth out the slightest irregularities in the front teeth or to cover minor discolorations. Cosmetics is part of modern dental practice, and any dentist who has kept up to date does bonding, bleaching, veneering, and other cosmetic services where there is a significant problem. Patients need a skilled general dentist who provides conservative dental health care, not one who is too intent on exploiting the desire of most people to look their best, even when looking best has little if anything to do with these high cost procedures.

Avoid the amalgam replacer. A few dentists are convinced that mercury in silver amalgam fillings poisons the body. They recommend replacement of amalgam fillings by composites, gold inlays, and porcelain crowns, citing studies of mercury vapor released from the amalgam every time a person chews. In truth, the amount of vapor released is so minute and the evidence of the safety of amalgam fillings is so overwhelming that there is no reason to be concerned.[14] Patients should avoid composite fillings on chewing surfaces of bicuspids and molars. Even though composites match natural tooth color, they are much less durable and do not seal the margins of posterior teeth as well as silver amalgam and other metallic fillings and they need to be resurfaced or replaced every few years. Dentists who advocate automatic replacement of amalgam fillings are unscientific and should be avoided.

Avoid the headache, backache, myofacial pain, and temporomandibular joint (TMJ/TMD) syndrome specialist. Many dentists attempt to cure headaches, jaw aches, and backaches with special diagnosis and treatment. They search for myofacial (muscle) pain trigger points and listen to joint movements with a stethoscope for detection of clicking and crepitus (grating) sounds. If you have no pain, treatment should be avoided. If muscle or TMJ discomfort is more than occasional, conservative treatment such as physiotherapy, avoidance of chewing gum, and avoiding excessive joint stretching movements is advisable.[15] An inexpensive soft plastic occlusal guard may also provide relief.[16] All these things should be done before a patient consents to special TMJ X-rays that are of little if any diagnostic value or to superexpensive orthotic, orthognathic, and dentocranial orthopedic appliances, most of which verge on quackery.

Special Needs Patients

More dentists are being trained to treat children and adults with behavioral, mental and physical disabilities, infants with severe dental decay, the mentally retarded including Down's Syndrome, cerebral palsy, advanced Parkinson's Disease, strokes and other crippling conditions with confinement to wheelchairs.

But the numbers are small and many areas of the country provide few dental services for people with these conditions.

Wheelchair access is, of course, essential and required by governmental agencies contracting with managed health care plans in California and other states. Therefore, many disabled patients can be treated in the dental office without any other special arrangements. Oral sedatives, tranquilizers, and muscle relaxants help to facilitate treatment, but the best sedative is still a good local anesthetic injection.

Children as young as 2 to 3 years of age with severe dental decay (Early Childhood Caries) can be sedated with oral medications and treated in the dental office by a pediatric dentist or a properly trained general practitioner. However, there is a trend for outpatient hospitalization of these infants, with administration of a general anesthetic by an anesthesiologist. Instead of costing a few hundred dollars for the fillings or extractions, the fee jumps to thousands of dollars when the child is hospitalized. Without dental insurance, the cost can be a major obstacle.

Some dentists arrange for an anesthesiologist to administer I-V sedation in their offices, which still adds about $600 to the fee but is much less costly than in a hospital. Other dentists work with oral surgeons who are qualified to administer I-V sedation in their own surgeries. In some cities there are dentists who treat special needs patients in their own dental centers that are equipped as well as a hospital outpatient facility. Any skilled general practitioner can treat the patient once I-V sedation has been administered. The key to safety is the well-trained anesthesiologist or oral surgeon administering sedation or general anesthesia in a setting that has all the equipment mandated for emergencies when things go wrong.

Finally, there is the institutionalized population, particularly the severely mentally retarded and the elderly in residential or nursing homes who are almost universally neglected. Some of these institutions arrange for dental hygienists or dentists to provide some care but, for the most part, it is few and far between. Even simple oral hygiene is neglected, although there is ample evidence that non-professional staff could be trained to teach and supervise toothbrushing.[17] Beyond that, there are few programs and little money to pay for dental care for those less fortunate than ourselves.

RECOMMENDATIONS

1. Choose a dentist that is accessible to all members of the family.
2. Do not be embarrassed about inquiring into the staff's training and experience.

3. Avoid dentists who indiscriminately replace old amalgam fillings or recommend posterior composite fillings on chewing surfaces.
4. Avoid *upgrades* and *add-ons.* Stick to basic dental care and don't be afraid to say No.
5. If extensive treatment is anticipated, comparison of basic fees charged by different dentists is relevant to the choice of dentist.
6. Choose a practice that minimizes frequency and amount of X-rays.
7. If an office appears unkempt and dingy, think elsewhere.
8. If the office staff does not respond reasonably to your *reasonable* needs, think negative alternatives.
9. Look for those dentists who practice conservative dentistry, prescribing the minimum treatment to maintain dental health.
10. To locate a dentist who caters to Special Needs patients, contact the local dental society, a dental school or a hospital with an outpatient facility equipped for dental care.

15

Financing Dental Care

FEE FOR SERVICE

About half the population of the United States has no dental insurance. They have to pay for all of their dental care "out-of-pocket." Even those with insurance are likely to have significant out-of-pocket costs. Thus, treatment is often put off until pain forces a visit to the dentist. Fear of the pain that may accompany treatment is another impediment, even among those with sufficient money to finance their own care.

Health care consumers should not be embarrassed about shopping around before embarking on extensive treatment. Many dentists will inform them over the telephone of their fees for X-rays, prophylaxis, fillings, root canal treatment, crowns, and dentures. You should also get an estimate of costs after a complete examination, recognizing that additional charges may be incurred if treatment is more extensive than anticipated. High fees do not necessarily correlate with high quality, but one should be wary of fees that are too low and particularly large-volume offices that accept whatever the insurance pays, no matter how little, as payment in full.

The following table on *Selected Dental Fees in the United States* presents average charges and the range of fees for most dental procedures. Fees vary widely from one part of the country to another and even within different parts of cities. They are usually higher in the northeastern and west coast states, and somewhat lower in the middle and southern states.

SELECTED DENTAL FEES IN THE UNITED STATES

ADA Code[1] and Procedure	Avg. Fee ($)[2]	Range($)[3]
DIAGNOSTIC		
0150 Comprehensive oral examination	50	0-80
0120 Periodic oral exam	30	0-45
0210 Complete X-ray series, including bitewings; may include examination fee.	65	45-95
0220 Single X-ray film	12	8-20
0230 Each additional X-ray film	8	5-15
0270 Bitewings-2 films	25	20-40
0274 Bitewings-4 films	35	25-45
0330 Panoramic film	45	30-90
0350 Orthodontic survey, including photographs	90	75-125
0470 Diagnostic casts (study models)	40	25-85
PREVENTIVE		
1110 Prophylaxis, adult	55	35-70
1120 Prophylaxis, child	30	25-50
1201 Topical fluoride (includes prophylaxis)	45	35-70
1351 Sealant, per tooth	20	15-45
SPACE MAINTAINER		
1510 Fixed, unilateral	145	95-300
1515 Fixed, bilateral	195	150-350
1525 Removable, bilateral	195	150-350
RESTORATIVE (FILLINGS)		
2110 Amalgam, 1-surface, primary tooth	40	30-75
2120 Amalgam, 2-surfaces, primary	50	35-100
2130 Amalgam, 3-surfaces, primary	60	45-125
2131 Amalgam, 4-surfaces, primary	60	50-150
2140 Amalgam, 1-surface, permanent tooth	65	35-90
2150 Amalgam, 2-surfaces, permanent	75	45-125
2160 Amalgam, 3-surfaces, permanent	85	55-145
2161 Amalgam, 4-surfaces, permanent	95	65-175
2330 Composite, 1-surface	70	45-120
2331 Composite, 2-surfaces	85	55-130
2332 Composite, 3-surfaces	90	70-175
INLAY/ONLAY		
2520/2542 Gold inlay/onlay, 2-surface	400	275-600
2530/2543 Gold inlay/onlay, 3-surface	475	300-675
2620/2642 Porcelain-ceramic, 2-surfaces	495	350-750
2630/2643 Porcelain-ceramic, 3-surfaces	550	450-800

SELECTED DENTAL FEES IN THE UNITED STATES

(continued)

ADA Code[1] and Procedure		*Avg. Fee ($)[2]*	Range($)[3]
CROWNS			
2710	Plastic (laboratory processed)	250	195-500
275	Porcelain with noble metal	475	350-850
2790	Full gold crown, noble metal	475	350-850
2810	3/4 gold crown, high noble metal	425	325-700
	(Base metals cost $50-75 less.)		
2830	Stainless steel crown, primary tooth	125	65-200
2892	Prefabricated post and core	95	75-210
2932	Plastic, prefabricated	90	65-250
2950	Crown buildup	90	65-175
2960	Labial resin veneer, chairside	225	175-450
2961	Labial resin veneer, laboratory	295	195-600
2962	Labial porcelain veneer, laboratory	450	300-750
ENDODONTICS (ROOT CANAL THERAPY)			
3110	Pulp cap	25	15-60
3220	Pulpotomy	85	50-125
3310	Anterior tooth, 1 root canal	275	200-500
3320	Bicuspid, 1-2 root canals	350	250-600
3330	Molar, 3-4 root canals	450	350-950
3410	Apicoectomy, anterior, separate procedure	275	225-460
3430	Retrograde filling, per root	95	40-250
3450	Root amputation	175	125-250
3920	Hemisection	175	125-375
PERIODONTICS			
4210	Gingivectomy, per quadrant	250	175-450
4211	Gingivectomy, per tooth	125	95-225
4260	Osseous surgery, per quadrant	550	450-1200
4340	Periodontal root planing, full mouth	460	300-900
4341	Periodontal root planing, per quadrant	150	95-225
4360/9940	Periodontal occlusal (night) guard	195	150-500
4910	Periodontal prophylaxis	95	60-125
FULL AND PARTIAL DENTURES			
5110/5120	Upper/lower denture, each	600	350-1200
5211/5212	Partial upper/lower, each, acrylic plastic	325	225-600
5213/5214	Partial upper/lower, each, chrome base	675	400-1200
5730/5731	Upper/lower denture reline (chairside)	175	95-275
5740/5741	Upper/lower partial reline (chairside)	200	125-350
5750/5751	Upper/lower denture reline (laboratory)	250	200-375

SELECTED DENTAL FEES IN THE UNITED STATES
(continued)

ADA Code[1] and Procedure		Avg. Fee ($)[2]	Range($)[3]
5760/5761	Upper/lower partial reline (laboratory)	250	200-375
5820	Temporary plastic stayplate	225	150-375
FIXED BRIDGES			
6240	Porcelain with noble metal pontic	475	350-850
6750	Porcelain with noble metal abutment crown	475	350-850
6790	Full crown abutment with noble metal (Base metals cost $50-75 less.)	475	350-850
ORAL SURGERY			
7110	Routine extraction	75	60-125
7210	Surgical extraction, erupted tooth	125	95-225
7220	Soft tissue impaction	150	95-225
7230	Partial bony impaction	195	125-300
7240	Full bony impaction	250	175-375
ORTHODONTICS			
	Full dentition, fixed bands, *2* years	3000	2500-4800
	Retainer (each)	125	95-175
MISCELLANEOUS			
9110	Palliative (emergency) treatment	45	0-90
9220	General anesthesia in dental office	175	125-250
9230	Analgesia (nitrous oxide)	45	0-95
9310	Specialist consultation	45	0-125
9972	Teeth whitening (bleaching), both arches	350	200-800

[1] American Dental Association. "Current Dental Terminology (CDT-3)," version 2000.

[2] A year 2000 estimate based on a number of fee schedules and surveys of fees that are subject to the biases of sampling and exaggerations, which dentists frequently list on dental insurance claims.

[3] The high side of the range represents fees charged by a minority of practitioners in high-cost areas. A few dentists charge even higher fees.

Prioritizing Treatment

Most dental treatment is elective, which means that it can be done at the convenience of the patient and the doctor. A good dentist prioritizes treatment. He or she explains the procedures that should be done at once to prevent further deterioration of the teeth and gums and those procedures that can be phased in over time.

DENTAL CARE PRIORITY SYSTEM

I. VERY URGENT-FUNCTIONAL AND SOCIAL DISABILITY
    Pain and acute infection
    Suspected cancer
    Caries (decay) into or near the pulp
    Teeth requiring extraction
    Disfiguring conditions-missing or badly decayed anterior teeth
II. MODERATELY URGENT (those conditions requiring care in the near future)
    Chronic or subacute periodontal (pyorrhea) conditions
    Heavy calculus (tartar) deposits
    Extensive penetration of caries (decay) into dentin
    Sufficient missing posterior teeth to require replacement—fewer than eight opposing posterior teeth present
    Space maintenance for children
    Replacement of ill-fitting prosthetic appliances
III. NONURGENT (those conditions requiring care, but postponable for a period of time)
    Periodontal surgery
    Beginning caries (decay)
    Replacement of missing teeth where fewer than required for Class I or Class II priorities
    Inlays or crowns on teeth previously restored with large amalgams, composites, or stainless steel crowns
IV. MAINTENANCE (no special conditions requiring remedial treatment)
    Patients placed on routine prophylaxis and recall care

Adapted from *Group Practice and the Future of Dental Care* by Charles R. Jerge, W. E. Marshall, Max H. Schoen, and Jay W. Friedman. Philadelphia: Lea & Febiger, 1974.

Budget Payments

Both patients and dentists prefer to have treatment completed as quickly as possible, the former to "get it over with," the latter to maximize their incomes. To expedite the process, dentists usually will work out a budget plan that allows patients to proceed directly with treatment. A substantial down payment may be required, perhaps a third of the cost of expensive treatment such as crowns and bridges. The down payment will more than cover the dentist's out-of-pocket laboratory expenses. There is a trend toward credit card financing of dental care. While convenient, it is also very costly. Credit card interest charges are high, often 17 percent or more. It makes more sense to pay as you go unless an interest-free payment plan can be arranged directly with the dental office.

Dental Insurance a Fringe Benefit of Employment

By the year 2000, the average annual expenditure per person for dental services exceeded $200, with a total expenditure for the 281.4 million population at about $60 billion.[1] The number of persons with some type of dental insurance has steadily increased to 52 percent, still leaving about 135 million with no dental coverage whatsoever.

But what does insurance actually do? Dental insurance pays for about half of total expenditures for dental care. Those with insurance save from 50 to 100 percent of out-of-pocket cost, depending on the quality of their insurance and the type of treatment. Commercial insurance companies account for 70 percent of the dentally insured population, with the remainder insured by Blue Cross/Blue Shield, dental service corporations sponsored by state dental associations (Delta Dental Plans), union welfare fund plans, and HMOs.

If your employer does not offer a dental plan, you may be able to purchase dental insurance on the open market, but it will have limited benefits and significant copayments for most services. Thus, it is more likely to be a discount plan rather than true insurance. Individuals looking for dental insurance usually need immediate and extensive treatment. Insurance companies would rather have a group to insure, which spreads the risk among everyone regardless of immediate need. After all, a fire insurance company would not last long if it insured only houses on fire. Therefore, dental insurance is usually available only as part of a fringe benefit package offered by an employer to all employees, but not always covering all members of the family.

As an alternative, reduced fee-for-service plans are offered in some of the larger metropolitan areas. To qualify, a small membership fee is charged, $4 to $6 per month, which then allows the family members to receive care at reduced fees from the participating panel of dentists. These plans are attractive on the surface, but there is an inherent risk of patients being sold a bill of goods, what the dental trade calls *add-ons and upgrades.* It is not uncommon for the dentist to employ a dental assistant as a "treatment counselor" who advises patients to get the better white fillings in their back teeth instead of those dirty old amalgams at an additional charge of $85 to $175 per filling. You may be told that in addition to a cleaning you need subgingival scaling at an extra charge of $60 per quadrant or $240 for the whole mouth. Then, to get rid of those nasty bacteria, you need a gum irrigation treatment that costs another $60, consisting of an assistant squirting a useless bactericidal solution on your gums. Instead of saving money, you may have paid hundreds of dollars more than would have been charged by an ethical dentist. But even ethical dentists are not immune to the glittering lure of *add-ons* and *up-grades*, and you, the patient, can only protect yourself by sticking to the basic benefits of the dental plan.

Utilization

Estimates of the population over age 2 that has at least one visit to the dentist annually ranges from a low of 43 percent to a high of 65 percent.[2] The low figure suggests there has been no increase since the 1950s, whereas the high figure may be overly optimistic. Surely there has been an increase in utilization resulting from dental insurance as well as the public's greater awareness of the value of dental care. The average of these two figures, 54 percent, more likely represents annual utilization. But averages blur important variations. For example, nearly two-thirds of the white population and those with higher education and dental insurance have at least one annual dental visit, compared to one-third of Afro-American and Hispanic populations with less than 12 years of school.

The problem with an annual utilization rate is that it may represent, more or less, the same people every year. Left out in the cold is the other half of the population at risk of deteriorating dental health because of lack of surplus income to cover the cost, the lack of dental insurance, the fear of pain, and ignorance of the consequences of dental neglect.

A surprising 72 percent of the population age 5 to 17 reportedly visits the dentist annually. This figure drops dramatically to 43 percent for those over 65 years of age, many of whom have lost all their teeth but should still have check-ups for early detection of cancer.[3] The high utilization by children and adolescents may be somewhat excessive in light of the significant decrease in dental decay.[4] Not everyone needs to see a dentist or dental hygienist once a year. Children and adults who rarely develop cavities and form calculus very slowly need only 18-24 month check-ups.

Many people with significant dental disease continue to neglect their mouths even with dental insurance coverage. High deductibles, low annual limitations, and multiple copayments may require too much out-of-pocket cost for the average family with extensive and expensive dental treatment needs. Without insurance, the poor, the marginally well off, the elderly with minimal financial support and limited transportation, and the institutionalized populations are as neglected as ever.

Types of Insurance

Insurance is usually classified as governmental and private. Government-sponsored dental insurance is totally inadequate. It is usually restricted to welfare recipients and limited in coverage to the bare essentials of treatment. Many dentists refuse to participate in governmental programs because of their typically low fees.

Dental insurance is sold to employers by commercial insurance companies such as Aetna, Cigna and Prudential, by dental association sponsored Delta Dental Plans, and by Blue Cross/Blue Shield companies. Many union welfare benefit trust funds self-fund their dental plans for their members. Commercial insurance is characterized as for-profit, whereas the self-insured union plans are nonprofit. In the nonprofit plans, money not spent or money saved by good administration of quality assurance and cost containment policies remains within the fund where it may be used to improve benefits for members. With commercial insurance, money not spent for dental care becomes part of corporate profits.

Indemnity insurance. By definition, indemnity insurance indemnifies or repays the beneficiary for all or part of the cost of dental treatment. In practice, the payment is usually made directly to the dentist, with the patient required to pay an additional sum, a copayment, for most services.

Indemnity plans allow free choice of dentists. Insurance payments are based either on the Usual, Customary, and Reasonable (UCR) fees charged by dentists in the same geographic region or on a fixed fee schedule—a Table of Allowances (TOA).

If the insurance pays on the basis of a set fee or TOA, the dentist does not have to charge the patient additionally, but can accept the allowance as payment in full. A union may refer its members to dentists who accept the TOA, but most dentists do not, and patients are charged the difference between the TOA and the UCR fee. But if the TOA is high enough, you can try to find a dentist who will accept it.

In the end, there is little difference between the two systems. They are both inflationary. The fees doctors list on their fee schedules or claims statements, not necessarily the fees charged patients, are put into the computers. The insurance company usually pegs its payments to the ninetieth percentile of listed fees, which means that 90 percent of the doctors charge that amount or less. Since doctors do not know what the ninetieth percentile or top payment level is, they constantly test the system by submitting higher fees to be assured they are paid the maximum UCR benefit. Many commercial carriers pass out money to providers on demand, within contractual limitations and exclusions, without reviewing the necessity for treatment or the reasonableness of charges. When payments exceed premiums or profits are too small, premiums are increased.

Thus, UCR fees rise higher and higher, patient copayments keep increasing and insurance premiums are increased to maintain profits.

The Table of Allowances system follows a similar pattern. Some plans set their TOA at 70 or 80 percent of UCR fees, increasing the payments each year to conform to computer-inflated dental fees.

Some of the biggest insurance companies do not even bother to limit payments to the ninetieth percentile, doling out whatever dentists charge, subject to deductibles and annual limits. Payments of close to $200 for examination and X-rays have been made to the same dentist who charges $65 to uninsured patients. Insurance pays 50 percent of a $700 fee ($350) for a crown and the patient pays the other $350 to the same dentist who charges a noninsured patient a total of $450. Common logic would dictate that insurance companies try to limit payments to maximize profits, but insurance companies are in the money-handling business. If they pay out more, they can charge higher premiums. Some insurance companies or administrators are paid a percentage of money handled, passing additional costs on to the employers and patients. Thus, the more they pay out, the more they make; hardly an incentive to control costs.

As insurance companies allow the payment to dentists to creep up, the patient's share also creeps up. After all, the logic goes, if the insurance company is willing to raise the UCR fee from $200 to $250 for a service reimbursed at 50 percent, who are the consumers to argue that their own share should not go up an additional $25? In effect, the amount the patient pays is changed without any consultation, with no one to represent and protect the consumer.

Most indemnity programs pay 80 percent of the UCR fee, except for bridges and dentures, which are paid at 50 percent. Many plans pay 100 percent of preventive services (examination, X-rays, and prophylaxes), with or without an initial deductible in the range of $50 to $100. (See the table below.)

Whether dentists accept plan payments as payment in full or make an additional charge to patients, the net effect of insurance is to significantly increase dentists' earnings. Private dental insurance now accounts for nearly 50 percent of gross dental practice income.[5]

Copayments. It is often stated that if something is "free," you don't appreciate its true value. Yet, there is hardly a doctor who does not accept free samples, free trips, free gifts, and free treatment from his colleagues. To suggest that patients likewise do not appreciate free health care is to deny the obvious demand for and success of prepaid health plans. Requiring patients to pay for part of the cost out-of-pocket has nothing to do with appreciation and everything to do with underfinancing of health care.

Patient copayments obviously lower the cost of dental insurance, reducing the employer's contribution by shifting 20 to 50 percent of the cost to the consumer. Without copayments and plan limitations, dentists would do anything and everything they could to enlarge their incomes. Copayments therefore inhibit unnecessary utilization. But they should not be imposed on treatment necessary to maintain dental health and function.

If the insurance payment, the percent of UCR, is high enough, many doctors waive the copayments. Though illegal, this widespread practice eliminates the deterrence of copayments and encourages excessive treatment.

Preauthorization. Processing of insurance claims can be an administrative headache for the dental office. Preauthorization of benefits should be obtained for extensive and/or expensive work such as crowns and bridges so that everyone knows in advance what will be paid. Thus, forms must be submitted twice: first, to determine eligibility and the amount of the benefit payment; second, to receive payment after completion of treatment. Even if preauthorization is not required, it is advisable. **Preauthorization**—also called **predetermination of benefits**—avoids misunderstandings that can be extremely costly to the patient in the event what was thought to be covered turns out not to be or to be covered to a much lesser extent.

The volume of paperwork may require the dentist to hire a special insurance clerk who does nothing but process forms. Some dentists charge a nominal amount for filing insurance forms, but most absorb the cost, complaining nonetheless. Such complaints ignore the tradeoff of decreased collection costs, a higher percentage of fees collected, and the overall increase in their net income that are the direct consequences of the proliferation of dental insurance.

Direct reimbursement. The dental associations would like to eliminate preauthorization and the risk of review and limitation of benefits by insurance companies. They have been promoting, with little success, a system of **direct reimbursement**, in which the employee pays the dental bill and then is reimbursed directly by the employer for whatever was covered. Good for the dentist since it would eliminate what he or she considers to be third party or insurance company control, but not so good for the consumer on limited income who would have to lay out all the money in advance with no assurance that all or most of it would be reimbursed.

SELECTED FEATURES OF INDEMNITY AND CAPITATION PLANS [*]

	Indemnity[†]	*Capitation*
Choice of dentist	No restrictions	Panel dentists
Annual deductible	$25-50 per person	No deductible
Maximum benefit per year	$750-1500	No limitation
	Patient Pays *20% of UCR* ($)	*Patient Pays* *Copayment* ($)
Procedure		
Examination	0	0
X-rays	0	0
Prophylaxis (2 per year)	0	0
Filling	10-30	0-10
Extractions (simple)	15-25	0-10
Root canal therapy		
Anterior - 1 root	40-100	0-45
Bicuspid - 2 roots	50-120	0-90
Molar - 3 roots	70-150	0-135
Periodontal root planing, per quadrant	20-45	0-35
Periodontal surgery, per quadrant	90-240	50-250
	50% UCR	
Fixed bridge, per tooth	175-425	50-325
Partial denture	200-600	75-325
Full denture	175-600	75-400
Orthodontics	1200-2500	500-2500

*Refer to the table on <u>Selected Dental Fees in the United States</u> at the beginning of this chapter for average fees charged. Some capitation plans exclude fixed bridges if large numbers of teeth are missing. Specialty services, most commonly orthodontics, may also be excluded.

†Some indemnity plans waive the deductible charge for examination, X-rays, and prophylaxis, paying benefits for these services at 100 percent of UCR fees.

IRRESPONSIBILITY OF INDEMNITY INSURANCE

The principles of **quality assurance** and **cost containment** have been reduced to pious platitudes printed in the indemnity plan brochures. "We screen our dentists to assure quality of care," they say, while accepting any dentist willing to be listed on their panel. "We limit out-of-pocket payments and assure reasonable costs," they write in bold print while encouraging dentists to increase their incomes by *upgrades* and *add-ons*. Truth in promotional materials is honored essentially in the breach. [These criticisms apply not only to indemnity insurance but also to managed care plans that accept any dentist on their panels and have so many copayments they resemble indemnity insurance. These managed care plans also encourage *upgrades* and *add-ons* to compensate for the low capitation payments to dentists.]

The problems with dental insurance are political as much as economic. Everyone understands a program limitation such as maximum benefits or dollars covered each year or per lifetime. Everyone recognizes that some services may be paid at 80 percent, others at 50 percent, some even at 100 percent. But few insurance companies are willing to risk the wrath of the dentists by denying payment for FUN (functionally unnecessary) treatment. Virtually none are willing to protect the consumer from the cheating and overcharging and poor quality of treatment, which would anger the dental profession even more. The failure of indemnity insurance to control costs and protect the consumer has been a major impetus for the expansion of HMOs and managed health care plans. Unfortunately, many of these plans utilize the same dentists who are abusing indemnity insurance, so that little is changed.

Predetermination of Benefits-Indirect Review

Predetermination is not necessary for routine examination, prophylaxis and minor treatment. But it is strongly advisable where extensive and/or expensive treatment is contemplated. Failure to preauthorize treatment does not mean that insurance payment will be denied. The insurance company will cover its part of the cost for necessary treatment whether or not it has been authorized. But some treatment such as crowns on teeth that can be filled or bridges on sound teeth may not be covered and the consumer needs to know in advance in order to make an informed decision as to whether or not to proceed.

Except for emergency care, which does not require predetermination, treatment can be scheduled after authorization of covered benefits at the convenience of the patient and the dentist, since it makes little difference when a filling, a crown or a bridge is done. Unless there is acute pain or infection, root canal treatment or periodontal therapy can also be phased in at a later date. Dentists do not have to wait for preauthorization to provide immediate palliative treatment, which can include a temporary filling or the first stage of root canal treatment that gets rid of the infection and eliminates the pain.

Once the patient is examined, the dentist submits a treatment plan to the insurance company, which lists all the procedures to be performed. The dentist documents the need for treatment by including diagnostic X-rays and, if appropriate, periodontal pocket measurements. Sometimes study models (plaster casts of the teeth) and photographs are submitted to document conditions not evident in X-rays. This information helps an experienced dental consultant approve necessary treatment and prevent obvious FUN treatment. This type of indirect review is 80 to 90 percent accurate, quite good by any standard.[6] The accuracy would likely be no higher if different dentists were to perform a clinical examination on the same patient, since dentists do not always agree on what is necessary treatment. Occasionally, a clinical examination is requested by the dental plan's consultant to obtain another opinion, but usually the indirect review is sufficient to determine benefits.

Quality Assurance—a Second Opinion

On the surface, predetermination of benefits by means of indirect review may seem like pure cost containment, a way to increase the profits of the insurance company. To be sure, the savings are extraordinary, amounting to $5,000 or $6,000 or more per consultant hour, since doctors are notorious for overtreating patients. Over the course of a year, millions of dollars are saved by this process. But from a wider consumer advocate viewpoint, the purpose is to protect the patient from FUN treatment that not only squanders funds and increases costs but can also be injurious and life-threatening.

The indirect review provides an automatic second opinion for the patient, which should be viewed as quality assurance as well as cost containment. The initial review may be done by a dentist or a trained dental assistant working under the supervision of a dentist who is responsible for the final decisions. A good reviewer can pick up missed cavities, "abscesses," and other conditions that have been overlooked by an attending dentist. More often, however, treatment will not be authorized for filling of nonexistent cavities, placement of crowns on teeth that can be easily filled, replacement of missing teeth with fixed bridges in the absence of a functional problem, gum treatments in the absence of gum disease, and extraction of sound teeth. Payment should also be denied for the one-third of X-rays that are of such poor diagnostic quality that they benefit only the dentist who is paid for them.

The fact that a service is listed as a covered benefit does not justify *carte blanche* authorization. Extractions may be a covered benefit, but the removal of sound teeth, sometimes at the insistence of a patient who does not fully understand the consequences, represents mutilating dental surgery. Unfortunately, limitation of program benefits to necessary and essential treatment does not limit a practitioner if the patient is willing and able to pay for additional services.

Despite abuses, nearly three-fourths of all treatment plans are authorized without change by reviewers because they are diagnostically accurate and rational. The review system then seems a positive measure.

Right of Appeal

All insurance plans have an appeals process. Yet even when benefits are denied for crowns, bridges, or periodontal treatment, relatively few appeals are made by dentists or patients, whether out of tacit admission that the treatment prescribed was not necessary or resignation and frustration with the system. The dentist may then try to convince the patient to pay himself. Recognizing that the attending dentist has the advantage of having physically examined the patient, a difference of opinion between the dentist and the reviewer should not be ignored. Denials are often reversed when the dentist submits additional information to support his diagnosis, which may include detailed description of the condition, study models, photographs, and X-rays of the teeth in question.

Whenever extensive and expensive treatment is contemplated, the dentist should submit for predetermination of benefits so that everyone knows beforehand what will be covered, what will not, and what the patient's share of the cost will be. If there is a significant difference of opinion, a clinical examination by an independent dentist, agreed upon by all parties, should be requested. Although the necessity for some treatment, even after it is done, can be determined beyond doubt with the additional documentation described above, a successful appeal is best assured when the pretreatment conditions of the mouth have not been altered.

Post-treatment Review—Another Type of Second Opinion

Let us assume that you are satisfied with the treatment that has just been completed. Your mouth feels comfortable, the sensitivity to hot and cold of some of the treated teeth has disappeared, and you are pleased enough to recommend your dentist to friends. Does that mean you have received good dental treatment? Most likely yes, but not always.

There is no reason to believe something is wrong unless you are experiencing discomfort. But installed crowns often have defective margins, which are filled with cement when they are put in place so that the teeth are not sensitive. As far as you know, everything is all right. As the cement dissolves, decay begins. If you are lucky, the tooth will become sensitive to hot and cold liquids or sweets or toothbrushing, and you will have it examined. Quite often nothing is felt even as the decay endangers the nerve. Years may pass before the "cavity" is discovered or the tooth begins to ache. By then, you will be blamed for neglecting your teeth, eating sweets, failing to brush and floss properly, and for being neurotic because you suspect (How could you?) your dentist did poor work.

Poor work should be detected at the next dental examination or by a dental hygienist during a prophylaxis. The problem is that the dentist who did the poor work may not detect the defects or may prefer to overlook them. The dental hygienist is the employee of the dentist and is not likely to risk his or her job to protect the patient. This is a difficult problem for dental hygienists employed by dentists who neglect periodontal disease or consistently do substandard crowns and bridges.

Poor treatment may be detected when a dentist submits a new treatment plan to the insurance company. New X-rays will be sent in that provide a "post-treatment" picture of previous fillings, crowns, fixed bridges and root canal therapy. Major defects show up in these X-rays. Even if ignored by the dentist who performed the poor treatment, the defects will be seen by the insurance consultant. One problem is connecting the defects to the dentist. Unless payments made for prior treatment is stored in a computer file, the consultant cannot readily identify the responsible dentist. Another problem is the reluctance of dental consultants to criticize other dentists. They are too willing to accept excuses such as "it was a difficult case" or "the patient was uncooperative," which might be true, but does not excuse deficient and negligent treatment.

A patient is not likely to be informed by a dental plan that he or she received negligent treatment. However, denial of insurance benefits for replacement of *multiple* fillings within two years or for replacement of a crown or bridge within five years due to open margins can be taken as confirmation that the original treatment was deficient.

Prepayment, Capitation, Health Maintenance Organizations, Managed Health Care

Indemnity insurance allows the patient to select any doctor, giving it a major advantage over capitation plans, which limit choice to panels or their own group practices. As long as there were few complaints about poor indemnity coverage or high out-of-pocket payments, as long as everyone was willing to go along with annual increases in premiums, there was little incentive to consider alternative dental care delivery systems. Sooner or later the cycle of increased costs and increased premiums had to be broken either by sharply curtailing benefits or by turning toward capitation or managed health care plans.

Prepaid health plans are thus referred to as an alternative health care delivery system. The term *Health Maintenance Organization* (HMO) was coined in the *1970s.*[7] The latest euphemism is *managed health care.* The plans are based on monthly payments to panel doctors for each plan member, called capitation, instead of fees for services rendered. Some dental plans collect capitation payments from the employers and pay the participating dentists discounted fees. The problem with this arrangement is that the dentists are still paid by fee-for-service, which rewards FUN treatment.

Dentistry was a relative latecomer to organized health care systems. Like medical associations, the dental associations resisted dental insurance as the first step toward "socialized dentistry."[8] They also opposed group dental practices associated with the early prepaid medical plans.

Except for a few programs designed for children and a few large medical HMOs with dental facilities, capitation dental plans were few and far between until the early 1970s. While indemnity dental insurance grew rapidly, covering over 90 million by 1997, prepaid dental HMO and PPO plans have grown even more rapidly in the past ten years, now numbering over 50 million members.[9]

Managed Health Care

Shifting the Risk. The basic principles of prepayment or capitation have always been to finance health care in advance and to inhibit FUN treatment, thereby reducing costs. The doctor receives a fixed monthly income and assumes the financial risk for the provision of care. Doing more than is necessary costs time and money and reduces profits. The idea is to maintain health rather than simply treat disease, hence the term *Health Maintenance Organization* (HMO). The hope is that serious illnesses and their consequences, and the overall cost of care, can be reduced by preventive or early remedial care. This is just the opposite of fee-for-service indemnity insurance, which rewards overtreatment and facilitates overcharging.

Having failed for want of trying to control indemnity costs, the big insurance companies have jumped on the "managed health care" bandwagon, with the result that half the population with health insurance is now enrolled in these types of commercial plans.

As noted, the insurance company contracts with dentists who agree to accept a fixed monthly payment for each subscriber. They also agree to a set of patient copayments for treatment not covered 100 percent by the capitation payment. Then the dental plan is sold to the employer who is guaranteed a fixed monthly cost for each employee, which not only includes the amount that will be paid to the dentist but also the insurance company's administrative costs, broker fees, and the company's profit. The employer-purchaser saves 30 to 40 percent of the cost of indemnity insurance. Small wonder, then, that employers have joined with insurance companies to promote managed health care plans. They are the major beneficiaries.

Excessive copayments. Savings to employers does not necessarily mean a reduction in the overall cost of health care. What is not covered by capitation is paid by consumers. Some managed dental plans have so many copayments that they resemble "limited indemnity" rather than prepayment. Dentists, recognizing they are also caught in this economic squeeze, protect themselves by minimizing nonchargeable services such as prophylaxis for which there are no copayments, and maximizing those services that require patient copayments, as well as promoting add-ons and upgrades.

Advantages lost. Most dentists view capitation as a subversion of the fee-for-service system for which their world was designed. Many join the plans out of resignation, fearing that if they do not, other dentists will, and they will be left out in the cold. Even those dentists who support the ideals of capitation have come to question the takeover by commercial insurance companies. They fear that many insurance companies reduce dentists' monthly capitation income and increase the number and size of copayments so that the presumed advantages of capitation to the dentist—steady income and fewer collection problems—will be lost.

Many dentists in capitation plan networks limit the number of early morning or late afternoon prime-time hours for plan patients. Just as dentists have to protect themselves from exploitation by commercial insurance plans, patients must protect their interests by insisting on timely and appropriate care.

Indemnity or capitation—which plan to choose?

Until recently, few employees had a choice since only indemnity dental insurance was offered. With the growth of managed health care plans and HMOs, two or more plans may be available. There is no one best plan for everyone. Among the major factors to consider are disposable income, that is, the amount of money a family can afford to spend out-of-pocket, the relationship with the family's present dentist, if any, and access to other plan dentists.

Costs Versus Choice

Capitation plans costs less but restrict choice of dentists. An indemnity plan allows a family to choose different dentists, perhaps one for the children, another for the plan member, and a third for his or her spouse. Unless the indemnity plan is unusually *rich* and has minimal or no deductibles or annual limits and pays a high percentage of the more expensive fees, out-of-pocket costs will be significantly greater. (See the table below.)

If what you have to pay out-of-pocket is the decisive factor, a capitation or managed health care plan that has minimal copayments should be selected. If free choice of dentist is more important, indemnity insurance may be better for you. Should the initial selection prove unsatisfactory, the alternative plan can be selected at the next annual reenrollment period. Transfers within the year may be allowed for special problems, and some plans allow transfers at any time with no restrictions. A few capitation plans permit different members of a family to choose different dentists on the capitation panel.

Exclusions and Limitations

The better capitation plans have fewer and lower copayments and less restrictive exclusions and limitations. (See preceding table on *Selected Features Of Indemnity And Capitation Plans*.) Both types of plans exclude cosmetic services such as crowns (caps) and veneer facings on the front teeth that have no other purpose than to improve appearance. Temporomandibular joint (TMJ) therapy, hospitalization for dental treatment, implants placed in the jawbones to support bridges and dentures, "full mouth rehabilitation," including crowns on all teeth worn down by attrition, are also common exclusions. If there is need for a lot of expensive treatment such as crowns and bridges, indemnity insurance that has an annual maximum benefit limitation of $750 to $1,000 will be unsatisfactory.

Indemnity insurance usually has a lifetime benefit for orthodontic treatment, but this is not too significant since few people undergo straightening of teeth more than once. If orthodontic treatment is anticipated, capitation plans usually cost less, but choice will be restricted to a panel orthodontist.

The Myth of Quality Assurance and Cost Containment

It has already been pointed out that managed care plans accept almost "any willing provider" on their panels. One of the reasons is that the governmental regulatory agencies, often the state department of health or a specific managed health care department, insist on wide geographical access. The standard for access is a primary care doctor within a 15 minute drive or, for specialists, a 30 minute drive. Initial appointments for routine examinations should be available within 3 to 4 weeks, follow-up appointments within two weeks. Ideally, you should not have to wait more than 30 minutes to be seen after arrival for your appointment, but don't count on it.

These are good but not necessarily realistic standards because of the bourgeoning populations and an increasing shortage of dentists. Not a problem in Beverly Hills or downtown New York City where there may be an oversupply of dentists. But in the newer concentrated immigration population centers as well as the older "ghetto" areas of the larger cities there are likely to be too few dentists, at least some of whom may not practice to the desired standard. In the more sparsely settled areas, dentists are also in small supply. To comply with the standards set forth by the regulatory agencies, these plans have no choice but to accept any dentist willing to join their panels.

Indemnity insurance plans are not bound by these standards. Patients can go to any dentist they choose where they are likely to be given priority over the capitated managed care patient. It is not unusual for someone with indemnity insurance to be given prime time appointments on the same day or within a few days, whereas the capitated patient will be put off for weeks. Economically this makes sense for the dentists, but what does it say of their ethics?

Are a 15 minute drive and a maximum 30 minute waiting room wait realistic? People will drive longer to have dinner out or to see a movie. They will stand in line longer without complaining to buy a ticket to the theater or a sports arena. They tie up half a day waiting at home for a serviceman to repair a washing machine. Non-emergencies, to be sure, but so are most doctor appointments. This is not an argument for longer drives or waiting time but rather for recognition that imposition of unrealistic standards raises unrealistic expectations without resolving the problem of poor distribution and shortages of health care providers.

Thus, the claim that quality is assured by careful selection of "quality dentists" is a myth. The plans look for at least average quality dental offices to participate, provided they can be found. If not, they accept what is found—any willing provider—giving lip service to improving the substandard dental practices that round out their networks.

The offices in the managed health care networks are reviewed every year or two by dental auditors to assure that adequate standards are being maintained. Most of the deficiencies have to do with record keeping, seldom with the quality of treatment. Negative reports are more likely to be ignored after promises of correction. The process resembles a ritual intended to give the appearance of quality assurance without really improving the quality of care.

Malpractice Insurance

Most dentists carry professional liability insurance to protect themselves against legal suits brought by patients who believe they have been injured or have received poor quality treatment.

What should you do when convinced you have been the recipient of defective treatment?

First have a frank discussion with your dentist. Perhaps the dentist was the one to point out the deficiencies and will probably volunteer to redo the work at no charge. Everyone makes mistakes, and the dentist who recognizes it and is willing to make necessary corrections deserves the patient's confidence. But if you have lost confidence and do not want to return for retreatment, you should request a refund to pay another dentist for the corrections. A responsible dentist will cooperate.

Or, you may request the assistance of the local dental society, most of which have a peer review committee to mediate such problems. Dentist-members of the peer review committee will perform the examination or arrange an independent examination. If treatment is found faulty, they will recommend that the original dentist refund an appropriate amount. The dentist who is not a member of the dental society, however, is not bound by the decisions of the peer review committee.

You may also consider taking your case to Small Claims Court if you think you can prove you have been overcharged or have received shoddy treatment. You do not need an attorney to plead your case here, but you do need clear evidence that you have been wronged.

If you suspect that extensive treatment must be redone because the dentist was negligent or incompetent or if you were injured in the process, consultation with an attorney may be appropriate.

Finding a dentist willing to testify as an "expert witness" on behalf of an injured patient can be difficult. Most dentists—and physicians—are reluctant to testify against a colleague. Nevertheless, if the case is well founded, if significant harm has been done, competent experts can be found. It is in the interest of the profession as well as the general public to expose and punish incompetent dentists.

One of the most frequent malpractice complaints stems from failure of dentists to inform, much less to treat, long-term patients with advanced periodontal disease. Other cases involve poor root canal fillings, injury such as paresthesia (permanent numbness of the lip or tongue) following removal of wisdom teeth, and improper treatment of infections and postsurgical complications. Although there is a large amount of defective crown and bridgework, it is not surprising more cases do not derive from this source because the amount of recovery is usually too small for the case to be taken on by an attorney.

Our society has become more litigious. Dissatisfied patients are more likely to sue doctors than ever before, not in small part due to a significant increase in the supply of attorneys. Regardless of the merits of the grievance, it is very hard to collect on dental malpractice. The money involved is usually small compared to the tens of thousands of dollars, if not millions, at stake in medical malpractice cases. Payments to patients for defective crowns or bridges or root canal treatment may amount to only a few thousand dollars, far too little to whet the appetites of attorneys. Lawyers are reluctant to invest a lot of time when the pot to be divided at the end is likely to be so small.

Unsuccessful treatment is not always an indication of poor treatment. There are not solutions to all problems. A good dentist will explain the risks and the limitations of treatment. But when a patient has sufficient reason to believe the dentist is the cause of the problem, he or she is entitled to pursue all legal means to be adequately compensated.

RECOMMENDATIONS

1. Don't be rushed into expensive and extensive treatment.
2. Prevent "buyer's remorse" by refusing impulsive acceptance of expensive add-ons and upgrades.
3. Get a written statement of all services, charges and/or copayments for extensive treatment, including alternative treatment options.
4. Don't sign agreements to pay for extensive treatment until you are sure that is what you want.
5. Avoid excessive credit card charges by budgeting treatment over time, based on the priority of need.
6. If you have dental insurance, expensive treatment should be preauthorized so you will know your out-of-pocket costs in advance. Otherwise, you may have to pay more than you bargained for.
7. If you suspect poor quality treatment, don't hesitate to get a second opinion.
8. Unless you have suffered serious injury, you will have difficulty getting a lawyer to handle your case. But your dental insurance plan or the local dental society may be able to help you get poor treatment redone at no additional cost.

A Final Caveat

The romanticized image of health care as a tender, caring relationship between doctor and patient was relevant to the time in history when that was the most they had to offer each other. As medical services became more technical, the business of health care became more complex. As health care became more effective in treating a wider range of illnesses, the healing profession's promise of TLC—*tender loving care*—in return for a respected place in the community was replaced by a less personal technical expertise. The romanticized dedication of the doctor to his or her poor and poor paying patients gave way to an implied contract to provide professional competency in exchange for an income competitive with that of most successful managers and business people. One cannot fault medical and dental practitioners for demanding to be paid well in a society whose general health is gauged by the gross national product rather than by the quality of life its citizens enjoy. Possibly if medical and dental education was not so costly, the nation might be able to recruit future physicians and dentists from among the children of other than financially successful people. If recently trained doctors were not so weighted down with debt, they would not be forced to emphasize income over social service, which is the bedrock of the healing professions. But as current trends continue, it is not surprising that consumers of health care services have become more ambivalent towards the providers of these services, placing faith in their expertise, yet fearful they might be exploited.

The purpose of this book is not to discourage you from taking advantage of the excellent dental care available in this country. Rather, it is to make you a better informed, more alert, and more assertive consumer of this care. A market system works for the betterment of both producer and consumer only when the consumer brings continual, knowledge-based pressure for an improved product at a reasonable cost. The role of the consumer will continue to be the most important factor in bringing about professional improvement.

By becoming informed consumers of dental services, by taking responsibility for the decisions that affect our dental health, by asking the right questions and settling for nothing less than accurate, nonevasive answers, we play a vital role in determining the level of care all citizens are offered, in what settings we are offered it, and at what costs.

Appendix—
Common Dental Complaints and Problems

Bad Breath

Mouth odors: due to poor oral hygiene, large cavities, periodontal disease, gingivitis, food retention under dentures and bridges, ulcerations and infections of the gums, abscess, tobacco, alcohol, mouth breathing, uncontrolled diabetes, certain foods such as garlic, and—mostly—digestive problems.

Denture Sores

Mucosal ulcerations: due to pressure spots, rough or sharp edges, overextended base, improper bite, excessive looseness, thin, fragile gums, sharp bone edges beneath the gums, poor denture hygiene.

Discolored Teeth

Brown stains: coffee, tea, and tobacco in excessive amounts combined with poor oral hygiene and infrequent professional prophylaxis (cleaning).

Gray shade: may be due to tetracycline taken by the mother during pregnancy or the child under age eight while the front teeth are still developing. Teeth may be lightened by bleaching.

Green gum line stains: frequently present on baby teeth and newly erupted permanent teeth because remnants of the covering membrane are still attached to the enamel after eruption. Usually wears off naturally or may be polished off in the dental office.

Mottled enamel: speckled, spotted, or broad bands of light, white to dark brown stains due to excessive fluorides in water ingested during the first eight years of life. May be reduced by bleaching, if not too severe.

Single tooth: dark yellow, opaque, gray, brown, black discoloration due to degeneration of the nerve tissue or to incomplete removal of the nerve during root canal treatment. May be reduced or eliminated by bleaching. May also be due to decay around an existing filling or to a large amalgam filling darkening the translucent enamel. Teeth also tend to darken with age as enamel wear allows yellowish dentin to show through.

Loose Dentures

Unstable artificial teeth: characteristic of full dentures, usually due to underextended denture base (too small), insufficient posterior seal (postdam) on an upper denture, inadequate bony ridge support (flat jawbone more common in the lower jaw), overextended base (too large), improper bite, dry mouth (insufficient saliva), nervous habits such as excessive tongue, lip, and cheek movements, partial denture clasps too loose or improperly designed.

Myofacial Pain

Pandora's Box I: pain and muscle spasms of the facial Dysfunction and masticatory muscles. May be triggered by jaw movements and chewing, or occur spontaneously because of clenching, bruxing, excessive gum chewing, and tension. Noninvasive palliative treatment is recommended. Usually disappears spontaneously, often after an extensive length of time.

Sensitive Teeth

Abrasion or attrition: physical wearing away of the enamel at the gum line, usually as a V-shaped indentation due to excessive and improper toothbrushing; wearing away of the top or biting surface of enamel by a heavy bite, coarse diet, or grinding (bruxism) of teeth.
Dental decay: cavity on the top or side of the tooth with a break through the enamel. Sensitivity to touch, sweets, heat, and cold.
Erosion: sensitivity to heat, cold, touch, and sweets at the gum line where the enamel has dissolved, leaving a smooth, concave or cupped-out area. Cause unknown if not directly related to excessive exposure to acids in

fruits, fruit juices, or soft drinks, or to regurgitation of stomach acids such as in bulemia.

Fractured enamel: When the fracture exposes dentin, the tooth may be sensitive to hot and cold temperatures, sweets, and touch.

Loose or broken filling: sensitivity to touch, hot and cold temperatures, biting, sweets. Defective filling may be due to the fracture of the material, new decay around the edges, dissolving of composite or synthetic porcelain filling, and faulty placement of the filling.

Loose tooth: sensitivity to pressure due to periodontal disease or traumatic injury. Baby teeth may hurt with chewing as they loosen during exfoliation (shedding).

Thermal change: sensitivity to heat and cold. May be due to a cavity, gum recession and root exposure, erosion, attrition, inflammation of the nerve, fracture, grinding, and excessive gum chewing.

Traumatic occlusion: tooth fits improperly against opposing teeth and feels *high* and is sensitive to biting pressure. May also become sensitive to thermal changes. Tooth may become loose with or without toothache, and the nerve may degenerate.

Root exposure: due to natural pathological gum recession, improper tooth brushing, poor oral hygiene. Sensitivity to thermal changes, touch, sweets.

Rough edges: enamel fracture due to decay or trauma, loose or fractured filling, defective filling, broken natural or artificial tooth.

Swollen and Bleeding Gums

Inflammation of the gums: due to tartar, poor oral hygiene, abscess, periodontal disease, cyst, pregnancy, diabetes, drug therapy, leukemia, poor-fitting bridges, dentures, and fillings; also, teething (eruption of baby and permanent teeth, especially wisdom teeth).

Temporomandibular Joint (TMJ) Pain

Pandora's Box II: may be due to muscle tension, traumatic injury such as blows, excesslive yawning, third molar surgery, grinding, clenching of teeth, excessive gum chewing, arthritic degeneration of the joint (grossly overdiagnosed). Noninvasive palliative greatment is recommended. Usually disappears spontaneously.

Toothache

Inflammation and infection of the dental nerve: due to decay, deep fillings, grinding and clenching, excessive gum chewing, periodontal abscess, split tooth, traumatic injury, tight partial denture clasp, heart attack.

Notes

1. Lifetime Dental Health

1. N. O. Harris and A. G. Christen, *Primary Preventive Dentistry,* 2nd ed. (Norwalk, Conn.: Appleton & Lange, 1987).
2. I. D. Mandel, "Maintaining Oral Health," chap. in D. F. Tapley et al, eds., *The Columbia University College of Physicians and Surgeons Complete Home Medical Guide,* Revised Edition (New York: Consumer Reports Books, 1989): 728-48.
3. K. J. Anusavice, "Chlorhexidine, Fluoride Varnish, and Xylitol Chewing Gum," *General Dentistry* 46 (1998): 34-8, 40.
4. G. H. Hildebrandt and B. S. Sparks, "Maintaining Mutans Streptococci Suppression With Xylitol Gum," *Journal of the American Dental Association* 131 (2000): 909-16.
5. J. D. B. Featherstone, "The Science and Practice of Caries Prevention," *Journal of the American Dental Association* 131 (2000): 887-98.
6. U.S. Department of Health and Human Services, *Oral Health in America: a Report of the Surgeon General. Rockville, MD:* U.S. Department of Health and Human Services, National Institute of Dental and Craniofacial Research, National Institutes of Health, 2000: 165-66.
7. G. J. Christensen, "Improving Treatment Plan Acceptance," *Journal of the American Dental Association* 130 (1999): 1629-31.

2. Dental Anatomy

1. J. B. Woelfel, *Dental Anatomy* (Philadelphia: Lea & Febiger, 1984).

3. Dental Caries (Decay)

1. U.S. Department of Health and Human Services, *Oral Health in America: a Report of the Surgeon General. Rockville, MD*: U.S. Department of Health and Human Services, National Institute of Dental and Craniofacial Research, National Institutes of Health, 2000: 2.

2. M. J. Kanellis, "Caries Risk Assessment and Prevention: Strategies for Head Start, Early Head Start, and WIC," *Journal of Public Health Dentistry*, 60 (3) (2000): 210-17.
3. H. C. Gift, "Oral Health Outcomes Research-Challenges and Opportunites," in G. D. Slade, editor, *Measuring Oral Health and Quality of Life* (Chapel Hill: University of North Carolina Department of Ecology, 1997.)
4. Health Care Financing Administration (HCFA),"National Health Expenditures, 1998," Washington, Health Care Financing Administration, 2000.
5. P. W. Caufield, G. R. Cutter, and A. P. Dasanayake, "Initial Acquisition of Mutans Streptococci by Infants: Evidence for a Discrete Window of Infectivity," *Journal of Dental Research* 72 (1993): 37-45.
6. J. D. B. Featherstone, "The Science and Practice of Caries Prevention," *Journal of the American Dental Association* 131 (2000): 887-98.
7. I. D. Mandel, "Dentistry at the Millennium: Overtreatment and Undertreatment," *Dental Abstracts*: 44 (6) (1999): 250-51.
8. Workshop on Guidelines for Sealant Use: Recommendations, *Journal of Public Health Dentistry* 55 (5) Special Issue (1995): 263-73.
9. L. W. Ripa, *Baby Bottle Tooth Decay (Nursing Caries)* (Washington, D. C.: Dental Health Section, American Public Health Association, 1988).

4. *Prevention and Treatment of Dental Caries (Decay)*

1. U.S. Department of Health and Human Services, *Oral Health in America: a Report of the Surgeon General. Rockville, MD*: U.S. Department of Health and Human Services, National Institute of Dental and Craniofacial Research, National Institutes of Health, 2000: 161.
2. J. B. McKinlay and S. M. McKinlay, "Medical Measures and the Decline of Mortality," chap. in P. Conrad and R. Kern, eds., *The Sociology of Health and Illness,* 2d ed. (New York: St. Martin's Press, 1986): 10-23.
3. Review of Fluoride Benefits and Risks: Report of the Ad Hoc Subcommittee on Fluoride of the Committee to Coordinate Health and Related Programs: (Washington, D. C.: U.S. Department of Health and Human Services, Public Health Service, 1991).
4. J. D. B. Featherstone, "The Science and Practice of Caries Prevention," *Journal of the American Dental Association* 131 (2000): 887-98.
5. American Dental Association, Council on Scientific Affairs, "Intervention: Fluoride Supplementation," *Journal of the American Dental Association* 126 (1995): 19-S.

6. Conference Report: A Joint IADR/ORCA International Symposium, "Fluorides: Mechanisms of Action and Recommendations for Use," March 21-24, 1989. *Journal of Dental Research* 68 (1989): 1215-16.

7. E. M. Bentley, R. P. Ellwood, and R. M. Davies, "Fluoride Ingestion from Toothpaste by Young Children," *British Dental Journal* 186 (1999): 460-62.

8. Council on Dental Therapeutics, American Dental Association, "Status Report: Effect of Acidulated Phosphate Fluoride on Porcelain and Composite Restorations," *Journal of the American Dental Association* 116 (1986): 115.

9. Preventing Tooth Decay: A Guide to Implementing Self-applied Fluoride Programs in School, DHEW Pub.No. (NIH) 77-1196 (Washington, D. C.: U.S. Department of Health and Human Services, Public Health Service, 1977).

10. J. D. B. Featherstone.

11. U.S. Department of Health and Human Services, *Oral Health in America*: 199.

12. E. D. Beltrán-Aguilar, J. W. Goldstein, and S. A. Lockwood, "Fluoride Varnishes: a Review of Their Clinical Use, Cariostatic Mechanism, Efficacy and Safety," *Journal of the American Dental Association* 131 (2000): 589-94.

13. L. M. Kaste, R. H. Selwitz, R. J. Oldakowski, J. A. Brunelle, D. M. Winn, and L. J. Brown, "Coronal Caries in the Primary and Permanent Dentition of Children and Adolescents 1-17 Years of Age: United States, 1988-1991," *Journal of Dental Research* 75 Special Issue (1996): 631-41.

14. "Workshop on Guidelines for Sealant Use," *Journal of Public Health Dentistry* 55 (1955) (5) Special Issue.

15. U.S. Department of Health and Human Services, *Oral Health in America*: 166.

16. J. W. Friedman, "The New Zealand School Dental Service: A Lesson in Radical Conservatism," *Journal of the American Dental Association* 85 Special Issue (1972): 609-17.

17. R. R. Lobene and A. Kerr, *The Forsyth Experiment: An Alternative System for Dental Care* (Cambridge, Mass.: Harvard University Press, 1979).

18. L. M. Silverstone, "Fluorides and Remineralization, "chap. in Shy Wei, ed., *Clinical Use of Fluorides* (Philadelphia: Lea & Febiger, 1985): 153-75.

19. E. D. Beltram and B. A. Burt, "The Pre- and Posteruptive Effects of Fluoride in the Caries Decline," *Journal of Public Health Dentistry* 48 (1988): 233-40.

20. E. Johansen, "Remineralization of Carious Lesions in Elderly Patients," *Gerodontics* 3 (1987): 47-50.
21. W. B. Eames, "When Not to Restore," *Journal of the American Dental Association* 117 (1988): 429-32.
22. D. B. Mahler and J. H. Engle, "Clinical Evaluation of Amalgam Bonding in Class I and II Restorations," *Journal of the American Dental Association* 131 (2000): 43-49.
23. B. M. Eley, "The Future of Dental Amalgam: a review of the literature," *British Dental Journal* 183 (1997): 11-14.
24. M. J. Wahl, "Amalgam-Resurrection and Redemption. Part 1. The Clinical and Legal Mythology of Anti-amalgam," *Quintessence International* 32 (7) Special Report (2001): 525-535; Part 2, 33 (3): 696-710
25. T. E. Donovan, "Adhesive Restorative Dentistry: A Conservative Approach," *Journal of the California Dental Association* 13 (1985): 13-20.
26. B. Köhler, C-G Rasmusson, and P. Ödman, "A Five-year Clinical Evaluation of Class II Composite Resin Restorations," *Journal of Dentistry* 28 (2000): 111-16.
27. P. Phantumvanit, Y. Songpaisan, T. Pilot, and J. E. Frencken, "Atraumatic Restorative Treatkent (ART): a Three-year Community Field Trial in Thailand-Survival of One-surface Restorations in the Permanent Dentition," *Journal of Public Health Dentistry* 56 (3) Special Issue (1996): 141-45.
28. R. L. Leung and I. Comfortes, "Porcelain Inlays and Onlays," *Journal of the California Dental Association* 16 (September 1988): 38-43.
29. Council on Dental Materials, Instruments and Equipment, American Dental Association, "Biologic Effects of Nickel-containing Dental Alloys," *Journal of the American Dental Association* 104 (1982): 501-4.
30. J. B. Lamster, D. I. Kalfus, P. J. Steigerwald, and A. I. Chasens, "Rapid Loss of Alveolar Bone Associated with Nonprecious Alloy Crowns in Two Patients with Nickel Hypersensitivity," *Journal of Periodontology* 58 (1987): 386-92.
31. B. L. Marshak, H. Helft, and R. Filo, "Factors Mitigating Against the Use of Dowels in Endodontically Treated Teeth," *Quintessence International* 19 (1988): 417-21.

5. *Common Diseases of the Gum and Soft Tissues of the Mouth*

1. F. A. Carranza, Jr., *Glickman's Clinical Periodontology*, 7th ed. (Philadelphia: W. B. Saunders, 1990).

2. F. A. Carranza, Jr., and D. A. Perry, *Clinical Periodontology for the Dental Hygienist* (Philadelphia: W B. Saunders, 1986).
3. U.S. Naval Dental School, *Color Atlas of Oral Pathology* (Philadelphia: Lippincott, 1956).
4. R. J. Genco and H. Löe, "The Role of Systemic Conditions and Disorders in Periodontal Disease," *Journal of Periodontology* 2 (2000): 98-116.
5. B. D. Johnson and D. Engel, "Acute Necrotizing Ulcerative Gingivitis: A Review of Diagnosis, Etiology and Treatment," *Journal of Periodontology* 57 (1986): 141-50.
6. S. L. Zunt, "Recurrent Apthous Ulcers: Prevention and Treatment," *Journal of Practical Hygiene* 10 (4) (2001): 17-23.
7. U.S. Department of Health and Human Services, *Oral Health in America: a Report of the Surgeon General. Rockville, MD*: U.S. Department of Health and Human Services, National Institute of Dental and Craniofacial Research, National Institutes of Health, 2000: 67-70.
8. P. B. Robertson and J. S. Greenspan, eds., *Oral Manifestations of AIDS* (Littleton, Mass.: PSG Publishing Co., 1988).
9. UNAIDS/WHO, Joint United Nations Programme on AIDS, "Report on Global HIV/AIDS Epidemic" (1998).
10. G. T. Clark, S. Nachnani, and D. V. Messadi, "Detecting and Treating Oral and Nonoral Malodors," *Journal of the California Dental Association* 25 (1997): 133-44.
11. P. R. Klokkevold, "Oral Malodor: A Periodontal Perspective," *Journal of the California Dental Association* 25 (1997): 153-59.
12. D. P. Lu, "Halitosis: an Etiologic Classification, a Treatment Approach and Prevention," *Journal of Oral Surgery, Oral Medicine and Oral Pathology* 54(5) (1982): 521-26.
13. S. Nachnani, "The Effects of Oral Rinses on Halitosis," *Journal of the California Dental Association* 25 (1997): 145-50.

Additional References

S. N. Bhaskar, *Synopsis of Oral Pathology*, 2d ed. (St. Louis: C. V. Mosby Company, 1965).

F. H. Lovejoy, Jr., ed., *The New Child Health Encyclopedia* (New York: Consumer Reports Books, 1987).

S. W. Redding and M. Montgomery, eds., *Dentistry in Systemic Disease* (Portland, Ore.: JBK Publishing, 1990).

J. A. Regezi and J. J. Sciubba, *Oral Pathology* (Philadelphia: W. B. Saunders, 1989).

6. *Chronic Destructive Periodontal Disease*

1. C. H. Drisko, "Trends in Surgical and Nonsurgical Periodontal Treatment," *Journal of the American Dental Association (Special Supplement)* 131 (2000): 31S-38S.
2. W. Becker, B. E. Becker, and L. E. Berg, "Periodontal Treatment Without Maintenance," *Journal of Periodontology* 55 (1984): 505-9.
3. J. MN. Albander, J. A. Brunelle, A. Kingman, "Destructive Periodontal Disease in Adults 30 Years of Age and Older in the United States, 1988-1994," *Journal of Periodontology* 70 (1999): 13-29.
4. P. P. Hujoel, MN. Drangsholt, C. Spiekerman, et al, "Periodontal Disease and Coronary Heart Disease Risk," *Journal of the American Medical Association* 284 (2000): 1406-10.
5. E. Hausmann, "Potential Pathways for Bone Resorption in Human Periodontal Disease," *Journal of Periodontology* 45 (1974): 338-43.
6. R. M. Frank and J. C. Voegel, "Bacterial Bone Resorption in Advanced Cases of Human Periodontitis," *Journal of Periodontal Research* 13 (1978): 251-61.
7. J. N. M. Heersche and D. A. Deporter, "The Mechanism of Osteoclastic Bone Resorption: A New Hypothesis," *Journal of Periodontal Research* 14 (1979): 266-67.
8. F. A. Carranza, Jr., *Glickman's Clinical Periodontology,* 7th ed. (Philadelphia: W. B. Saunders, 1990): 243.
9. T. J. O'Leary, E. P. Barrington, and R. Gottsgen, "Periodontal Therapy-a Summary Status Report 1987-1988," *Journal of Periodontology* 59 (1988): 306-10.
10. H. Hanamura et al., "Periodontal Status and Bruxism," *Journal of Periodontology* 58 (1987): 137-76.
11. N. P. Lang, T. Orsanic, F. A. Gusberti, and B. E. Siegust, "Bleeding on Probing: A Predictor for the Progression of Periodontal Disease," *Journal of Clinical* Periodontology 13 (1986): 590-96.

7. *Primary Prevention of Periodontal Disease*

1. C. H. Drisko, "Trends in Surgical and Nonsurgical Periodontal Treatment," *Journal of the American Dental Association (Special Supplement)* 131 (2000): 31S-38S.
2. N. P. Lang, B. R. Cumming, and H. Löe, "Toothbrushing Frequency as It Relates to Plaque Development and Gingival Health," *Journal of Periodontology* 44 (1973): 396-405.

3. D. A. Boab and R. H. Johnson, "The Effect of a New Electric Toothbrush on Supragingival Plaque and Gingivitis," *Journal of Periodontology 60* (1989): 336-41.

4. R. L. Boyd, P. Murray, and P. B. Robertson, "Effect on Periodontal Status of Rotary Electric Toothbrushes vs. Manual Toothbrushes During Periodontal Maintenance. I. Clinical Results. II. Microbiological Results." *Journal of Periodontology* 60 (1989): 390-401.

5. R. C. Graves, J. A. Disney, and J. W. Stamm, "Comparative Effectiveness of Flossing and Brushing in Reducing Interproximal Bleeding," *Journal of Periodontology* 60 (1989): 243-47.

6. "Toothpastes," *Consumer Reports* 51 (1986): 144-49.

7. D. M. Lamberts, R. C. Wunderlich, and R. G. Caffesse, "The Effect of Waxed and Unwaxed Dental Floss on Gingival Health," *Journal of Periodontology* 53 (1982): 393-400.

8. "Dental Irrigators," *Consumer Reports* 49 (1984): 141-43.

9. S. G. Ciancio, M. L. Mather, J. J. Zarnbom, and H. S. Reynolds, "Effect of a Chemotherapeutic Agent Delivered by an Oral Irrigation Device on Plaque, Gingivitis, and Subgingival Microflora," *Journal of Periodontology* 60 (1989): 310-15.

10. W. J. Killoy, "Local Delivery of Antimicrobials: A New Era in the Treatment of Adult Periodontitis," *Compendium of Continuing Education in Dentistry (Special Issue)* 20 (4) (1999): 13-18.

11. L. M. Weaks, N. B. Lescher, C. M. Baines, and S. V. Holroyd, "Clinical Evaluation of the Prophy-jet as an Instrument for Routine Removal of Tooth Stain and Plaque," *Journal of Periodontology* 55 (1984): 496-98.

12. J. Jowsey, B. L. Riggs, and P. J. Kelly, "Fluoride in the Treatment of Osteoporosis," chap. in E. Johnsen, D. R. Taves, and T. O. Olsen, eds., *Continuing Evaluation of the Use of Fluorides* (Boulder, Colo.: Westview Press, 1979).

13. C. H. Drisko, "Root Instrumentation. Power-driven Versus Manual Scalers, which one?" *Dental Clinics of North America* 42 (1998): 229-44.

14. J. Lindhe and S. Nyman, "Long-term Maintenance for Patients Treated for Advanced Periodontal Disease," *Journal of Periodontology* 55 (1984): 504-14.

15. W. Becker, B. E. Becker, and L. E. Berg, "Periodontal Treatment Without Maintenance," *Journal of Periodontology* 55 (1984): 505-9.

8. Treatment of Periodontal Disease

1. J. M. Albander, J. A. Brunelle, A. Kingman, "Destructive Periodontal Disease in Adults 30 years of Age and Older in the United States, 1988-1994," *Journal of Periodontology* 67 (1999): 13-29.
2. R. C. Oliver, L. J. Brown, and H. Löe, "An Estimate of Periodontal Treatment Needs in the U.S. Based on Epidemiologic Data," *Journal of Periodontology* 60 (1989): 371-80.
3. C. H. Drisko, "Trends in Surgical and Nonsurgical Periodontal Treatment," *Journal of the American Dental Association (Special Supplement)* 131 (2000): 31S-38S.
4. J. Lindhe, S. Nyman, and T. Karping, "Scaling and Root Planing in Shallow Pockets," *Journal of Clinical Periodontology* 9 (1982): 415-18.
5. T. P. Hughes and R. G. Caffesse, "Gingival Changes Following Scaling, Root Planing and Oral Hygiene: A Biometric Evaluation," *Journal of Periodontology* 49 (1978): 245-52.
6. S. H. Kestenberg and E. R. Young, "Potential Problems Associated with Occupational Exposure to Nitrous Oxide," *Journal of the Canadian Dental Association* 54 (1988): 277-86.
7. C. H. Devore, M. J. Hicks, and J. A. Claman, "A System for Ensuring Success of Long-term Supportive Periodontal Therapy," *Journal of Dental Hygiene* 63 (1989): 214-20.
8. N. P. Lang, T. Orsanic, F. A. Gusberti, and B. E. Siegust, "Bleeding on Probing: A Predictor for the Progression of Periodontal Disease," *Journal of Clinical Periodontology* 13 (1986): 590-96.
9. C. D. Overholser, "Longitudinal Clinical Studies with Antimicrobial Mouth Rinses," *Journal of Clinical Periodontology* 15 (1988): 517-19.
10. C. H. Drisko, "Trends in Surgical and Nonsurgical Periodontal Treatment," *Journal of the American Dental Association (Special Supplement)* 131 (2000): 31S-38S.
11. B. L. Pihlstrom, R. B. McHugh, T. H. Oliphant, and C. Ortiz-Campos, "Comparison of Surgical and Non-surgical Treatment of Periodontal Disease: A Review of Current Studies and Additional Results After 6 Years," *Journal of Clinical Periodontology* 10 (1983): 524-41.
12. A. Badersten, R. Nilveus, and J. Egelberg, "Effect of Non-surgical Periodontal Therapy. II. Severely Advanced Periodontitis," *Journal of Clinical Periodontology* 11 (1984): 63-76.
13. W. Becker, B. E. Becker, and L. E. Berg, "Periodontal Treatment Without Maintenance," *Journal of Periodontology* 55 (1984): 505-9.
14. J. F. Collins and L. Perkins, "Clinical Evaluation of the Effectiveness of Three Dentrifices in Relieving Dentin Sensitivity," *Journal of Periodontology* 55 (1984): 720-25.

15. S. C. Steinberg and A. D. Steinberg, "Phenytoin-induced Gingival Overgrowth Control in Severely Retarded Children," *Journal of Periodontology* 53 (1982): 429-33.
16. F. A. Carranza, Jr., *Glickman's Clinical Periodontology*, 7th ed. (Philadelphia: W. B. Saunders, 1990): 852-56.
17. Ibid., 883-90.

9. Cosmetic Dentistry and Orthodontics

1. H. S. Horowitz, "Indexes for Measuring Dental Fluorosis," *Journal of Public Health Dentistry* 46 (1986): 179-83.
2. U.S. Department of Health and Human Services, *Oral Health in America: a Report of the Surgeon General. Rockville, MD*: U.S. Department of Health and Human Services, National Institute of Dental and Craniofacial Research, National Institutes of Health, 2000: 161.
3. J. Kaneko, "Bleaching Effect of Sodium Percarbonate on Discolored Pulpless Teeth in Vitro," *Journal of Endodontics 26* (2000): 25-28.
4. D. Viscio, A. Gaffar, S. Fakhry-Smith, and T. Xu, "Present and Future Technologies of Tooth Whitening," *Compendium of Continuing Education in Dentistry* 21 Supplement No 28 (2000): S36-S43.
5. V. B., Haywood, "Current Status of Nightguard Vital Bleaching," *Compendium of Continuing Education in Dentistry* 21 Supplement No. 28 (2000): S10-S17.
6. G. Kugel, "Nontray whitening,"*Compendium of Continuing Education in Dentistry* (2000): 21:524-28.
7. R. E. Goldstein, *Change Your Smile* (Chicago: Quintessence International, 1984).
8. G. A. Maryniuk, "In Search of Treatment Longevity-A 30-Year Perspective," *Journal of the American Dental Association* 109 (1984): 739-44.
9. A. Geiger, B. Wasserman, and L. Turgeon, "Relationship of Occlusion and Periodontal Disease. VII. Relationship of Crowding and Spacing to Periodontal Destruction and Gingival Inflammation," *Journal of Periodontology* 45 (1974): 43-49.
10. J. L. Ackerman, "Orthodontics: Art, Science, or Transscience?" *Angle Orthodontist* 44 (1974): 243-50.
11. S. R. Cohen, "Follow-up Evaluation of 105 Patients with Myofacial Pain Dysfunction Syndrome," *Journal of the American Dental Association* 97 (1978): 825-28.
12. *TMD: Temporomandibular Disorders.* NIH Pub. No. 96-3487 Bethesda, Md.: National Institutes of Health, National Institute of Dental Research, 1996).

13. R. A. Dionne, "Antidepressants for Chronic Orofacial Pain, *Compendium of Continuing Education in Dentistry"* 21 (October 2000): 822-28. *See also* L. E. Ta, J. P. Phero, H. Hale-Donze, et al. "Clinical Evaluation of Patients with Failed TMJ Implants," *American Pain Society*, Atlanta (2000).

14. D. C. Dixon, et al., "The Validity of Transcranial Radiography in Diagnosing TMJ Anterior Disk Displacement," *Journal of the American Dental Association* 108 (1984): 615-18.

15. R. G. Kaplan, "Mandibular Third Molars and Postretention Crowding," *American Journal of Orthodontics* 66 (1974): 411-30.

16. S. E. Bishara and G. Andreason, "Third Molars: A Review," *American Journal of Orthodontics* 83 (1983): 131-37.

17. T. M. Graber, *Orthodontics* (Philadelphia: W. B. Saunders, 1966), 490.

18. J. A. Gibilisco, ed., *Stafne's Oral Radiographic Diagnosis,* 5th ed. (Philadelphia: W. B. Saunders, 1985): 132.

19. L. E. Pearson, "Gingival Height of Lower Central Incisors, Orthodontically Treated and Untreated," *Angle Orthodontist* 38 (1968): 377-79.

20. V. Sassouni and G. C. Sotereanos, *Diagnosis and Treatment of Dentofacial Abnormalities* (Springfield, Mass.: Charles W. Thomas, 1974).

21. Dixon et al.; Kaplan.

22. J. W. Friedman, "The Case for the Preservation of Third Molars," *Journal of the California Dental Association* 5 (1977): 50-56.

23. J. W. Friedman, "Containing the Cost of Third Molar Extractions: A Dilemma for Health Insurance," *Public Health Reports* 98 (1983): 376-84.

24. P. Yablon, M. C. Wolf, and K. P. Maykow, "Third Molar Teeth: Differing Concepts Between Oral Surgeons and Other Dentists," *New York State Dental Journal* 54 (1988): 27-31.

25. Graber: 718.

26. J. E. Marceau and B. P. Trottier, "Third Molar Development Following Second Molar Extractions," *Journal of Pedodontics* 8 (1983): 34-51.

27. D. W. Liddle, "Second Molar Extraction in Orthodontic Treatment," *American Journal* of *Orthodontics* 72 (1977): 599-616.

28. R. L. Holt, *Straight Teeth* (New York: William Morrow, 1980), 283.

29. C. Kurz and J. C. Gonnan, "Lingual Orthodontics: A Status Report," *Journal of Clinical Orthodontics* 17 (1983): 310-21.

30. K. A. Atchison, L. S. Luke, and S. C. White, "Contribution of Pretreatment Radiographs. to Orthodontists' Decision Making," *Oral Surgery, Oral Medicine, Oral Pathology* 71 (1991): 238-45.

31. Geiger, Wasserman, and Turgeon.

0. Replacement of Missing Teeth-Bridges and Dentures

1. D. A. Shugars, J.A. Bader, S. W. Phillips, Jr., B. A. White, and C. F. Brantley, "The Consequences of Not Replacing a Missing Posterior Tooth," *Journal of the American Dental Association* (2000): 1317-22.
2. J. W. Friedman, "PSROs in Dentistry," *American Journal of Public Health* 65 (1975): 1298-1303.
3. C. A. McCollum, Jr., "Oral Surgery for Children," chap. in S. B. Finn, *Clinical Pedodontics*, 4th ed. (Philadelphia: W. B. Saunders, 1973): 393.
4. A. C. Elias and A. Sheiham, The relationship between satisfaction with mouth and number and position of teeth, *Journal of Oral Rehabilitation*: 25 (1998): 649.
5. R. A. Simonsen, V. Thompson, and G. Barrack, *Etched Cast Restorations: Clinical and Laboratory Techniques* (Chicago: Quintessence International, 1983).
6. D. Henderson and V. L. Steffel, *McCraken's Removable Partial Prosthodontics* (St. Louis: C. V. Mosby, 1981).
7. J. G. Green, T. M. Durham, and T. A. King, "Management of Patients with Swallowed Dental Objects," *American Journal of Dentistry* 1 (1988): 147-50.
8. U.S. Department of Health and Human Services, *Oral Health in America: a Report of the Surgeon General. Rockville, MD*: U.S. Department of Health and Human Services, National Institute of Dental and Craniofacial Research, National Institutes of Health, 2000: 66-67.
9. J. W. Friedman, "Dentistry in the Geriatric Patient: Mutilation by Consensus," *Geriatrics* 23 (1968): 98-107.
10. J. B. Farmer and M. E. Connelly, "Palateless Dentures: Help for the Gagging Patient," *Journal of Prosthetic Dentistry* 52 (1984): 691-94.
11. U.S. Department of Health and Human Services, 67-70.
12. T. D. Taylor, "Prosthodontic Problems and Limitations Associated with Osseointegration," *Journal of Prosthetic Dentistry* 79 (1998): 74-78.
13. D. E. Jennings, "Treatment of the Mandibular Compromised Ridge. A Literature Review," *Journal of Prosthetic Dentistry* 61 (1989): 575-59.
14. G. Sandberg, T. Stenberg and K. Wikblad, "Ten Years of Patients' Experiences with Fixed Implant-Supported Prostheses," *Journal of Dental Hygiene* 74 (3) (2000): 210-18.

11. Endodontics - Root Canal Treatment

1. L S. Cohen and R. C. Burns, eds., *Pathways of the Pulp* (St. Louis: C. V. Mosby, 1976).

2. J. I. Ingle and J. F. Tainter, *Endodontics*, 3rd ed. (Philadelphia: Lea & Febiger, 1985).
3. Ibid., 235.
4. J. A. Gibilisco, ed., *Stafne's Oral Radiographic Diagnosis*, 5th ed. (Philadelphia: W. B. Saunders, 1985): 80-81.
5. Ibid.: 201-5.
6. H. Berk and A. A. Krakow, "Efficient Vital Pulp Therapy," *Dental Clinics of North America* 9 (1965): 373-85.
7. R. Johnson, A. Yaari, R. Berkowitz, and G. F. Currier, "Techniques of Pulp Therapy for Primary and Immature Permanent Teeth," *The Compendium of Continuing Education in Dentistry* 1 (1980): 27-35.
8. J. H. Camp, "Pulp Therapy for Primary and Young Permanent Teeth, *Dental Clinics of North America* 28 (1984): 651-68.
9. L. K. Bakland, "Management of Traumatically Injured Pulps in Immature Teeth Using MTA," *Journal of the California Dental Association* 28 (2000): 855-58.
10. J. W. Friedman, "Evaluation of the Delivery of Endodontic Services to the Public," *Journal of Endodontics* 3 (1987): 84-88.
11. Ingle and Tainter: 238-41.
12. G. N. Glickman and K.A. Koch, "21st-Century Endodontics," *Journal of the American Dental Association (Special Supplement)* 131 (2000): 39S-46S.
13. P. J. Ashkenaz, "One-visit Endodontics," D*ental Clinics of North America* 28 (1984): 853-63.
14. Ingle and Tainter: 227.
15. N. Chivian, "Endodontics: An Overview," *Dental Clinics of North America* 28 (1984): 637-49.
16. E. N. Green, "Hemisection and Root Amputation," *Journal of the American Dental Association* 112 (1986): 511-18.
17. Ingle and Tainter: 812.
18. J. L. Gutman, "When to Use Posts," D*entist* 67 (1989): 24, 32, 40.
19. J. L. Gutman, "Restoring Endodontically Treated Teeth," *Texas Dental Journal* 114 (1997): 14-23.
20. C. A. McCollum, Jr., "Oral Surgery for Children," chap. in S. B. Finn, *Clinical Pedodontics*, 4th ed. (Philadelphia: W B. Saunders, 1973): 393.

12. Oral Surgery - Extractions

1. American Dental Association 1998 Survey of Dental Practice.
2. Council on Dental Care Programs, American Dental Association, "Code on Dental Procedures and Nomenclature," *Journal of the American Dental Association* 104 (1982): 351-56.

3. J. W. Friedman, "The Case for Preservation of Third Molars, "*Journal of the California Dental Association* 5 (1977): 50-56.
4. J. W. Friedman, "Containing the Cost of Third Molar Extractions: A Dilemma for Health Insurance," *Public Health Reports* 98 (1983): 376-84.
5. I. Slodov, R. G. Behrents, and D. P. Dobrowski, "Clinical Experience with Third Molar Orthodontics," A*merican Journal of Orthodontics and Dento-facial Orthopedics* 96 (1989): 453-61.
6. M. R. Patwardham, "A Radiographic Study of Prevalence of Pathology Associated with Third Molars" (Los Angeles: University of California, 1979). Unpublished.
7. C. R. Brann and M. R. Shepherd, "Factors influencing nerve damage during lower third molar surgery. *British Dental Journal* 186 (1999): 514-16.
8. M. P. Coplans and I. Curson, "Deaths Associated with Dentistry," *British Dental Journal* 153 (1982): 357-62.
9. T. J. Pallasch, "Antibiotic Prophylaxis: The Clinical Significance of Its Recent Evolution," *Journal of the California Dental Association* 25 (1999): 619-32.
10. G. 0. Kruger, ed., *Textbook of Oral Surgery* (St. Louis: C.V. Mosby, 1974): 107-8.
11. D. P. Kipp, B. H. Goldstein, and W. W. Weiss, "Dysthesia After Mandibular Third Molar Surgery," *Journal of the American Dental Association* 100 (1980): 185-92.
12. Friedman, "Containing the Cost of Third Molar Extractions."
13. Coplans and Curson: 198-201.

13. Drugs and Anesthetics

1. For a complete description of drugs, their effects and side effects, see *Physicians Desk Reference* (PDR), annual edition (Oradell, N.J.: Medical Economics Company, Inc.).
2. T. J. Pallasch, "Global Antibiotic Resistance and Its Impact on the Dental Community," *Journal of the California Dental Association*, 28 (2000): 215-33.
3. T. J. Pallasch, "Antibiotics for Acute Orofacial Infections," *Journal of the California Dental Association* (1993): 34-44.
4. P. B. Robertson and J. S. Greenspan, eds., *Perspectives on Oral Manifestations of AIDS* (Littleton, Mass.: PSG Publishing Company, Inc., 1988).
5. The Public Citizen Health Research Group, "Generic Versus Brand Name Drugs: Same Effects, Lower Prices," *Health Letter* 4 (1988): 10.

6. S. H. Kestenberg and E. R. Young, "Potential Problems Associated with Occupational Exposure to Nitrous Oxide," *Journal of the Canadian Dental Association* 54 (1988): 277-86.

14. How to Choose a Good Dentist

1. J. W. Friedman and K. A. Atchison, "The Standard of Care: An Ethical Responsibility of Public Health Dentistry," *Journal of Public Health Dentistry* 53 (3) (1993): 165-69.
2. J. L. Schwartz, *Medical Plans and Health Care* (Springfield, Illinois: Charles C. Thomas, 1968)
3. U. S. Department of Health and Human Services, *Oral Health in America: a Report of the Surgeon General. Rockville, MD*: U. S. Department of Health and Human Services, National Institute of Dental and Craniofacial Research, National Institutes of Health, 2000: 232.
4. UCLA Center for Health Policy Research and the Kaiser Family Foundation, "Racial and Ethnic Disparities in Access to Health Insurance and Health Care," (2000).
5. J. W. Friedman, "The Value of Free Choice in Health Care," *Medical Care* 3 (1965): 121-27.
6. C. E. Jerge, W. E. Marshall, M. H. Schoen, and J. W. Friedman, eds., *Group Practice and the Future of Dental Care* (Philadelphia: Lea & Febiger, 1974).
7. R. W. Phelon, J. W. Kushman, J. R. Freed, and J. A. Gershen, "Dental Care Quality and Commercialism: A Pilot Study," (1988). Unpublished.
8. "Public Information Release," American Dental Association, Bureau of Public Information, April 29, 1979.
9. S. E. DeAngelis and V. Goral, "Utilization of Local Anesthesia by Arkansas Dental Hygienists and Dentists' Delegation/Satisfaction Relative to this Function,"*Journal of Dental Hygiene* 74 (2000):196-204.
10. For an example of expanded function regulations, see California Dental Practice Act (Sacramento: Board of Dental Examiners, Department of Consumer Affairs, 1990).
11. D. G. Boggs and M. A. Shork, "Determination of optimal time elapse for recall of patients in an incremental dental care program," *Journal of the American Dental Association* 90 (1975): 644-53.
12. M. L. Kantor, S. J. Zeichner, R. W. Valachovic, and A. B. Reiskin, "Efficacy of Dental Radiographic Practices: Options for Image Receptors, Examination Selection, and Patient Selection," *Journal of the American Dental Association* 119 (1986): 259-68.
13. J. W. Friedman, *A Guide for the Evaluation of Dental Care* (Los Angeles: University of California, School of Public Health, 1972).

14. "The Mercury Scare," *Consumer Reports* 51 (1986.): 150-52.
15. *TMD: Temporomandibular Disorders.* NIH Pub. No. 96-3487 Bethesda, Md.: National Institutes of Health, National Institute of Dental Research, 1996).
16. C. A. Pettengill, M. R. Growney, Jr., R. Schoff, and C. R. Kenworthy, "A Pilot Study Comparing the Efficacy of Hard and Soft Stabilizing Appliances in Treating Patients with Temporomandibular Disorders," *Journal of Prosthetic Dentistry* 79 (1998): 165-68.
17. B. Lange, C. Cook, D. Dunning, M. L. Froeschie and D. Kent, "Improving the Oral Hygiene of Institutionalized Mentally Retarded Clients," *Journal of Dental Hygiene* 74 (2000): 205-9.

15. Financing Dental Care

1. U. S. Department of Health and Human Services, *Oral Health in America: a Report of the Surgeon General. Rockville, MD*: U. S. Department of Health and Human Services, National Institute of Dental and Craniofacial Research, National Institutes of Health, 2000: 4, 227-32.
2. Ibid., 80-86.
3. D. A. Dawson and P. F. Adams, *Current Estimates from the National Interview Survey, United States, 1986.* National Center for Health Statistics. Vital and Health Statistics, Series 10, No. 164. DHHS Pub. No. (PHS) 87-1592 (Washington, D.C.: U.S. Government Printing Office, 1987).
4. *The Prevalence of Dental Caries in United States Children- 1986-1987- the National Dental Caries Prevalence Survey.* NIH Pub. No. 89-2247 (Bethesda, Md.: National Institutes of Health, National Institute of Dental Research, 1989).
5. U. S. Department of Health and Human Services: 229.
6. J. W. Friedman, *A Guide for the Evaluation of Dental Care* (Los Angeles: University of California, School of Public Health, 1972).
7. H. Luft, *Health Maintenance Organizations: Dimensions and Performance* (New York: Wiley & Sons, 1981).
8. M. I. Roemer and J. W. Friedman, *Doctors in Hospitals* (Baltimore: Johns Hopkins Press, 1971).
9. U. S. Department of Health and Human Services: 230.

Glossary

Acknowledgment is given to the following publications used in the preparation of the glossary: *Dental Science Handbook,* a joint Project of the American Dental Association and the National Institute of Dental Research, U.S. Department of Health, Education and Welfare, U.S. Government Printing Office, 1969; "Definitions of Prepaid Dental Care Terms" in the *Directory of Prepaid Dental Care Plans,* 1967, U. S. Department of Health, Education and Welfare, U.S. Government Printing Office, 1968; *1986-87 Source Book of Health Insurance Data,* Health Insurance Association of America, Washington, D.C.

Abrasion. Mechanical wearing away of tooth surfaces. *See* Attrition.

Abscess. Pus formation in the bone or soft tissues. *See* Cyst, Granuloma.

Abutment. The natural tooth supporting or holding in place a fixed or removable bridge.

Acid taste. Sour taste.

Adhesion. Sticking together of two materials or parts such as scar tissue adhesions.

Administrator. The person in charge of the business and administrative functions of an organization; the organization responsible for administering a health insurance plan. *See* Third party, Fourth party.

ADS. Attending Dentist Statement. The billing form sent to the insurance company for predetermination or payment of benefits based on fees listed for the procedures performed or to be performed. *Syn.* Claims statement.

Adverse selection. The tendency of persons with poorer than average health expectations to incur greater than average health care costs, thereby raising the cost of insurance for everyone.

Aesthetics. *See* Esthetics.

Alloy. A combination of two or more metals to form a compound metallic material such as silver amalgam fillings, cast gold onlays and crowns.

Alveolar bone or process. *See* Bone, alveolar; socket.

Alveolectomy. The surgical removal of a portion of the alveolar process, usually at the time of extractions, to eliminate bulges or sharp edges to allow placement of a denture.

Amalgam. A metallic alloy formed mostly of silver and tin mixed with mercury into a soft plastic material that sets hard in a few hours after placement inside a tooth cavity.

Analgesia. In dentistry refers to inhalation of nitrous oxide gas wherein the patient remains conscious but is less sensitive to minor pain.

Anaphylaxis. Hypersensitivity of the body to a drug or foreign protein, which results in an allergic reaction. Such reactions range from localized inflammation, itching, and fever to severe shock with collapse, convulsions, and death.

Anesthesia, general. Inhalation and/or injection of chemicals to induce unconsciousness and complete loss of feeling.

Anesthesia, local. Injection of a chemical to reduce or eliminate sensations of pain in a particular area of the body while the patient remains fully conscious.

Anterior. Toward the front or midline of the mouth.

Anterior teeth. The incisor and cuspid teeth; the six upper and six lower front teeth.

Antibiotic. Drugs such as penicillin, erythromycin, and tetracycline administered by injection, taken orally, or applied topically for the treatment of bacterial infections.

ANUG. The abbreviation for acute necrotizing ulcerative gingivostomatitis, a severe, noncontagious infection of the gums. *Syn.* Trench mouth; Vincent's infection.

Apex. The end or tip of the root of a tooth.

Apical. The part of the tooth that is near the end or tip of the root.

Apicoectomy. Surgical removal of the root tip in conjunction with root canal therapy or performed separately to eliminate an area of infection.

Arch. A structure that is curved like an arc; the teeth in each jaw are set in an arc, the dental arch. Also, refers to the bone supporting the teeth. The dental jawbones are called the maxillary (upper) arch and the mandibular (lower) arch. *See* Dental arch.

Artery. A vessel transporting blood from the heart to the structures of the body; supplies the tissues with oxygen, nutrients, blood cells, and so forth.

Articular Disc. The cartilaginous disk interposed between the ball joint of the mandible and its socket (glenoid fossa) in the skull. *Syn.* Disc.

Articulation. Parts joined together by a joint; in dentistry, refers to the movable temporomandibular joints on either side that attach the lower jaw to the skull and permit jaw movements. *See* Occlusal articulation.

Articulator. A mechanical device that simulates the movements of the upper and lower jaws for the construction of onlays, crowns, bridges, and dentures, and other prosthetic devices; resembles a hinge that allows plaster casts of the teeth to be articulated. *See* Articulation.

Assignment of benefits. Permission of the beneficiary of an insurance plan for benefits to be paid directly to the provider of services such as the doctor, the clinic, or the hospital.

Atrophy. Resorption of the dental ridge bone, leaving flat surfaces. Also refers to loss of muscle mass due to insufficient function and exercise.

Attrition. Abnormal wearing away of tooth surface by rubbing or grinding teeth together. *See* Abrasion.

Audit. Review of records and/or treatment to verify what was done.

Baby bottle tooth decay (BBTD). *See* Early childhood caries (ECC). *Syn.* Nursing caries.

Baby teeth. *See* Deciduous teeth.

Bacteremia. Presence of bacteria in the blood.

Beneficiary. A person eligible for benefits under a dental plan. *Syn.* Covered person; eligible dependent; eligible member; enrollee; plan member. *See* Eligibility.

Benefits. Payments for services provided by a dental plan. *See* Coverage; indemnification; schedule (Table) of allowances.

Bicuspids. The two double-cusped permanent teeth in each quadrant between the cuspids and molars.

Bite. The force that brings the lower teeth up against the upper teeth; usually refers to the cutting, grinding, shearing action of the teeth and to the articulating relationships of the upper and lower teeth or jaws as in "the bite."

Bite guard. A plastic shield that fits over the chewing surfaces of the teeth like an athlete's mouthpiece to protect the teeth and jaw joints from excessive pressure of bruxism, clenching, and so forth. *Syn.* Night guard; occlusal guard; occlusal splint; periodontal splint.

Bitewing X-ray. The type of diagnostic dental X-ray film (radiograph) of the crowns of the posterior upper and lower teeth taken together on a single film to detect cavities and the fit of fillings and crowns; also useful in evaluating periodontal bone loss.

Bleaching. Application of bleaching agents, usually hydrogen peroxide, to a discolored tooth to restore its natural color or lighten the natural shade.

Bonding. Etching of enamel to attach composite filling material or veneers to the outer surface of a tooth.

Bone. The calcified material of the skeleton. Contains an outer, hard shell or plate (cortical bone) and an inner matrix (cancellous bone) interspersed with marrow, connective tissue, blood vessels, and channels for nerves. The outer plate of bone is covered by the periosteum, a sheet of dense, tough connective tissue.

Bone, alveolar. The part of the jawbones that surrounds and holds the roots of teeth.

Bone augmentation. Placement of synthetic or specially prepared natural bone beneath the gums to build up the ridge for support of an artificial denture or to fill in voids around teeth. *See* Graft, bone.

Bone, cancellous. The main portion or bulk of bone that forms the matrix or latticework containing the marrow spaces.

Bone, cortical. The hard outer shell or plate of bone surrounding the medullary (marrow) spaces.

Bridgework. A fixed (cemented) or removable prosthetic appliance that replaces missing teeth by attachment to other teeth. *Syn.* Fixed bridge; fixed partial denture; permanent bridge; removable partial denture.

Brittle. Lacking in "give," elasticity, or plasticity, Breaks easily on sharp impact or bending forces.

Bruxism. Grinding, gnashing, clenching of teeth.

Buccal. Refers to the cheek. *See* Buccal cavity; buccal surface.

Buccal cavity. The space inside the mouth between the teeth or dental arch and the cheek. Also, a cavity (decay) on the outer surface of the tooth.

Buccal surface. The cheek and lip surfaces of the teeth. Same as the labial (lip) surface of anterior teeth.

Bucco-lingual. The dimension or width of the tooth from tongue side to cheek side.

Buildup. A cement, composite, or amalgam filling placed in a tooth with a large cavity or fracture, sometimes with pins for added retention, prior to shaping (grinding) the tooth for a crown or onlay.

Bur. A dental drill or bit.

By report (B/R). The written report explaining a charge for an unlisted procedure or an increase in the usual fee.

Calcification. The maturation or hardening of bone and teeth by deposition of calcium salts.

Calculus. Calcified bacterial plaque that forms from mineral salts in the saliva and deposits on the crowns and roots of teeth. Calculus stones occasionally block the ducts of the salivary glands. *Syn.* Scale; tartar.

Canal, root. *See* Root canal.

Cancer. A malignant tumor or overgrowth of tissue that, if not treated early and successfully, can cause death. *See* Tumor.

Cap. Covering all or part of a structure. Usually refers to an artificial crown on a natural tooth to restore its shape, appearance, and function. *See* Crown.

Capitation. Payment for group dental care and/or insurance on the basis of a head count or the number of persons covered by the dental plan. Usually refers to monthly payments to a closed panel plan or an HMO or managed care plan to cover basic services at no charge and more expensive services at reduced rates.

Caries, dental. Decalcification and disintegration of tooth structure by microorganisms. *Syn.* Carious lesion, cavity, dental decay.

Cariogenic. Substances that promote dental decay.

Cariogenic diet. A diet that contains a lot of sugar in natural and processed form that promotes dental decay.

Carious lesion. *See* Caries, dental.

Cartilage. A specialized semihard fibrous connective tissue that separates the bony surfaces of movable joints, providing a "lubricating" or sliding surface that reduces frictional wear.

Cavitron. An ultrasonic vibrating instrument with a water spray coolant that is used to scale or remove calculus and plaque from tooth surfaces.

Cavity. A carious lesion or hole in a tooth. *See* Caries, dental.

Cellulitis. Inflammation and swelling of connective tissue resulting from fluids being forced into the tissue rather than draining or being discharged on the surface.

Cement base. A substance that hardens like mortar and serves as a thermal insulator to protect the pulp beneath a filling or crown. *See* Buildup.

Cementoenamel junction. The point at which the enamel shell of the crown terminates on the root of the tooth.

Cementum. A thin layer of calcified connective tissue that has the hardness of bone and covers; the root surfaces of the tooth for attachment to the alveolar bone.

Cephalograph. A lateral (sideview) X-ray film of the entire head.

Ceramco. The trade name for a brand of porcelain-metal crown or bridge. Used generically to refer to all porcelain-metal restorations.

Cervix. The neck portion of the tooth at the junction of the crown and root. *See* Cementoenamel junction.

Claims statement. The listing (bill of particulars) of services provided on the dental insurance form that is submitted to the insurance company for payment. *See* ADS-Attending Dentist Statement.

Classification. Refers to the type of procedure or service performed such as a simple extraction, surgical extraction, or bony impaction. The type of crooked teeth such as a Class I, II, or III malocclusion. The type of filling.

Cleft lip. A congenital fissure or channel running through the upper lip to the nose resulting from the failure of the embryonic parts of the lip to unite properly during uterine development. Can be closed in early infancy by surgery.

Cleft palate. A congenital fissure or channel running through the middle of the palate resulting from failure of the embryonic parts of the palate to fuse together during uterine development. Can be closed surgically in early infancy or by means of a plastic bulb (obturator).

Clenching. *See* Bruxism.

Clicking, joint. *See* Crepitation.

Closed panel. A group of dentists who provide care for a special population.

Coinsurance. The portion or percentage of the fee, ranging from 10 to 50 percent, paid by the insuree (beneficiary), the balance of which is paid by the insurance plan. *Syn.* Copayment; surcharge.

Composite filling. A restoration or filling composed of a plastic resin material that resembles the natural tooth.

Consent. *See* Informed consent.

Consultant. *See* Dental consultant.

Consultation. *See* Second opinion.

Contact points. The points of contact - front and back or side to side - between two adjacent teeth in the same dental arch.

Contagious. A disease that can be transmitted from one person to another.

Contract. A formal, legally binding agreement, verbal or written, between the patient and the provider (dentist, physician, hospital, and so forth) to pay for specified services and appliances for an agreed upon amount of money over a specified period of time. The written document of agreement defining the dental insurance plan, its coverage and copayments, and the benefits to be provided for or paid on behalf of the program beneficiaries.

Conversion privilege. The right of an insured person to convert to a different plan without providing evidence of insurability, or to convert to an individual, self-paying policy upon termination of group coverage.

Coordination of benefits (COB). When both spouses have insurance, the secondary insurance pays the difference between the primary insurance plan's benefit and the charge up to the maximum benefit provided by the secondary insurance, not to exceed the actual charge. *See* Dual insurance.

Copayment. The amount paid out-of-pocket by the patient, with the remainder paid by insurance. *See* Coinsurance.

Cosmetic treatment. The placement of crowns (caps) and veneers on teeth, bleaching or other services solely to improve appearance. *Syn.* Esthetic treatment.

Coverage. Plan benefits that define eligibility, the extent and limitation of services, annual dollar coverage, and the amount of beneficiary copayments. *See* Eligibility; schedule of allowances.

Crepitation. Grating, clicking, crackling or popping sounds of the temporomandibular joints sometimes heard on opening and closing the mouth. *Syn.* Crepitus

Crevice. *See* Gingival crevice.

Crown. The portion of the tooth covered with enamel. The restoration of the natural crown with an artificial crown. *Syn.* Cap.

CT scan. Computerized radiographic imaging to provide a three-dimensional picture of internal structures.

Curettage. Scraping the gums or other areas, such as tooth sockets after extraction, or cyst cavities, with a sharp instrument to remove inflamed and diseased tissue.

Curette. A spoon-shaped instrument with sharp cutting or scraping edges. *See* Scaler.

Cuspids. The large single-cusped teeth at the corners of the mouth, located between the incisors and bicuspids. *Syn.* Canine teeth; eye teeth.

Cusps. The raised, round parts on the top or chewing surfaces of teeth.

Cyst. An abnormal cavity in the bone, soft tissues, glands, and so forth, containing fluid or semifluid material in an epithelium-lined sac.

Decalcification. *See* Enamel, decalcified.

Decay. *See* Caries, dental.

Deciduous teeth. The child's first set of 20 teeth that are replaced by permanent teeth. *Syn.* Baby teeth; milk teeth; primary teeth.

Deductible. The amount of charges paid by the insured before benefits by the insurance company become payable.

Dental arch. The curving structure formed by the crowns of the teeth in their normal position in the jawbone. The residual ridge of jawbone that supports a denture after the natural teeth are lost. *Syn.* Maxillary or upper arch, mandibular or lower arch.

Dental caries. *See* Caries, dental.

Dental consultant. A dentist to whom a patient is referred by the primary dentist for further diagnosis and recommendations. A dentist employed by an insurance company, trust fund, or administrator to supervise and review dental treatment plans and claim statements and to perform audits of the quality of treatment. *See* Referral; second opinion.

Dental floss. Waxed or unwaxed nylon string that is inserted between the teeth and moved up and down to remove food particles and bacterial plaque deposits. *See* Flossing.

Dental hygienist. A person qualified to clean and scale teeth (prophylaxis), to plane smooth the root surfaces, to teach and supervise oral hygiene, to provide basic and maintenance periodontal disease therapy. May also take diagnostic X-rays and place sealants; in teeth.

Dental plaque. *See* Plaque, dental.

Dentin. The bulk of tooth structure that is covered by a crown of enamel and a thin veneer of cementum along the root.

Dentition. The natural teeth in the dental arch. *See* Dental arch.

Dentition, mixed. The presence of both deciduous (baby) and permanent teeth in the dental arches during the child's development.

Dentition, permanent. The 32 teeth that form the adult dentition. *Syn.* Permanent teeth, Secondary teeth.

Dentoenamel junction. The area at which the enamel is joined to the dentin.

Denture adhesive. A commercial powder or paste placed in a denture to help hold it in place.

Deposits. *See* Calculus; plaque, dental.

Diastema. A space between two adjacent teeth in the same arch.

Die. The laboratory model or replication of a tooth that has been prepared to receive a crown or onlay.

Direct reimbursement. A plan advocated by the dental association in which the employee would pay the dental bill and then be reimbursed directly by the employer for whatever was covered.

Disc. *See* Articular disc.

Distal. Away from the midline of the face toward the back of the mouth.

Distal surface. The side surface of the tooth away from the midline of the face. Opposite to the mesial surface.

Dowel post. A metal post that is placed into a root canal when the tooth is broken off at or near the gum line; it extends above the tooth to provide additional support for an artificial crown. *See* Buildup.

Dry mouth. A condition caused by inadequate secretion of saliva by the salivary and parotid glands. *Syn.* Xerostomia.

Dry socket. A condition that occurs following an extraction when the blood clot disintegrates.

Dual choice. An option given an individual between two or more dental plans, usually a choice between a prepaid capitation closed panel plan and fee-for-service indemnity insurance.

Dual insurance. The result of both spouses having dental insurance so family members are covered by both insurance plans. *See* Coordination of benefits.

Early childhood caries. Rampant decalcification and carious destruction (decay) of the baby teeth, usually the upper incisors, caused by excessive suckling on nursing bottles. *Syn.* Baby bottle tooth decay; nursing caries

Edentulism. The absence of all teeth. May be complete or partial loss of teeth.

Eligibility. Refers to coverage by a dental plan for a specified period of time. *See* Beneficiary.

Enamel. The highly calcified shell covering the crown of the tooth.

Enamel, decalcified. Enamel that has been partly or completely dissolved, characterized by a chalky, soft surface in contrast to the porcelain-like hardness of sound enamel.

Enamel, hypocalcified. Enamel that is poorly calcified during the development of the tooth.

Enamel, mottled. Enamel that contains light to dense or dark bands or spots of white, yellow, brown, or black discoloration. May also be chalky and pitted. *See* Fluorosis.

Endodontics. The branch of dentistry concerned with the treatment of injuries and disease of the dental pulp or "nerve." *Syn.* Endodontia. *See* Root canal therapy.

Endodontist. A dentist with additional training who specializes in endodontics.

Epithelium. The tissue that covers the internal and external surfaces of the body such as the outer layer of the skin, the gums, and the mucous membranes of the mouth.

Equilibration, occlusal. Spot grinding of the chewing surfaces of the teeth to equalize the bite, to relieve "high" points of interference so that the teeth fit and slide together evenly. *Syn.* Occlusal adjustment.

Erosion, dental. Chemical dissolution of enamel and dentin, usually at the neck of the tooth just below the dentoenamel junction, resulting in a groove or saucer-shaped depression. *See* Abrasion.

Esthetics. Having to do with appearance. *Syn.* Cosmetics. *See* Composite filling; veneer.

Exclusion. A condition or person listed in the policy for which there is no insurance coverage.

Exfoliation, dental. The physiological process by which the root(s) of a deciduous (baby) tooth is resorbed or dissolved and the crown shed to be replaced by the erupting permanent tooth underneath.

Exodontics. The area of dentistry pertaining to the extraction of teeth. *Syn.* Exodontia.

Experience rating. Determining the premium rate for a group policy wholly or partially on the basis of the group's cost experience.

Explanation of Benefits (EOB). The reason for limitation of the insurance payment, usually stated on the record of the paid claims statement.

Explorer. A needle-point instrument used to probe the smooth surfaces, pits, and grooves of teeth.

Fee-for-service. The charge for a specific procedure or item of service such as a cleaning, filling, or crown.

Fee schedule. A list of specific fees or maximum dollar amounts that will be charged or paid for each dental procedure. *See* Schedule of allowances.

Fibroma. A benign tumor composed of fibrous tissue.

Fissure. A cleft or groove. Usually refers to a fault at the center of chewing surfaces where the cuspal planes of enamel have not coalesced perfectly during formation.

Fissure sealant. A special composite material that seals enamel pits and fissures (grooves) to prevent decay. *Syn.* Sealant.

Fixed fee schedule. *See* Fee schedule.

Flipper. A removable acrylic (plastic) partial denture for the temporary replacement of anterior teeth.

Floss. *See* Dental floss.

Flossing. Using dental floss to remove food debris and plaque deposits.

Fluoridation. The addition of fluoride to the public water supply to an optimum concentration.

Fluoride, topical. The application of a solution or gel containing fluoride to teeth. May be applied by a dentist, a dental assistant, a hygienist, or self-applied.

Fluorosis. Dark brown discoloration of tooth enamel that also may be pitted, caused by excessive fluorides in natural drinking water or excessive ingestion of fluorine compounds. *See* Enamel, mottled.

Follicle, dental. The small sac within the jawbone in which the tooth develops. The womb of the tooth.

Foramen, apical. The natural opening at or near the tip (apex) of the dental root through which the blood vessels and nerves pass into the root canal and pulp chamber.

Fourth party. An independent administrative organization that is employed by an insurance company or self-insured benefit trust fund to administer its dental plan. *See* Administrator; third party.

Frenectomy. Cutting and removal of a thick band of tissue that sometimes separates the two upper front teeth (central incisors) or limits tongue movement.

Frenum. A string-like fold of tissue that limits the movement of the lips, tongue, and cheeks.

Frenum release. A simple surgical incision that eliminates a "frenum pull" that is causing gingival recession.

FUN treatment. Acronym for treatment that is functionally unnecessary.

Gingiva. The fibrous tissue and mucous membrane that covers the alveolar process of the jawbone and attaches to the cementum at the neck of the teeth. *Syn.* Gums.

Gingival crevice. The circumferential space or trough between the gingiva or gum tissue and the crown or root of the tooth. *See* Periodontal pocket.

Gingival papilla. The triangular or pyramid-shaped wedge of gum tissue that fills the space between adjacent teeth.

Gingival recession. The movement of the gum away from the neck of the crown in the direction of the root, exposing the root surface.

Gingival sulcus. *See* Gingival crevice.

Gingivectomy. Surgical removal of loose gum tissue to its lower level of attachment to the tooth. *See* Periodontal surgery.

Gingivitis. Inflammation of the gingiva or gums.

Gingivoplasty. Surgical reshaping and reduction of thickened gum tissue to its normal size and contour.

Graft, bone. Natural or synthetic bone that is inserted around the root of a tooth or onto the alveolar ridge. *See* Bone augmentation.

Graft, soft tissue. Gum or palatal tissue that is removed from one area of the mouth to replace gum tissue lost from another area or to thicken the attached gingiva.

Granulation tissue. *See* Tissue, granulation.

Granuloma, dental. Abnormal tissue at the apex or tip of the root, usually surrounded by a fibrous sac and caused by an infected or degenerated tooth pulp. *See* Abscess; cyst.

Group contract. A contract of insurance made with an employer or other entity that covers a group of persons identified as individuals by reference to their relationship to the entity.

Group dental practice. A dental practice conducted by two or more dentists sharing staff personnel and facilities and patient care responsibilities.

Group, insured. All the persons eligible to receive health care benefits according to the contractual agreement.

Gums. *See* Gingiva.

Halitosis. Bad breath.

Handpiece. The dentist's drill.

Harelip. *See* Cleft lip.

Health Maintenance Organization (HMO). An organization that provides comprehensive health care services by a fixed group of health care practitioners often working together in a facility for a specified group at a fixed capitation payment.

Hygienist. *See* Dental hygienist.

Hyperemia. An increase in the amount of blood present in a particular part of the body.

Hypocalcification. *See* Enamel, hypocalcified.

Iatrogenic. A condition or injury produced inadvertently by a physician or dentist.

Impaction. A tooth that fails to erupt into its normal position in the dental arch but remains fully or partially embedded and covered over by bone or gum tissue.

Implant. A metal post, blade, or framework set into or against the dental ridge or jawbone beneath the gum with an extension above the gum for attachment of an artificial. crown, bridge, or denture.

Impression, dental. An imprint in. a material from which a reproduction of a part of the mouth or tooth can be made of a hard plaster or other substance. *See* Model, die.

Incidence. The occurrence of a disease or event in a population measured over a specific period of time such as the number of new cavities per 100 children per year.

Incisal surface. The cutting edge of the incisors and cuspid teeth.

Incisors. The four upper and four lower single-cusped front teeth designed for incising or cutting food.

Indemnification. Reimbursement to the beneficiary or insured person in the amount allowed by the insurance plan for the covered expense, usually as a percentage of the fee or on the basis of a Schedule of Allowances. *Syn.* Indemnity.

Independent Practice Association (IPA). An arrangement whereby a third party payor such as an insurance company or a self-insured benefit trust fund contracts with individual medical or dental practitioners who furnish services at their private office at lower than usual fees in return for prompt payment and a certain volume of patients.

Individual insurance. Policies that provide protection to the policyholder and/or his family. Sometimes called Personal Insurance, as distinct from group insurance.

Infection. Disease caused by growth of pathogenic microorganisms in the body such as bacteria, viruses, yeasts, parasites.

Informed consent. Agreement to dental treatment based on a true understanding of the reasons for treatment, anticipated results, risks of failure or injury, and cost.

Inlay, gold. A custom-fabricated cast gold alloy restoration that is cemented into a previously prepared cavity in a tooth. *See* Onlay.

Insurance, dental. A contract whereby specified payment is made for dental services out of a fund derived from pooled premiums paid by or on behalf of all beneficiaries.

Interproximal. Between the mesial and distal surfaces of the teeth.

Interproximal filling. A filling that is inserted on the mesial or distal surface of a tooth.

Intravenous (I-V) sedation. Injection of a barbiturate or tranquilizer such as diazepam (Valium) into a vein to induce a light general anesthesia in which the patient remains semiconscious, though often with no memory of the experience afterward. *Syn.* Twilight sleep. *See* Pentothal.

Jacket. Refers to an artificial crown or cap on an anterior tooth. *See* Crown.

Joint, temporomandibular (TMJ). *See* Temporomandibular joint.

Labial. Toward the lips, as in the labial surface of an incisor or cuspid tooth facing the inner surface of the lips. *Syn.* Facial; buccal.

Laminate veneer. *See* Veneer.

Leukoplakia. White, irregular patches on the mucous membranes of the tongue or cheek, usually caused by chronic irritation. These areas may become malignant.

Ligament, periodontal. *See* Periodontal ligament.

Lingual. Related to the tongue, as in the surface of a tooth that faces the tongue.

Lingual nerve. The sensory nerve supplying half of the tongue that usually becomes numb when the lower jaw is anesthetized by a local injection.

Malignancy. A condition that is life-threatening. Usually refers to a malignant tumor. *See* Cancer.

Malocclusion. Literally "bad occlusion." Any condition in which the position of the teeth or jaws does not conform to a theoretical ideal.

Malpractice. Literally "bad practice." Improper treatment or treatment of such poor quality that bodily harm is done.

Mandible. The horseshoe-shaped lower jawbone that contains the lower teeth.

Mandibular. Refers to the mandible, as in the mandibular (lower) teeth.

Mastication. The act of chewing food to allow swallowing and digestion. *Syn.* Chewing.

Matrix. A mold in which anything is formed. Usually a thin band of metal or plastic wrapped around the tooth during the placement of a filling such as amalgam or composite.

Maxilla. The upper jawbone that contains the upper teeth.

Maxillary. Refers to the maxilla, as in the maxillary teeth.

Maximum benefit. The maximum amount of money that will be paid by insurance in a given year or in a lifetime for covered services.

Medicaid. State programs of public assistance to persons regardless of age whose income and resources are insufficient to pay for health care.

MediCare. The hospital insurance system and the supplementary medical insurance for the aged (and sometimes disabled) created by the 1965 amendments to the Social Security Act.

Mesial. Toward the midline of the dental arch or face.

Mesial surface. The side of the tooth facing the front or midline.

Midline. The vertical center of the face, jaws, and teeth.

Milk teeth. Primary or baby teeth. *See* Deciduous teeth.

Mixed dentition. *See* Dentition, mixed.

Mobility. The degree of looseness of a tooth.

Model. A duplicate of mouth structures, usually the teeth, made of plaster of paris or dental stone. *See* Die; impression, dental; mold; study model.

Molars. The multicusped posterior teeth located behind the bicuspids that are designed for grinding food in preparation for swallowing.

Mold. The impression form from which a model is made. Also, the term used to specify the particular shape of manufactured teeth. *See* Impression, dental; model.

Mottled enamel, mottled teeth. *See* Enamel, mottled.

Muco-osseous surgery. Periodontal gum and bone surgery in the treatment of periodontal disease or pyorrhea.

Mucosa, oral. The lining surface of the oral cavity or mouth.

Mucus. The syrupy secretion of the mucous glands contained in submandibular, sublingual, and minor salivary glands.

Myofacial pain. Discomfort and pain in the facial muscles and the muscles controlling jaw movement.

Myofacial pain dysfunction (MPD). A catchall for myofacial pain, headaches, and neck and shoulder muscle discomfort and pain. *See* Temporomandibular disorders (TMD).

Necrosis. Death of tissue.

Neoplasm. Any abnormal growth of tissue. *See* Cancer; fibroma; tumor.

Nerve. A cordlike structure that conveys impulses. May be sensory to provide the five senses: hearing, taste, touch, sight, and smell; or motor to produce muscle action. *See* Pulp, dental.

Night guard. *See* Bite guard; splint.

Nitrous oxide. A gas that is inhaled to induce analgesia or general anesthesia. Frequently referred to as "laughing gas."

Nonvital tooth. A tooth in which the pulp or dental nerve is degenerated or "dead."

Novocaine. A generic term for a local injection of a proprietary anesthetic such as Novocain, Xylocaine, or Lidocaine.

Nursing caries. *See* Early childhood caries (ECC); baby bottle tooth decay (BBTD); rampant caries.

Occlusal adjustment. *See* Equilibration, occlusal.

Occlusal articulation. The functional relationship or fitting together of the upper and lower teeth. *See* Articulation.

Occlusal groove. The central groove or sulcus of the chewing surface of a tooth.

Occlusion, abnormal. *See* Malocclusion.

Occlusion, centric. The position of the upper and lower teeth in contact when the jaws are closed.

Occlusion, dental. The relationship between the maxillary (upper) and mandibular (lower) teeth when they come together and contact during the various movements of the mandible.

Onlay. A gold or porcelain inlay extended to cover the cusps for greater protection of the tooth. *See* Inlay.

Open panel. Refers to a dental plan in which the patient can choose any licensed dentist.

Optional services. Alternative or additional treatment that is not a covered benefit of insurance.

Orthodontics. The branch of dentistry concerned with correction of malocclusion. *Syn.* Orthodontia.

Orthodontist. A dentist who has received additional training and specializes in the treatment of malocclusions.

Orthognathic surgery. Surgical reduction or lengthening of the jawbone to improve appearance and function, usually in conjunction with orthodontic treatment.

Orthopedic splint. A plastic splint like a bite guard that is adjusted at frequent intervals to "open the bite" and reposition the temporomandibular joints (TMJ). *See* Bite guard; splint.

Osteomyelitis. Inflammation of bone that extends into the marrow.

Out-of-pocket expense. Payments made by the patient that are not reimbursed (indemnified) by an insurance plan.

Overbite. The overlapping of mandibular teeth by the maxillary teeth. Usually refers to the anterior or incisor teeth, but posterior teeth also overlap in normal position. A normal anterior overbite ranges from one to four millimeters.

Palate. The roof of the mouth consisting of a hard anterior part, the *hard palate,* and a soft movable posterior part, the *soft palate.*

Palate, cleft. *See* Cleft palate.

Panograph. *A* large panoramic radiograph of the upper and lower jaws that does not require placement of film in the mouth. *Syn.* Pantomogram, panorex.

Papilla, gingival. *See* Gingival papilla.

Papilloma. *See* Fibroma.

Pathogenic. Any disease-producing microorganism or material. A condition, habit, or malfunction that interferes with normal function and causes physical injury.

Pediatric dentist. A dentist who has received additional training and specializes in the treatment of children. *Syn.* Pedodontist.

Pedodontics. The branch of dentistry concerned with the diagnosis and treatment of dental diseases and conditions in children. *Syn.* Pediatric dentistry; pedodontia.

Pedodontist. A dentist specializing in the treatment of children. *See* Pediatric dentist.

Peer review. An examination or review of a dentist's treatment, fees, or behavior by his or her peers, who are other qualified dentists, as by a peer review committee of the dental association.

Pentothal. A barbiturate used in I-V sedation. *Syn.* Twilight sleep. *See* Intravenous sedation.

Percussion. Tapping on a part of the body (the tooth in dentistry) to aid in diagnosis.

Periapical. The area immediately surrounding the apex or tip of the root of a tooth.

Pericoronitis. Inflammation and infection of the gum tissue surrounding a tooth.

Periodontal disease. The general term for inflammatory and degenerative diseases of the supporting and attachment structures of the teeth and alveolar bone. *Syn.* Pyorrhea.

Periodontal ligament. The thin, slightly elastic fibrous membrane that surrounds the root of the tooth and attaches it to the bony alveolar socket.

Periodontal pocket. A pathologic deepening of the gingival crevice produced by destruction of the attachment of the gingiva to the root surface and of the adjacent alveolar bone.

Periodontal surgery. Surgery performed on the gums and bone surrounding the teeth.

Periodontics. The branch of dentistry concerned with the treatment of periodontal disease or pyorrhea. *Syn.* Periodontia.

Periodontist. A dentist who has received additional training and specializes in the treatment of periodontal disease.

Periodontitis. Inflammation of the structures surrounding teeth and attaching them to their sockets, which includes the gingiva (gums), periodontal ligaments, and alveolar bone.

Pins. *See* Buildup.

Pit, dental. A small depression in the enamel, usually at the junction of several grooves on the occlusal surface.

Plaque, dental. A gel-like deposit of material on the surface of the tooth that harbors bacterial growth and acid formation beneath its surface, causing dental decay. On the tooth's outer surface, it produces the toxic products that initiate periodontal disease.

Plastic filling. *See* Composite filling.

Pocket. *See* Periodontal pocket.

Pontic. The artificial tooth on a fixed bridge suspended between the natural abutment teeth.

Popping, joint. *See* Crepitation

Porcelain fused to metal crown. *Abbr.* PFM or PMC. The most popular type of crown restoration consisting of a cast metal cap over which porcelain is bonded to restore the natural shape and color of a tooth. *Syn.* Ceramco crown; microbond crown.

Post. *See* Dowel post.

Practitioner. Anyone who works at or practices a profession. Usually a dentist, physician, optometrist, lawyer, and so forth.

Preauthorization. Verifying the eligibility of the patient for insurance and the extent of financial coverage prior to commencement of elective (nonemergency) treatment. *See* Treatment, elective.

Precancerous. An abnormal condition or area of tissue that may turn into cancer.

Predetermination of benefits. *See* Preauthorization.

Preexisting condition. A condition that existed prior to eligibility for insurance.

Preferred Provider Organization (PPO). An arrangement whereby a third party payor such as an insurance company or a self-insured benefit trust fund contracts with a group of medical or dental providers who furnish services at lower than usual fees in return for prompt payment and a certain volume of patients.

Premolars. *See* Bicuspids.

Prepaid dental plan. An arrangement by which payments are made by a third party such as an insurance company or a self-insured trust fund in advance to a panel of dentists practicing independently or in groups, who provide some services at no additional out-of-pocket cost to the patient, and other services at reduced charges or copayments. *See* Health Maintenance Organization (HMO), Independent Practice Association (IPA), Preferred Provider Organization (PPO).

Prepayment. *See* Prepaid dental plan.

Prevalence. The number of cases of a condition or disease that is present in the population at any given time.

Prevention. *See* Treatment, preventive.

Procedure. The treatment or service performed, such as prophylaxis, filling, crown, extraction, denture.

Prognosis. An evaluation of the probable outcome of a disease or condition and its treatment.

Prophylactic. A remedy or treatment that is intended to prevent a disease or prevent a condition from worsening. *See* Treatment, preventive.

Prophylaxis, dental. Cleaning of teeth to remove stains, calculus, and plaque deposits.

Prosthesis, dental. An artificial appliance constructed to replace missing teeth or to restore a damaged part of the mouth such as a fixed bridge or a partial or full denture.

Prosthetic appliance. *See* Prosthesis, dental.

Prosthodontics. The branch of dentistry concerned with the construction of artificial appliances to replace missing teeth or other parts of the oral cavity and face. *Syn.* Prosthodontia.

Prosthodontist. A specialist in prostbodontic treatment.

Provider. Usually the dentist or physician performing or supervising treatment and who receives payment. May also be a therapist or the "clinic" or hospital.

Proximal surface. The side of a tooth that is in contact with or faces an adjacent tooth in the same dental arch. Refers to the mesial or distal surface of the tooth. *Syn.* Interproximal surface.

Pulp chamber. The opening in the center of the crown of a tooth, appearing tubular in the anterior teeth (incisors and cuspids) and bulbous in posterior molar teeth. It is continuous with the longer, narrower root canals that extend to the apex (tip) of the root. The pulp chamber and root canals contain the pulp or nerve tissue.

Pulp, dental. Commonly called the "nerve" of the tooth, it is comprised of nerve fibrils, blood and lymph vessels, connective tissue, and cells contained within the pulp chamber and root canals.

Pulpectomy. Removal of the entire pulp from the pulp chamber and root canals.

Pulpitis. Inflammation of the dental pulp or nerve. *Syn.* Toothache, pulpalgia.

Pulpotomy. A partial pulpectomy in which only the crown portion of the pulp contained in the pulp chamber is removed.

Pyorrhea. *See* Periodontal disease.

Quadrant. One-fourth of the mouth. One-half of the upper or lower dental arch.

Radiograph, dental. An X-ray film of the teeth and jaws, resembling the negative of a photograph. *Syn.* Roentgenogram; X-ray.

Radiolucent. A substance such as tissue, bone, or teeth that permits X-rays, to varying degrees, to pass through to form an image on the X-ray film. The more lucent the substance, the darker its image on the film.

Radiopaque. A substance that blocks X-rays, such as metal crowns and amalgam fillings, which appear white on the film.

Rampant decay. Dental caries throughout the dentition, affecting numerous teeth simultaneously. *See* Early Childhood Caries (ECC); baby bottle tooth decay (BBTD); nursing caries.

Recession. *See* Gingival recession.

Referral. Transfer of a patient from the primary dentist to another dentist, usually a specialist, for treatment.

Relative value. A unit of measurement that assesses the difficulty, time, and expense of one procedure or service compared with another in order to determine a fee.

Resorption. The dissolving and loss of a substance such as alveolar bone, roots, or dentin due to disease or abnormal pressure.

Restoration, dental. A filling, crown, onlay, bridge, or denture that restores or replaces lost tooth structure or the whole tooth.

Retainer. The part of a bridge or partial denture that holds it in place, usually a crown or a clasp. The appliance used to hold teeth in position until they are firmly set in bone following orthodontic treatment.

Review. *See* Audit; dental consultant; peer review.

Ridge augmentation. *See* Bone augmentation; graft, bone.

Root. The part of a tooth that fits into and is attached to the tooth socket in the jaw bone.

Root canal. The tubular canal inside the tooth's root that extends from the pulp chamber to the apex of the root.

Root canal therapy. Removing the nerve or pulp tissue and filling the pulp chamber and root canals with an inert material such as gutta percha. *Syn.* Nerve treatment. *See* Pulpectomy.

Root planing. Scaling and smoothing of root surfaces to the depth of periodontal pockets to remove calculus and plaque deposits.

Rubber dam. A thin sheet of rubber that covers the mouth through which the teeth protrude to keep them dry during treatment.

Saliva. The clear, slightly acid, mucous-serous secretions of the parotid submandibular, sublingual, and minor salivary glands into the oral cavity.

Scale. The act of cleaning tooth surfaces with a scaler. Also, calculus deposits on the teeth. *Syn.* Calculus; tartar.

Scaler. A hand-held instrument used in a scraping motion to remove calculus and plaque deposits from the crowns and roots of teeth. May also be an ultrasonic instrument. *See* Cavitron; curettage.

Schedule of allowances. A list of specified amounts that will be paid toward the cost of dental services. *Syn.* Table of allowances. *See* Fee schedule.

Sealant. A composite material that is etched into defective pits and fissures to prevent dental decay.

Second opinion. An independent consultation or examination by another doctor to evaluate a diagnosis, treatment plan, or the treatment itself.

Shedding. *See* Exfoliation, dental.

Shot. Euphemism for a local anesthetic injection.

Silicate. An obsolete filling material that has been replaced by composites. *Syn.* Synthetic porcelain.

Socket. A hollow or depression into which a corresponding part fits. In dentistry, usually refers to a tooth socket.

Socket, dry. *See Dry* socket.

Space maintainer. An appliance used to prevent adjacent teeth from drifting or moving into the space created by loss of a tooth. *Syn.* Spacer.

Spacer. *See* Space maintainer.

Splint. A device to reinforce teeth. *See* Bite guard; splinting.

Splinting. Temporary or permanent reinforcement of loose teeth, or joining adjacent teeth together for additional support of a long bridge.

Study model. A duplicate of mouth structures, usually the teeth, made of plaster of paris or dental stone. *See* Model.

Subgingival scaling. Removal of plaque and calculus from tooth surfaces beneath the gums.

Sulcus. *See* Gingival crevice; periodontal pocket.

Supragingival scaling. Removal of plaque and calculus from tooth surfaces at the margin of, or above, the gums.

Surcharge. *See* Coinsurance; copayment.

Surface, filling. The number of surfaces that comprise a filling, such as a one-surface, two-surface, three-surface, or four-surface filling.

Surface, proximal. *See* Proximal surface; mesial surface; distal surface.

Suture. The act of closing a surgical or accidental wound or cut with stitches. Also, the material used.

Table of allowances. *See* Schedule of allowances.

Tartar. *See* Calculus; plaque; scale.

Teeth, deciduous. The first set of 20 baby teeth. *Syn.* Milk teeth; primary teeth; baby teeth.

Teeth, permanent. The second set of 32 teeth.

Temporomandibular disorders (TMD). A group of conditions, often painful, that affect the jaw joint and the muscles that control chewing. *Syn.* Temporomandibular joint syndrome; TMJ. *See* Myofacial pain disorders (MPD).

Temporomandibular joint (TMJ). The bilateral joints formed by the ball-shaped condyle of the mandible and the glenoid fossa or socket of the skull.

Temporomandibular joint syndrome. *See* Temporomandibular disorders (TMD).

T.E.N.S. Transcutaneous electrical nerve stimulation. The application of minute electrical currents to the outer surface of the skin.

Third molar. The last four of the 32 permanent teeth that erupt between 16 and 25 years of age. *Syn.* Wisdom teeth.

Third party. The entity that pays for part or all of the cost of dental care on behalf of the eligible beneficiaries according to the benefits of the dental plan. May be an insurance company, an employer, or a self-insured health benefit trust fund. *See* Fourth party.

Tissue. An aggregation of similar specialized cells united in the performance of a particular function. In dentistry, usually refers to gingival or gum tissue, granulation tissue, nerve tissue, and mucosal tissue.

Tissue, granulation. Young, vascularized connective tissue formed from blood elements in the process of healing ulcers and wounds such as in tooth sockets following extractions.

Temporomandibular dysfunction (TMD). *See* TMJ syndrome.

TMJ syndrome. Chronic pain in the temporomandibular joint(s) and musculature.

Tomography. A special type of radiography that produces an X-ray film in one plane while blurring or eliminating images from structures in other planes.

Tongue. The movable, muscular organ on the floor of the mouth that aids in chewing, swallowing, and speech, and provides almost the entire sense of taste through taste buds imbedded in its upper surface.

Tongue thrust. An abnormal positioning of the tongue against or between the front teeth during swallowing and speech.

Tooth. *See* Teeth.

Toothache. *See* Pulpitis.

Topical fluoride. *See* Fluoride, topical.

Torus. A benign outgrowth of bone, usually in the center of the hard palate or along the inside of the mandible.

Treatment. The actions performed to remedy a particular disease or condition.

Treatment, elective. Treatment that does not require immediate attention and that can be scheduled at the convenience of both the provider and the patient.

Treatment plan. The list of services to be rendered based on the dentist's examination and diagnosis and agreed to by the patient.

Treatment, preventive. The management and care of a patient to prevent the occurrence of a disease or undesirable condition.

Trench mouth. Severe, noncontagious infection of the gum, technically called acute necrotizing ulcerative gingivostomatitis. *Syn.* ANUG; Vincent's infection.

Tumor. An abnormal mass of new tissue that has no physiologic use. It may be benign (harmless) or malignant (harmful and life-threatening). *See* Cancer.

Twilight sleep. *See* Intravenous sedation.

Usual, customary, and reasonable (UCR) fee. The ordinary fee charged in a community or area for a specific service.

Veins. The blood vessels that conduct blood to the heart.

Veneer. A cosmetic facing that covers the visible surface of the tooth.

Vincent's infection. *See* ANUG; Trench mouth.

Wisdom teeth. *See* Third molars.

Xeroradiography. A system for reducing the amount of X-ray exposure that results in a xeroradiograph, which looks more like a black and white photographic print than a conventional X-ray film.

Xerostomia. *See* Dry mouth.

X-ray. The beam of electrons emitted by an X-ray (Roentgen ray) tube to form an image on a sensitized film. *See* Radiograph, dental.

Index